CAMBRIDGE MONOGRAPHS ON
APPLIED AND COMPUTATIONAL
MATHEMATICS

Series Editors
P. G. CIARLET, A. ISERLES, R. V. KOHN, M. H. WRIGHT

23   Curve and Surface Reconstruction

The Cambridge Monographs on Applied and Computational Mathematics reflects the crucial role of mathematical and computational techniques in contemporary science. The series publishes expositions on all aspects of applicable and numerical mathematics, with an emphasis on new developments in this fast-moving area of research.

State-of-the-art methods and algorithms as well as modern mathematical descriptions of physical and mechanical ideas are presented in a manner suited to graduate research students and professionals alike. Sound pedagogical presentation is a prerequisite. It is intended that books in the series will serve to inform a new generation of researchers.

Curve and Surface Reconstruction: Algorithms with Mathematical Analysis

TAMAL K. DEY

The Ohio State University

CAMBRIDGE
UNIVERSITY PRESS

CAMBRIDGE UNIVERSITY PRESS
Cambridge, New York, Melbourne, Madrid, Cape Town, Singapore,
São Paulo, Delhi, Dubai, Tokyo, Mexico City

Cambridge University Press
32 Avenue of the Americas, New York, NY 10013-2473, USA

www.cambridge.org
Information on this title: www.cambridge.org/9780521863704

First published 2007

A catalog record for this publication is available from the British Library

Library of Congress Cataloging in Publication data

Dey, Tamal K. (Tamal Krishna), 1964–
    Curve and surface reconstruction : algorithms with mathematical analysis / Tamal K. Dey.
        p. cm. — (Cambridge monographs on applied and computational mathematics ; 23)
    Includes bibliographical references and index.
    ISBN-13: 978-0-521-86370-4 (hardback)
    ISBN-10: 0-521-86370-8 (hardback)
    1. Curves on surfaces – Mathematical models.   2. Surfaces – Mathematical models.
3. Surfaces, Models of.   I. Title.   II. Series.

    QA565.D49 2006
    516.3'62–dc22

                                                                2006017359

ISBN 978-0-521-86370-4 Hardback

To my parents Gopal Dey and Hasi Dey and to all my teachers who taught me how to be a self-educator.

Contents

Preface

The subject of this book is the approximation of curves in two dimensions and surfaces in three dimensions from a set of sample points. This problem, called *reconstruction*, appears in various engineering applications and scientific studies. What is special about the problem is that it offers an application where mathematical disciplines such as differential geometry and topology interact with computational disciplines such as discrete and computational geometry. One of my goals in writing this book has been to collect and disseminate the results obtained by this confluence. The research on geometry and topology of shapes in the discrete setting has gained a momentum through the study of the reconstruction problem. This book, I hope, will serve as a prelude to this exciting new line of research.

To maintain the focus and brevity I chose a few algorithms that have provable guarantees. It happens to be, though quite naturally, they all use the well-known data structures of the Voronoi diagram and the Delaunay triangulation. Actually, these discrete geometric data structures offer discrete counterparts to many of the geometric and topological properties of shapes. Naturally, the Voronoi and Delaunay diagrams have been a common thread for the materials in the book.

This book originated from the class notes of a seminar course "Sample-Based Geometric Modeling" that I taught for four years at the graduate level in the computer science department of The Ohio State University. Graduate students entering or doing research in geometric modeling, computational geometry, computer graphics, computer vision, and any other field involving computations on geometric shapes should benefit from this book. Also, teachers in these areas should find this book helpful in introducing materials from differential geometry, topology, and discrete and computational geometry. I have made efforts to explain the concepts intuitively whenever needed, but I have retained the mathematical rigor in presenting the results. Lemmas and theorems have been used to state the results precisely. Most of them are equipped with proofs that bring out the insights. For the most part, the materials are self-explanatory. A motivated graduate student should be able to grasp the concepts through a careful reading. The exercises are set to stimulate innovative thoughts, and readers are strongly urged to solve them as they read.

The first chaper describes the necessary basic concepts in topology, Delaunay and Voronoi diagrams, local feature size, and ε-sampling of curves and surfaces. The second chapter is devoted to curve reconstruction in two dimensions. Some general results based on ε-sampling are presented first followed by two algorithms and their proofs of correctness. Chapter 3 presents results connecting surface geometries and topologies with ε-sampling. For example, it is shown that the normals and the topology of the surface can be recovered from the samples as long as the input is sufficiently dense. Based on these results, an algorithm for surface reconstruction is described in Chapter 4 with its proofs of guarantees. Chapter 5 contains results on undersampling. It presents a modification of the algorithm presented in Chapter 4. Chapter 6 is on computing watertight surfaces. Two algorithms are described for the problem. Chapter 7 introduces the case where sampling is corrupted by noise. It is shown that, under a reasonable noise model, the normals and the medial axis of a surface can still be approximated from a noisy input. Using these results a reconstruction method for noisy samples is presented in Chapter 8. The results in Chapter 7 are also used in Chapter 9 where a method to smooth out the noise is described. This smoothing is achieved by projecting the points on an implicit surface defined with a variation of the least squares method. Chapter 10, the last chapter, is devoted to reconstruction algorithms based on Morse theoretic ideas. Discretization of Morse theory using Voronoi and Delaunay diagrams is the focus of this chapter.

A book is not created in isolation. I am indebted to many people without whose work and help this book would not be a reality. First, my sincere gratitude goes to Nina Amenta, Dominique Attali, Marshall Bern, Jean-Daniel Boissonnat, Frederic Cazals, Frédéric Chazal, Siu-Wing Cheng, Herbert Edelsbrunner, David Eppstein, Joachim Giesen, Ravi Kolluri, André Lieutier, and Edgar Ramos whose beautiful work has inspired writing this book. I thank my students Samrat Goswami, James Hudson, Jian Sun, Tathagata Ray, Hyuckje Woo, Wulue Zhao, and Luke Molnar for implementing and experimenting with various reconstruction algorithms, which provided new insights into the problem. Special mention is due the CGAL project that offered a beautiful platform for these experiments. Joachim Giesen, Joshua Levine, and Jian Sun did an excellent job giving me the feedback on their experiences in reading through the drafts of various chapters. Rephael Wenger, my colleague at Ohio State, provided many valuable comments about the book and detected errors in early drafts.

Last but not least, I thank my other half, Kajari Dey, and our children Soumi Dey (Rumpa) and Sounak Dey (Raja) who suffered for diminished family attention while writing this book, but still provided their unfailing selfless support. Truly, their emotional support and encouragement kept me engaged with the book for more than four years.

1

Basics

Simply stated, the problem we study in this book is: how to approximate a shape from the coordinates of a given set of points from the shape. The set of points is called a point sample, or simply a *sample* of the shape. The specific shape that we will deal with are curves in two dimensions and surfaces in three dimensions. The problem is motivated by the availability of modern scanning devices that can generate a point sample from the surface of a geometric object. For example, a range scanner can provide the depth values of the sampled points on a surface from which the three-dimensional coordinates can be extracted. Advanced hand held laser scanners can scan a machine or a body part to provide a dense sample of the surfaces. A number of applications in computer-aided design, medical imaging, geographic data processing, and drug designs, to name a few, can take advantage of the scanning technology to produce samples and then compute a digital model of a geometric shape with reconstruction algorithms. Figure 1.1 shows such an example for a sample on a surface which is approximated by a triangulated surface interpolating the input points.

The reconstruction algorithms described in this book produce a piecewise linear approximation of the sampled curves and surfaces. By approximation we mean that the output captures the topology and geometry of the sampled shape. This requires some concepts from topology which are covered in Section 1.1.

Clearly, a curve or a surface cannot be approximated from a sample unless it is dense enough to capture the features of the shape. The notions of features and dense sampling are formalized in Section 1.2.

All reconstruction algorithms described in this book use the data structures called *Voronoi diagrams* and their duals called *Delaunay triangulations*. The key properties of these data structures are described in Section 1.3.

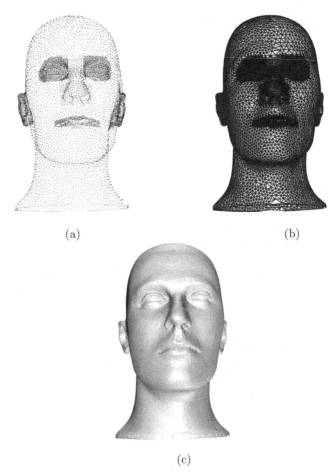

(a)   (b)

(c)

Figure 1.1. (a) A sample of MANNEQUIN, (b) a reconstruction, and (c) rendered
MANNEQUIN model.

1.1 Shapes

The term *shape* can circumscribe a wide variety of meaning depending on the
context. We define a shape to be a subset of an Euclidean space. Even this class
is too broad for our purpose. So, we focus on a specific type of shapes called
smooth manifolds and limit ourselves only up to three dimensions.

A global yardstick measuring similarities and differences in shapes is provided by *topology*. It deals with the connectivity of spaces. Various shapes are
compared with respect to their connectivities by comparing functions over them
called *maps*.

1.1.1 Spaces and Maps

In point set topology a *topological space* is defined to a be a point set $\mathbb{T}$ with a system of subsets $\mathcal{T}$ so that the following conditions hold.

1. $\emptyset, \mathbb{T} \in \mathcal{T}$,
2. $U \subseteq \mathcal{T}$ implies that the union of U is in $\mathcal{T}$,
3. $U \subseteq \mathcal{T}$ and U finite implies that the intersection of U is in $\mathcal{T}$.

The system $\mathcal{T}$ is the topology on the set $\mathbb{T}$ and its sets are *open* in $\mathbb{T}$. The *closed* sets of $\mathbb{T}$ are the subsets whose complements are open in $\mathbb{T}$. Consider the k-dimensional Euclidean space $\mathbb{R}^k$ and let us examine a topology on it. An *open ball* is the set of all points closer than a certain Euclidean distance to a given point. Define $\mathcal{T}$ as the set of open sets that are a union of a set of open balls. This system defines a topology on $\mathbb{R}^k$.

A subset $\mathbb{T}' \subseteq \mathbb{T}$ with a *subspace topology* $\mathcal{T}'$ defines a *topological subspace* where $\mathcal{T}'$ consists of all intersections between $\mathbb{T}'$ and the open sets in the topology $\mathcal{T}$ of $\mathbb{T}$. Topological spaces that we will consider are subsets of $\mathbb{R}^k$ which inherits their topology as a subspace topology. Let x denote a point in $\mathbb{R}^k$, that is, $x = \{x_1, x_2, \ldots, x_k\}$ and $\|x\| = (x_1^2 + x_2^2 + \cdots + x_k^2)^{\frac{1}{2}}$ denote its distance from the origin. Example of subspace topology are the k-ball $\mathbb{B}^k$, k-sphere $\mathbb{S}^k$, the halfspace $\mathbb{H}^k$, and the open k-ball $\mathbb{B}_o^k$ where

$$
\begin{aligned}
\mathbb{B}^k &= \{x \in \mathbb{R}^k \mid \|x\| \leq 1\} \\
\mathbb{S}^k &= \{x \in \mathbb{R}^{k+1} \mid \|x\| = 1\} \\
\mathbb{H}^k &= \{x \in \mathbb{R}^k \mid x_k \geq 0\} \\
\mathbb{B}_o^k &= \mathbb{B}^k \setminus \mathbb{S}^k.
\end{aligned}
$$

It is often important to distinguish topological spaces that can be covered with finitely many open balls. A *covering* of a topological space $\mathbb{T}$ is a collection of open sets whose union is $\mathbb{T}$. The topological space $\mathbb{T}$ is called *compact* if every covering of $\mathbb{T}$ can be covered with finitely many open sets included in the covering. An example of a compact topological space is the k-ball $\mathbb{B}^k$. However, the open k-ball is not compact. The *closure* of a topological space $\mathbb{X} \subseteq \mathbb{T}$ is the smallest closed set $\mathrm{Cl}\mathbb{X}$ containing $\mathbb{X}$.

Continuous functions between topological spaces play a significant role to define their similarities. A function $g \colon \mathbb{T}_1 \to \mathbb{T}_2$ from a topological space $\mathbb{T}_1$ to a topological space $\mathbb{T}_2$ is *continuous* if for every open set $U \subseteq \mathbb{T}_2$, the set $g^{-1}(U)$ is open in $\mathbb{T}_1$. Continuous functions are called *maps*.

Homeomorphism

Broadly speaking, two topological spaces are considered the same if one has a correspondence to the other which keeps the connectivity same. For example, the surface of a cube can be deformed into a sphere without any incision or attachment during the process. They have the same topology. A precise definition for this topological equality is given by a map called *homeomorphism*. A homeomorphism between two topological spaces is a map $h : \mathbb{T}_1 \to \mathbb{T}_2$ which is bijective and has a continuous inverse. The explicit requirement of continuous inverse can be dropped if both $\mathbb{T}_1$ and $\mathbb{T}_2$ are compact. This is because any bijective map between two compact spaces must have a continuous inverse. This fact helps us proving homeomorphisms for spaces considered in this book which are mostly compact.

Two topological spaces are *homeomorphic* if there exists a homeomorphism between them. Homeomorphism defines an equivalence relation among topological spaces. That is why two homeomorphic topological spaces are also called *topologically equivalent*. For example, the open k-ball is topologically equivalent to $\mathbb{R}^k$. Figure 1.2 shows some more topological spaces some of which are homeomorphic.

Homotopy

There is another notion of similarity among topological spaces which is weaker than homeomorphism. Intuitively, it relates spaces that can be continuously deformed to one another but may not be homeomorphic. A map $g : \mathbb{T}_1 \to \mathbb{T}_2$ is *homotopic* to another map $h : \mathbb{T}_1 \to \mathbb{T}_2$ if there is a map $H : \mathbb{T}_1 \times [0, 1] \to \mathbb{T}_2$ so that $H(x, 0) = g(x)$ and $H(x, 1) = h(x)$. The map H is called a *homotopy* between g and h.

Two spaces $\mathbb{T}_1$ and $\mathbb{T}_2$ are *homotopy equivalent* if there exist maps $g : \mathbb{T}_1 \to \mathbb{T}_2$ and $h : \mathbb{T}_2 \to \mathbb{T}_1$ so that $h \circ g$ is homotopic to the identity map $\iota_1 : \mathbb{T}_1 \to \mathbb{T}_1$ and $g \circ h$ is homotopic to the identity map $\iota_2 : \mathbb{T}_2 \to \mathbb{T}_2$. If $\mathbb{T}_2 \subset \mathbb{T}_1$, then $\mathbb{T}_2$ is a *deformation retract* of $\mathbb{T}_1$ if there is a map $r : \mathbb{T}_1 \to \mathbb{T}_2$ which is homotopic to ι_1 by a homotopy that fixes points of $\mathbb{T}_2$. In this case $\mathbb{T}_1$ and $\mathbb{T}_2$ are homotopy equivalent. Notice that homotopy relates two maps while homotopy equivalence relates two spaces. A curve and a point are not homotopy equivalent. However, one can define maps from a 1-sphere $\mathbb{S}^1$ to a curve and a point in the plane which have a homotopy.

One difference between homeomorphism and homotopy is that homeomorphic spaces have same dimension while homotopy equivalent spaces need not have same dimension. For example, the 2-ball shown in Figure 1.2(e) is homotopy equivalent to a single point though they are not homeomorphic. Any of

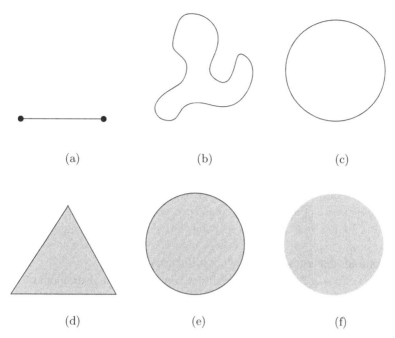

Figure 1.2. (a) 1-ball, (b) and (c) spaces homeomorphic to the 1-sphere, (d) and (e) spaces homeomorphic to the 2-ball, and (f) an open 2-ball which is not homeomorphic to the 2-ball in (e).

the end vertices of the segment in Figure 1.2(a) is a deformation retract of the segment.

Isotopy

Homeomorphism and homotopy together bring a notion of similarity in spaces which, in some sense, is stronger than each one of them individually. For example, consider a standard torus embedded in $\mathbb{R}^3$. One can knot the torus (like a knotted rope) which still embeds in $\mathbb{R}^3$. The standard torus and the knotted one are both homeomorphic. However, there is no continuous deformation of one to the other while maintaining the property of embedding. The reason is that the complement spaces of the two tori are not homotopy equivalent. This requires the notion of *isotopy*.

An *isotopy* between two spaces $\mathbb{T}_1 \subseteq \mathbb{R}^k$ and $\mathbb{T}_2 \subseteq \mathbb{R}^k$ is a map $\xi : \mathbb{T}_1 \times [0, 1] \to \mathbb{R}^k$ such that $\xi(\mathbb{T}_1, 0)$ is the identity of $\mathbb{T}_1$, $\xi(\mathbb{T}_1, 1) = \mathbb{T}_2$ and for each $t \in [0, 1]$, $\xi(\cdot, t)$ is a homeomorphism onto its image. An *ambient isotopy* between $\mathbb{T}_1$ and $\mathbb{T}_2$ is a map $\xi : \mathbb{R}^k \times [0, 1] \to \mathbb{R}^k$ such that $\xi(\cdot, 0)$ is the identity of $\mathbb{R}^k$, $\xi(\mathbb{T}_1, 1) = \mathbb{T}_2$ and for each $t \in [0, 1]$, $\xi(\cdot, t)$ is a homeomorphism of $\mathbb{R}^k$.

Observe that ambient isotopy also implies isotopy. It is also known that two spaces that have an isotopy between them also have an ambient isotopy between them. So, these two notions are equivalent. We will call $\mathbb{T}_1$ and $\mathbb{T}_2$ *isotopic* if they have an isotopy between them.

When we talk about reconstructing surfaces from sample points, we would like to claim that the reconstructed surface is not only homeomorphic to the sampled one but is also isotopic to it.

1.1.2 Manifolds

Curves and surfaces are a particular type of topological space called *manifolds*. A *neighborhood* of a point $x \in \mathbb{T}$ is an open set that contains x. A topological space is a *k-manifold* if each of its points has a neighborhood homeomorphic to the open k-ball which in turn is homeomorphic to $\mathbb{R}^k$. We will consider only k-manifolds that are subspaces of some Euclidean space.

The plane is a 2-manifold though not compact. Another example of a 2-manifold is the sphere $\mathbb{S}^2$ which is compact. Other compact 2-manifolds include *torus* with one through-hole and *double torus* with two through-holes. One can glue g tori together, called *summing g tori*, to form a 2-manifold with g through-holes. The number of through-holes in a 2-manifold is called its *genus*. A remarkable result in topology is that all compact 2-manifolds in $\mathbb{R}^3$ must be either a sphere or a sum of g tori for some $g \geq 1$.

Boundary

Surfaces in $\mathbb{R}^3$ as we know them often have boundaries. These surfaces have the property that each point has a neighborhood homeomorphic to $\mathbb{R}^2$ except the ones on the boundary. These surfaces are 2-manifolds with boundary. In general, a *k-manifold with boundary* has points with neighborhood homeomorphic to either $\mathbb{R}^k$, called the *interior points*, or the halfspace $\mathbb{H}^k$, called the *boundary points*. The boundary of a manifold M, bd M, consists of all boundary points. By this definition a manifold as defined earlier has a boundary, namely an empty one. The interior of M consists of all interior points and is denoted Int M.

It is a nice property of manifolds that if M is a k-manifold with boundary, bd M is a $(k-1)$-manifold unless it is empty. The k-ball $\mathbb{B}^k$ is an example of a k-manifold with boundary where bd $\mathbb{B}^k = \mathbb{S}^{k-1}$ is the $(k-1)$-sphere and its interior Int $\mathbb{B}^k$ is the the open k-ball. On the other hand, bd $\mathbb{S}^k = \emptyset$ and Int $\mathbb{S}^k = \mathbb{S}^k$. In Figure 1.2(a), the segment is a 1-ball where the boundary is a 0-sphere consisting of the two endpoints. In Figure 1.2(e), the 2-ball is a manifold with boundary and its boundary is the circle, a 1-sphere.

Orientability

A 2-manifold with or without boundary can be either *orientable* or *nonorientable*. We will only give an intuitive explanation of this notion. If one travels along any curve on a 2-manifold starting at a point, say p, and considers the oriented normals at each point along the curve, then one gets the same oriented normal at p when he returns to p. All 2-manifolds in $\mathbb{R}^3$ are orientable. However, 2-manifolds in $\mathbb{R}^3$ that have boundaries may not be orientable. For example, the Möbius strip, obtained by gluing the opposite edges of a rectangle with a twist, is nonorientable. The 2-manifolds embedded in four and higher dimensions may not be orientable no matter whether they have boundaries or not.

1.1.3 Complexes

Because of finite storage within a computer, a shape is often approximated with finitely many simple pieces such as vertices, edges, triangles, and tetrahedra. It is convenient and sometimes necessary to borrow the definitions and concepts from combinatorial topology for this representation.

An *affine combination* of a set of points $P = \{p_0, p_1, \ldots, p_n\} \subset \mathbb{R}^k$ is a point $p \in \mathbb{R}^k$ where $p = \Sigma_{i=0}^n \alpha_i p_i$, $\Sigma_i \alpha_i = 1$ and each α_i is a real number. In addition, if each α_i is nonnegative, the point p is a *convex combination*. The *affine hull* of P is the set of points that are an affine combination of P. The *convex hull* Conv P is the set of points that are a convex combination of P. For example, three noncollinear points in the plane have the entire $\mathbb{R}^2$ as the affine hull and the triangle with the three points as vertices as the convex hull.

A set of points is affinely independent if none of them is an affine combination of the others. A *k-polytope* is the convex hull of a set of points which has at least $k + 1$ affinely independent points. The affine hull aff μ of a polytope μ is the affine hull of its vertices.

A *k-simplex* σ is the convex hull of exactly $k + 1$ affinely independent points P. Thus, a vertex is a 0-simplex, an edge is a 1-simplex, a triangle is a 2-simplex, and a tetrahedron is a 3-simplex. A simplex $\sigma' = $ Conv T for a nonempty subset $T \subseteq P$ is called a *face* of σ. Conversely, σ is called a *coface* of σ'. A face $\sigma' \subset \sigma$ is *proper* if the vertices of σ' are a proper subset of σ. In this case σ is a *proper* coface of σ'.

A collection $\mathcal{K}$ of simplices is called a *simplicial complex* if the following conditions hold.

(i) $\sigma' \in \mathcal{K}$ if σ' is a face of any simplex $\sigma \in \mathcal{K}$.
(ii) For any two simplices $\sigma, \sigma' \in \mathcal{K}$, $\sigma \cap \sigma'$ is a face of both unless it is empty.

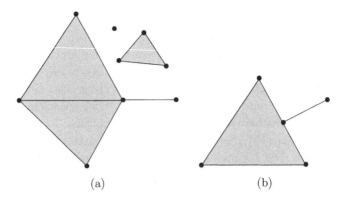

Figure 1.3. (a) A simplicial complex and (b) not a simplicial complex.

The above two conditions imply that the simplices meet nicely. The simplices in Figure 1.3(a) form a simplicial complex whereas the ones in Figure 1.3(b) do not.

Triangulation

A triangulation of a topological space $\mathbb{T}$ is a simplicial complex $\mathcal{K}$ whose underlying point set is $\mathbb{T}$. Figure 1.1(b) shows a triangulation of a 2-manifold with boundary.

Cell Complex

We also use a generalized version of simplicial complexes in this book. The definition of a cell complex is exactly same as that of the simplicial complex with simplices replaced by polytopes. A cell complex is a collection of polytopes and their faces where any two intersecting polytopes meet in a face which is also in the collection. A cell complex is a k-complex if the largest dimension of any polytope in the complex is k. We also say that two elements in a cell complex are *incident* if they intersect.

1.2 Feature Size and Sampling

We will mainly concentrate on smooth curves in $\mathbb{R}^2$ and smooth surfaces in $\mathbb{R}^3$ as the sampled spaces. The notation Σ will be used to denote this generic sampled space throughout this book. We will defer the definition of smoothness until Chapter 2 for curves and Chapter 3 for surfaces. It is sufficient to assume

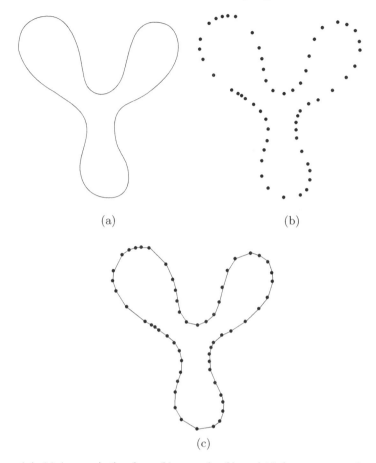

Figure 1.4. (a) A curve in the plane, (b) a sample of it, and (c) the reconstructed curve.

that Σ is a 1-manifold in $\mathbb{R}^2$ and a 2-manifold in $\mathbb{R}^3$ for the definitions and results described in this chapter.

Obviously, it is not possible to extract any meaningful information about Σ if it is not sufficiently sampled. This means features of Σ should be represented with sufficiently many sample points. Figure 1.4 shows a curve in the plane which is reconstructed from a sufficiently dense sample. But, this brings up the question of defining features. We aim for a measure that can tell us how complicated Σ is around each point $x \in \Sigma$. A geometric structure called the *medial axis* turns out to be useful to define such a measure.

Before we define the medial axis, let us fix some notations about distances and balls that will be used throughout the rest of this book. The Euclidean distance between two points $p = (p_1, p_2, \ldots, p_k)$ and $x = (x_1, x_2, \ldots, x_k)$ in $\mathbb{R}^k$ is the length $\| p - x \|$ of the vector $\overrightarrow{xp} = (p - x)$ where

$$\| p - x \| = \left\{ (p_1 - x_1)^2 + (p_2 - x_2)^2 + \cdots + (p_k - x_k)^2 \right\}^{\frac{1}{2}}.$$

Also, we have

$$\begin{aligned}
\| p - x \| &= \{ (p - x)^T (p - x) \}^{\frac{1}{2}} \\
&= \{ p^T p - 2p^T x + x^T x \}^{\frac{1}{2}} \\
&= \{ \| p \|^2 - 2p^T x + \| x \|^2 \}^{\frac{1}{2}}.
\end{aligned}$$

For a set $P \subseteq \mathbb{R}^k$ and a point $x \in \mathbb{R}^k$, let $d(x, P)$ denote the Euclidean distance of x from P; that is,

$$d(x, P) = \inf_{p \in P} \{ \| p - x \| \}.$$

We will also consider distances called *Hausdorff distances* between two sets. For $X, Y \subseteq \mathbb{R}^k$ this distance is given by

$$\max \{ \sup_{x \in X} d(x, Y), \sup_{y \in Y} d(y, X) \}.$$

Roughly speaking, the Hausdorff distance tells how much one set needs to be moved to be identical with the other set.

The set $B_{x,r} = \{ y \mid y \in \mathbb{R}^k, \| y - x \| \le r \}$ is a *ball* with center x and radius r. By definition $B_{x,r}$ and its boundary are homeomorphic to $\mathbb{B}^k$ and $\mathbb{S}^{k-1}$ respectively.

1.2.1 Medial Axis

The medial axis of a curve or a surface Σ is meant to capture the middle of the shape bounded by Σ. There are slightly different definitions of the medial axis in the literature. We adopt one of them and mention the differences with the others.

Assume that Σ is embedded in $\mathbb{R}^k$. A ball $B \subset \mathbb{R}^k$ is *empty* if the interior of B is empty of points from Σ. A ball B is *maximal* if every empty ball that contains B equals B. The *skeleton* Sk_Σ of Σ is the set of centers of all maximal balls. Let M_Σ^o be the set of points in $\mathbb{R}^k$ whose distance to Σ is realized by at least two points in Σ. The closure of M_Σ^o is M_Σ, that is, $M_\Sigma = \text{Cl}\, M_\Sigma^o$. The following inclusions hold:

$$M_\Sigma^o \subseteq Sk_\Sigma \subseteq M_\Sigma.$$

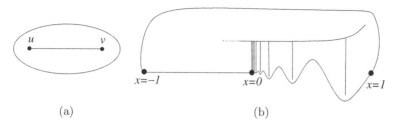

(a)   (b)

Figure 1.5. (a) The two endpoints on the middle segment are not in M_Σ^o, but are in Sk_Σ and M_Σ, and (b) right half of the bottom curve is $y = x^3 \sin \frac{1}{x}$. Sk_Σ does not include the segment in M_Σ at $x = 0$.

There are examples where the inclusions are strict. For example, consider the curve in Figure 1.5(a). The two endpoints u and v are not in M_Σ^o though they are in Sk_Σ. These are the centers of the curvature balls that meet the curve only at a single point. Consider the curve in Figure 1.5(b):

$$y = \begin{cases} 0 & \text{if } -1 \le x \le 0 \\ x^3 \sin \frac{1}{x} & \text{if } 0 < x \le 1. \end{cases}$$

The two endpoints $(-1, 0)$ and $(1, \sin 1)$ can be connected with a smooth curve so that the resulting curve Σ is closed, that is, without any boundary point, see Figure 1.5(b). The set M_Σ^o has infinitely many branches, namely one for each oscillation of the $y = x^3 \sin \frac{1}{x}$ curve. The closure of M_Σ^o has a vertical segment at $x = 0$, which is not part of Sk_Σ and thus Sk_Σ is a strict subset of M_Σ. However, this example is a bit pathological since it is known that a large class of curves and surfaces have $Sk_\Sigma = M_\Sigma$. All curves and surfaces that are at least C^2-smooth[1] have $Sk_\Sigma = M_\Sigma$. The example we considered in Figure 1.5(b) is a C^1-smooth curve which is tangent continuous but not curvature continuous.

In our case we will consider only the class of curves and surfaces where $Sk_\Sigma = M_\Sigma$ and thus define the *medial axis* of Σ as M_Σ. For simplicity we write M in place of M_Σ.

Definition 1.1. *The medial axis M of a curve (surface) $\Sigma \subset \mathbb{R}^k$ is the closure of the set of points in $\mathbb{R}^k$ that have at least two closest points in Σ.*

Each point of M is the center of a ball that meets Σ only tangentially. We call each ball $B_{x,r}$, $x \in M$, a *medial ball* where $r = d(x, \Sigma)$. If a medial ball $B_{x,r}$ is tangent to Σ at $p \in \Sigma$, we say $B_{x,r}$ is a medial ball *at p*.

---

[1] See the definition of C^i-smoothness for curves in Chapter 2 and for surfaces in Chapter 3.

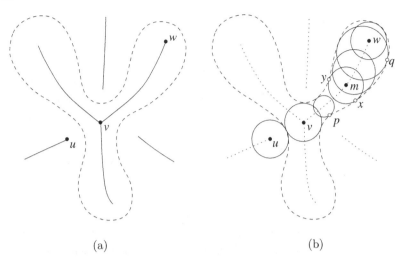

(a)   (b)

Figure 1.6. (a) A subset of the medial axis of the curve in Figure 1.4 and (b) medial ball centered at v touches the curve in three points, whereas the ones with centers u and w touch it in only one point and coincide with the curvature ball.

Figure 1.6(a) shows a subset of the medial axis of a curve. Notice that the medial axis may have a branching point such as v and boundary points such as u and w. Also, the medial axis need not be connected. For example, the part of the medial axis in the region bounded by the curve may be disjoint from the rest (see Figure 1.6(a)). In fact, if Σ is C^2-smooth, the two parts of the medial axis are indeed disjoint. The subset of the medial axis residing in the unbounded component of $\mathbb{R}^2 \setminus \Sigma$ is called the *outer* medial axis. The rest is called the *inner* medial axis.

It follows from the definition that if one grows a ball around a point on the medial axis, it will meet Σ for the first time tangentially in one or more points (see Figure 1.6(b)). Conversely, for a point $x \in \Sigma$ one can start growing a ball keeping it tangent to Σ at x until it hits another point $y \in \Sigma$ or becomes maximally empty. At this moment the ball is medial and the segments joining the center m to x and y are normal to Σ at x and y respectively (see Figure 1.6).

If we move along the medial axis and consider the medial balls as we move, the radius of the medial balls increases or decreases accordingly to maintain the tangency with Σ. At the boundaries it coincides with the radius of the *curvature ball* where all tangent points merge into a single one (see Figure 1.6(b)).

It will be useful for our proofs later to know the following property of balls intersecting the sampled space Σ. The proof of the lemma assumes that Σ

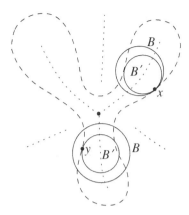

Figure 1.7. The ball B intersecting the upper right lobe is shrunk till it becomes tangent to another point other than x. The new ball B' intersects the medial axis. The ball B intersecting the lower lobe is shrunk radially to the ball B' that is tangent to the curve at y and also intersects the curve in other points. B' can further be shrunk till it meets the curve only tangentially.

is either a smooth curve or a smooth surface whose definitions are given in later chapters. Also, the proof uses some concepts from differential topology (critical point theory) some of which are exposed in Chapter 10. The readers may skip the proof at this point if they are not familiar with these concepts.

We say that a topological space is a k-ball or a k-sphere if it is homeomorphic to $\mathbb{B}^k$ or $\mathbb{S}^k$ respectively.

Lemma 1.1 (Feature Ball). *If a d-ball $B = B_{c,r}$ intersects a k-manifold $\Sigma \subset \mathbb{R}^d$ at more than one point where either (i) $B \cap \Sigma$ is not a k-ball or (ii) $\mathrm{bd}(B \cap \Sigma)$ is not a $(k-1)$-sphere, then a medial axis point is in B.*

Proof. First we show that if B intersects Σ at more than one point and B is tangent to Σ at some point, B contains a medial axis point. Let x be the point of this tangency. Shrink B further keeping it tangent to Σ at x. This means the center of B moves toward x along a normal direction at x. We stop when B meets Σ only tangentially. Observe that, since $B \cap \Sigma \neq x$ to start with, this happens eventually when B is maximally empty. At this moment B becomes a medial ball and its center is a medial axis point which must lie in the original ball B, refer to Figure 1.7.

Now consider when condition (ii) holds. Define a function $h \colon B \cap \Sigma \to \mathbb{R}$ where $h(x)$ is the distance of x from the center c of B. The function h is a scalar function defined over a smooth manifold. At the critical points of h where its gradient vanishes the ball B becomes tangent to Σ when shrunk appropriately. Let m be a point in Σ so that $h(m)$ is a global minimum. If there is more than one such global minimum, the ball B meets Σ only tangentially at more than one point when radially shrunk to a radius of $h(m)$. Then, B becomes a medial ball which implies that the original B contains a medial axis point, namely its center. So, assume that there is only global minimum m of h.

We claim that the function h has a critical point p in $\text{Int}(B \cap \Sigma)$ other than m where B becomes tangent to Σ. If not, as we shrink B centrally the level set $\text{bd}(B \cap \Sigma)$ does not change topology until it reaches the minimum m when it vanishes. This follows from the Morse theory of smooth functions over smooth manifolds.[2] Since m is a minimum, there is a small enough $\delta > 0$ so that $B_{c,h(m)+\delta} \cap \Sigma$ is a k-ball. The boundary of this k-ball given by $(\text{bd } B_{c,h(m)+\delta}) \cap \Sigma$ should be a $(k-1)$-sphere. This contradicts the fact that $\text{bd}(B \cap \Sigma)$ is not a $(k-1)$-sphere and remains that way till the end. Therefore, there is a critical point, say $y \neq m$ of h in $\text{Int}(B \cap \Sigma)$. At this point y, the ball $B_{c,\|y-c\|}$ becomes tangent to Σ, see also Figure 1.7. Now we can apply our previous argument to claim that B contains a medial axis point.

Next, consider when condition (i) holds. If condition (ii) also holds, we have the previous argument. So, assume that $\text{bd}(B \cap \Sigma)$ is a $(k-1)$-sphere and $B \cap \Sigma$ is not a k-ball. Again, we claim that the function h as defined earlier has a critical point other than m. If not, consider the subset of Σ swept by B while shrinking it till it meets Σ only at m. This subset is homeomorphic to a space which is formed by taking the product of $\mathbb{S}^{k-1}$ with the closed unit interval I in $\mathbb{R}$ and then collapsing one of its boundary to a single point, that is, the quotient space $(\mathbb{S}^{k-1} \times I)/(\mathbb{S}^{k-1} \times \{0\})$. This space is a k-ball which contradicts the fact that $B \cap \Sigma$ is not a k-ball to begin with. Therefore, as B is continually shrunk, it becomes tangent to Σ at a point $y \neq m$. Apply the previous argument to claim that B has a medial axis point.   ∎

Figure 1.8 illustrates the different cases of Feature Ball Lemma in $\mathbb{R}^2$.

1.2.2 Local Feature Size

The medial axis M with the distance to Σ at each point $m \in M$ captures the shape of Σ. In fact, Σ is the boundary of the union of all medial balls centering points of the inner (or outer) medial axis. So, as a first attempt to capture local feature size one may define the following two functions on Σ.

---

[2] See Milnor (1963) for an exposition on Morse theory.

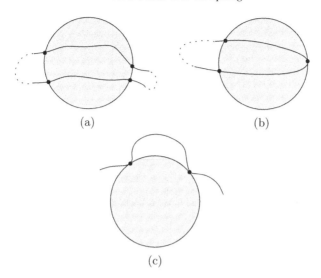

(a)   (b)

(c)

Figure 1.8. (a) $B \cap \Sigma$ is not a 1-ball, (b) $B \cap \Sigma$ is a 1-ball, but bd $B \cap \Sigma$ is not a 0-sphere, and (c) bd $B \cap \Sigma$ is a 0-sphere, but $B \cap \Sigma$ is not a 1-ball.

$\rho_i, \rho_o : \Sigma \to \mathbb{R}$ where $\rho_i(x)$, $\rho_o(x)$ are the radii of the inner and outer medial balls respectively both of which are tangent to Σ at x.

The functions ρ_i and ρ_o are continuous for a large class of curves and surfaces. However, we need a stronger form of continuity on the local feature size function to carry out the proofs. This property, called the *Lipschitz property*, stipulates that the difference in the function values at two points is bounded by a constant times the distance between the points. Keeping this in mind we define the following.

Definition 1.2. *The local feature size at a point $x \in \Sigma$ is the value of a function*

$$f : \Sigma \to \mathbb{R} \text{ where } f(x) = d(x, M).$$

In words, $f(x)$ is the distance of $x \in \Sigma$ to the medial axis M.

Figure 1.9 illustrates how the local feature size can vary over a shape. As one can observe, the local feature sizes at the leg and tail are much smaller than the local feature sizes at the middle in accordance with our intuitive notion of features. For example, $f(b)$ is much smaller than $f(a)$. Local feature size can be determined either by the inner or outer medial axis. For example, $f(c)$ is determined by the outer medial axis whereas $f(d)$ is determined by the inner one.

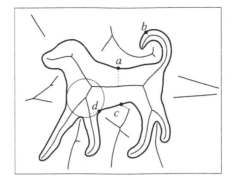

Figure 1.9. Local feature sizes $f(a)$, $f(b)$, $f(c)$, and $f(d)$ are the lengths of the corresponding dotted line segments.

It follows from the definitions that $f(x) \leq \min\{\rho_i(x), \rho_o(x)\}$. In Figure 1.9, $f(d)$ is much smaller than the radius of the drawn medial ball at d. Lipschitz property of the local feature size function f follows easily from the definition.

Lemma 1.2 (Lipschitz Continuity). $f(x) \leq f(y) + \|x - y\|$ *for any two points x and y in Σ.*

Proof. Let m be a point on the medial axis so that $f(y) = \|y - m\|$. By triangular inequality,

$$\|x - m\| \leq \|y - m\| + \|x - y\|, \quad \text{and}$$
$$f(x) \leq \|x - m\| \leq f(y) + \|x - y\|.$$

∎

1.2.3 Sampling

A *sample* P of Σ is a set of points from Σ. Once we have quantized the feature size, we would require the sample respect the features, that is, we require more sample points where the local feature size is small compared to the regions where it is not.

Definition 1.3. *A sample P of Σ is a ε-sample if each point $x \in \Sigma$ has a sample point $p \in P$ so that $\|x - p\| \leq \varepsilon f(x)$.*

The value of ε has to be smaller than 1 to have a dense sample. In fact, practical experiments suggest that $\varepsilon < 0.4$ constitutes a dense sample for reconstructing

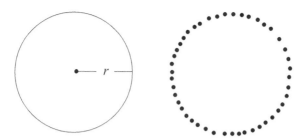

Figure 1.10. Local feature size at any point on the circle is equal to the radius r. Each point on the circle has a sample point within $0.2r$ distance.

Σ from P. A ε-sample is also a ε'-sample for any $\varepsilon' > \varepsilon$. The definition of ε-sample allows a sample to be arbitrarily dense anywhere on Σ. It only puts a lower bound on the density. Figure 1.10 illustrates a sample of a circle which is a 0.2-sample. By definition, it is also a 0.3-sample of the same.

A useful application of the Lipschitz Continuity Lemma 1.2 is that the distance between two points expressed in terms of the local feature size of one can be expressed in terms of that of the other.

Lemma 1.3 (Feature Translation). *For any two points x, y in Σ with $\|x - y\| \le \varepsilon f(x)$ and $\varepsilon < 1$ we have*

(i) $f(x) \le \frac{1}{1-\varepsilon} f(y)$ and
(ii) $\|x - y\| \le \frac{\varepsilon}{1-\varepsilon} f(y)$.

Proof. We have

$$f(x) \le f(y) + \|x - y\|$$
$$\text{or, } f(x) \le f(y) + \varepsilon f(x).$$

For $\varepsilon < 1$ the above inequality gives

$$f(x) \le \frac{1}{1 - \varepsilon} f(y) \text{ proving (i).}$$

Plug the above inequality in $\|x - y\| \le \varepsilon f(x)$ to obtain (ii). ∎

Uniform Sampling

The definition of ε-sample allows nonuniform sampling over Σ. A *globally uniform* sampling is more restrictive. It means that the sample is equally dense everywhere. Local feature size does not play a role in such sampling. There could be various definitions of globally uniform samples. We will say a sample

$P \subset \Sigma$ is *globally δ-uniform* if any point $x \in \Sigma$ has a point in P within $\delta >$ 0 distance. In between globally uniform and nonuniform samplings, there is another one called the *locally uniform sampling*. This sampling respects feature sizes and is uniform only locally. We say $P \subset \Sigma$ is *locally (ε, δ)-uniform* for $\delta > 1 > \varepsilon > 0$ if each point $x \in \Sigma$ has a point in P within $\varepsilon f(x)$ distance and no point $p \in P$ has another point $q \in P$ within $\frac{\varepsilon}{\delta} f(p)$ distance. This definition does not allow two points to be arbitrarily close which may become a severe restriction for sampling in practice. So, there is an alternate definition of local uniformity. A sample P is *locally (ε, κ)-uniform* for some $\varepsilon > 0$ and $\kappa \geq 1$ if each point $x \in \Sigma$ has at least one and no more than κ points within $\varepsilon f(x)$ distance.

$$\tilde{O}(\varepsilon) \; notation$$

Our analysis for different algorithms obviously involve the sampling parameter ε. To ease these analyses, sometimes we resort to $\tilde{O}$ notation which provides the asymptotic dependences on ε. A value is $\tilde{O}(\varepsilon)$ if there exist two constants $\varepsilon_0 > 0$ and $c > 0$ so that the value is less than $c\varepsilon$ for any positive $\varepsilon \leq \varepsilon_0$. Notice that $\tilde{O}$ notation is slightly different from the well-known big-O notation since the latter would require ε greater than or equal to ε_0.

1.3 Voronoi Diagram and Delaunay Triangulation

Voronoi diagrams and Delaunay triangulations are important geometric data structures that are built on the notion of "nearness." Many differential properties of curves and surfaces are defined on local neighborhoods. Voronoi diagrams and their duals, Delaunay triangulations, provide a tool to approximate these neighborhoods in the discrete domain. They are defined for a point set in any Euclidean space. We define them in two dimensions and mention the extensions to three dimensions since the curve and surface reconstruction algorithms as dealt in this book are concerned with these two Euclidean spaces. Before the definitions we state a nondegeneracy condition for the point set P defining the Voronoi and Delaunay diagrams. This nondegeneracy condition not only makes the definitions less complicated but also makes the algorithms avoid special cases.

Definition 1.4. *A point set $P \subset \mathbb{R}^k$ is nondegenerate if (i) the affine hull of any ℓ points from P with $1 \leq \ell \leq k$ is homeomorphic to $\mathbb{R}^{\ell-1}$ and (ii) no $k+2$ points are cospherical.*

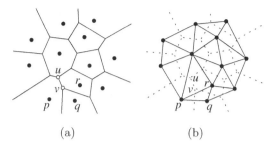

(a)   (b)

Figure 1.11. (a) The Voronoi diagram and (b) the Delaunay triangulation of a point set in the plane.

1.3.1 Two Dimensions

Let P be a set of nondegenerate points in the plane $\mathbb{R}^2$.

Voronoi Diagrams

The Voronoi cell V_p for each point $p \in P$ is given as

$$V_p = \{x \in \mathbb{R}^2 \mid d(x, P) = \|x - p\|\}.$$

In words, V_p is the set of all points in the plane that have no other point in P closer to it than p. For any two points p, q the set of points closer to p than q are demarked by the perpendicular bisector of the segment pq. This means the Voronoi cell V_p is the intersection of the closed half-planes determined by the perpendicular bisectors between p and each other point $q \in P$. An implication of this observation is that each Voronoi cell is a convex polygon since the intersection of convex sets remains convex.

Voronoi cells have *Voronoi faces* of different dimensions. A Voronoi face of dimension k is the intersection of $3 - k$ Voronoi cells. This means a k-dimensional Voronoi face for $k \leq 2$ is the set of all points that are equidistant from $3 - k$ points in P. A zero-dimensional Voronoi face, called *Voronoi vertex* is equidistant from three points in P, whereas a one-dimensional Voronoi face, called *Voronoi edge* contains points that are equidistant from two points in P. A Voronoi cell is a two-dimensional Voronoi face.

Definition 1.5. *The Voronoi diagram* Vor P *of P is the cell complex formed by Voronoi faces.*

Figure 1.11(a) shows a Voronoi diagram of a point set in the plane where u and v are two Voronoi vertices and uv is a Voronoi edge.

Some of the Voronoi cells may be unbounded with unbounded edges. It is a straightforward consequence of the definition that a Voronoi cell V_p is unbounded if and only if p is on the boundary of the convex hull of P. In Figure 1.11(a), V_p and V_q are unbounded and p and q are on the convex hull boundary.

Delaunay Triangulations

There is a *dual* structure to the Voronoi diagram Vor P, called the *Delaunay triangulation*.

Definition 1.6. *The Delaunay triangulation of P is a simplicial complex*

$$\text{Del } P = \{\sigma = \text{Conv } T \mid \bigcap_{p \in T \subseteq P} V_p \neq \emptyset\}.$$

In words, $k + 1$ points in P form a Delaunay k-simplex in Del P if their Voronoi cells have nonempty intersection. We know that $k + 1$ Voronoi cells meet in a $(2 - k)$-dimensional Voronoi face. So, each k-simplex in Del P is dual to a $(2 - k)$-dimensional Voronoi face. Thus, each Delaunay triangle pqr in Del P is dual to a Voronoi vertex where V_p, V_q, and V_r meet, each Delaunay edge pq is dual to a Voronoi edge shared by Voronoi cells V_p and V_q, and each vertex p is dual to its corresponding Voronoi cell V_p. In Figure 1.11(b), the Delaunay triangle pqr is dual to the Voronoi vertex v and the Delaunay edge pr is dual to the Voronoi edge uv. In general, when μ is a dual Voronoi face of a Delaunay simplex σ we say $\mu = \text{dual } \sigma$ and conversely $\sigma = \text{dual } \mu$.

A *circumscribing ball* of a simplex σ is a ball whose boundary contains the vertices of the simplex. The smallest circumscribing ball of σ is called its *diametric* ball. A triangle in the plane has only one circumscribing ball, namely the diametric one. However, an edge has infinitely many circumscribing balls among which the diametric one is unique, namely the one with the center on the edge.

A dual Voronoi vertex of a Delaunay triangle is equidistant from its three vertices. This means that the center of the circumscribing ball of a Delaunay triangle is the dual Voronoi vertex. It implies that no point from P can lie in the interior of the circumscribing ball of a Delaunay triangle. These balls are called *Delaunay*. A ball is *empty* if its interior does not contain any point from P. Clearly, the Delaunay balls are *empty*. The converse also holds.

Property 1.1 (Triangle Emptiness). *A triangle is in the Delaunay triangulation if and only if its circumscribing ball is empty.*

The triangle emptiness property of Delaunay triangles also implies a similar emptiness for Delaunay edges. Clearly, each Delaunay edge has an empty circumscribing ball passing through its endpoints. It turns out that the converse is also true, that is, any edge pq with an empty circumscribing ball must also be in the Delaunay triangulation. To see this, grow the empty ball of pq always keeping p, q on its boundary. If it never meets any other point from P, the edge pq is on the boundary of Conv P and is in the Delaunay triangulation since V_p and V_q has to share an edge extending to infinity. Otherwise, when it meets a third point, say r from P, we have an empty circumscribing ball passing through p, q, and r. By the triangle emptiness property pqr must be in the Delaunay triangulation and hence the edge pq.

Property 1.2 (Edge Emptiness). *An edge is in the Delaunay triangulation if and only if the edge has an empty circumscribing ball.*

The Delaunay triangulation form a planar graph since no two Delaunay edges intersect in their interiors. It follows from the property of planar graphs that the number of Delaunay edges is at most $3n - 6$ for a set of n points. The number of Delaunay triangles is at most $2n - 4$. This means that the dual Voronoi diagram also has at most $3n - 6$ Voronoi edges and $2n - 4$ Voronoi vertices. The Voronoi diagram and the Delaunay triangulation of a set of n points in the plane can be computed in $O(n \log n)$ time and $O(n)$ space.

Restricted Voronoi Diagrams

When the input point set P is a sample of a curve or a surface Σ, the Voronoi diagram Vor P imposes a structure on Σ. It turns out that this diagram plays an important role in reconstructing Σ from P. Formally, a restricted Voronoi cell $V_p|_\Sigma$ is defined as the intersection of the Voronoi cell V_p in Vor P with Σ, that is,

$$V_p|_\Sigma = V_p \cap \Sigma \quad \text{where } p \in P.$$

Similar to the Voronoi faces, we can define *restricted Voronoi faces* as the intersection of the restricted Voronoi cells. They can also be viewed as the intersection of Voronoi faces with Σ. In Figure 1.12(a), the white circles represent restricted Voronoi faces of dimension zero. The curve segments between them are restricted Voronoi faces of dimension one which are restricted Voronoi cells in this case. Notice that the restricted Voronoi cell $V_p|_\Sigma$ in the figure consists of two curve segments whereas $V_r|_\Sigma$ consists of a single curve segment.

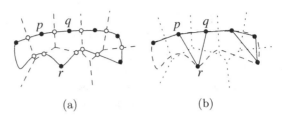

(a)   (b)

Figure 1.12. (a) Restricted Voronoi diagram for a point set on a curve and (b) the corresponding restricted Delaunay triangulation.

Definition 1.7. *The restricted Voronoi diagram* Vor $P|_\Sigma$ *of P with respect to* Σ *is the collection of all restricted Voronoi faces.*

Restricted Delaunay Triangulations.

As with Voronoi diagrams we can define a simplicial complex dual to a restricted Voronoi diagram Vor $P|_\Sigma$.

Definition 1.8. *The restricted Delaunay triangulation of P with respect to* Σ *is a simplicial complex* Del $P|_\Sigma$ *where a k-simplex with k + 1 vertices, $R \subseteq P$, is in this complex if and only if*

$$\bigcap V_p|_\Sigma \neq \emptyset, \ for \ p \in R.$$

In words, a simplex in Del P is in Del $P|_\Sigma$ if and only if its dual Voronoi face intersects Σ. The simplicial complex Del $P|_\Sigma$ is called the *restricted Delaunay triangulation* of P with respect to Σ. Figure 1.12(b) shows the restricted Delaunay triangulation for the restricted Voronoi diagram in (a). The vertex p is connected to q and r in the restricted Delaunay triangulation since $V_p|_\Sigma$ meets both $V_q|_\Sigma$ and $V_r|_\Sigma$. However, the triangle pqr is not in the triangulation since $V_p|_\Sigma$, $V_q|_\Sigma$ and $V_r|_\Sigma$ do not meet at a point.

1.3.2 Three Dimensions

We chose the plane to explain the concepts of the Voronoi diagrams and the Delaunay triangulations in the previous subsection. However, these concepts extend to arbitrary dimensions. We will mention these extensions for three dimensions which will be important for later expositions.

Voronoi cells of a point set P in $\mathbb{R}^3$ are three-dimensional convex polytopes some of which are unbounded. There are four types of Voronoi faces: Voronoi vertices, Voronoi edges, Voronoi facets, and Voronoi cells in increasing order of dimension starting with zero and ending with three. Four Voronoi cells meet

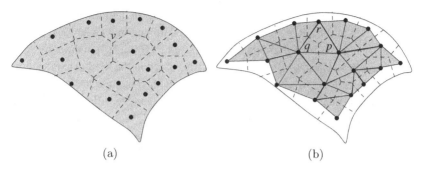

(a)   (b)

Figure 1.13. (a) The restricted Voronoi diagram and (b) the restricted Delaunay triangulation for a sample on a surface.

at a Voronoi vertex which is equidistant from four points in P. Three Voronoi cells meet at a Voronoi edge, and two Voronoi cells meet at a Voronoi facet.

The Delaunay triangulation of P contains four types of simplices dual to each of the four types of Voronoi faces. The vertices are dual to the Voronoi cells, the Delaunay edges are dual to the Voronoi facets, the Delaunay triangles are dual to the Voronoi edges, and the Delaunay tetrahedra are dual to the Voronoi vertices. The circumscribing ball of each tetrahedron is empty. Conversely, any tetrahedron with empty circumscribing ball is in the Delaunay triangulation. Further, each Delaunay triangle and edge has an empty circumscribing ball. Conversely, an edge or a triangle belongs to the Delaunay triangulation if there exists an empty ball circumscribing it.

The number of edges, triangles, and tetrahedra in the Delaunay triangulation of a set of n points in three dimensions can be $O(n^2)$ in the worst case. By duality the Voronoi diagram can also have $O(n^2)$ Voronoi faces. Both of the diagrams can be computed in $O(n^2)$ time and space.

We can define the restricted Voronoi diagram and its dual restricted Delaunay triangulation for a point sample on a surface in $\mathbb{R}^3$ in the same way as we did for a curve in $\mathbb{R}^2$. Figure 1.13 shows the restricted Voronoi diagram and its dual restricted Delaunay triangulation for a set of points on a surface. The triangle pqr is in the restricted Delaunay triangulation since $V_p|_\Sigma$, $V_q|_\Sigma$, and $V_r|_\Sigma$ meet at a common point v.

1.4 Notes and Exercises

The books by Munkres [71] and Weeks [81] are standard books on point set topology where the definitions of topological spaces and maps can be found in details. Munkres [72] and Stillwell [79] are good sources for algebraic and combinatorial topology where simplicial complexes and their use in triangulation of topological spaces are described. A number of useful definitions in topology are collected in the survey paper by Dey, Edelsbrunner, and Guha [29].

The concept of the medial axis was introduced by Blum [14] in the context of image analysis. Variants of this concept as discussed in the Medial axis section appeared later. Choi, Choi, and Moon [25] established that the medial axis of a piecewise real analytic curve is a finite graph. Chazal and Soufflet [21] extended this result to semianalytic curves. See Matheron [66], Wolter [82], and Chazal and Lieutier [20] for more expositions on the medial axis.

The concept of local feature size was first used by Ruppert [76] for meshing a polygonal domain with guaranteed qualities. His definition was somewhat different from the one described in this chapter. The local feature size as defined in this chapter and used throughout the book appeared in Amenta, Bern, and Eppstein [5].

The Voronoi diagrams and the Delaunay triangulations are well-known data structures named after Georges Voronoi [80] and Boris Delaunay [28] respectively. They are frequently used in various computational problems. A good source for the materials on the Delaunay triangulation is Edelsbrunner [43]. Voronoi diagrams are discussed in great detail in Okabe, Boots, and Sugihara [74]. Various references to the algorithms for computing Voronoi diagrams and Delaunay triangulations can be found in the *Handbook of Discrete and Computational Geometry* [50]. The concepts of the restricted Voronoi and Delaunay diagrams were used by Chew [24] for meshing surfaces. Edelsbrunner and Shah [48] formalized the notion.

Exercises

1. Construct an explicit deformation retraction of $\mathbb{R}^k \setminus \{0\}$ onto $\mathbb{S}^{k-1}$. Also, show $\mathbb{R}^k \cup \{\infty\}$ is homeomorphic to $\mathbb{S}^k$.

2. Deduce that homeomorphism is an equivalence relation. Show that the relation of homotopy among maps is an equivalence relation.

3. Construct a triangulation of $\mathbb{S}^2$ and verify that $v - e + f = 2$ where v is the number of vertices, e is the number of edges, and f is the number of triangles. Prove that the number $v - e + f$ (Euler characteristic) is always 2 for any triangulation of $\mathbb{S}^2$.

4. Let p be a vertex in Del P in three dimensions. Show that a point $x \in V_p$ if and only if $\|p - x\| \leq \|q - x\|$ for each vertex q where pq is a Delaunay edge.

5. Show that for any Delaunay simplex σ and its dual Voronoi face $\mu = \text{dual}\,\sigma$, the affine hulls aff μ and aff σ intersect orthogonally.

6. An edge e in a triangulation $T(P)$ of a point set $P \subset \mathbb{R}^2$ is called *locally Delaunay* if e is a convex hull edge or the circumscribing ball of one triangle incident to e does not contain the other triangle incident to e completely inside. Show that $T(P) = \text{Del } P$ if and only if each edge of $T(P)$ is locally Delaunay.

7. Given a point set $P \subset \mathbb{R}^2$, an edge connecting two points p, q in P is called a nearest neighbor edge if no point in P is closer to q than p is. Show that pq is a Delaunay edge.

8. Given a point set $P \subset \mathbb{R}^2$, an edge connecting two points in P is called *Gabriel* if its diametric ball is empty. The Gabriel graph for P is the graph induced by all Gabriel edges. Give an $O(n \log n)$ algorithm to compute the Gabriel graph for P where P has n points.

9. Let pq be a Delaunay edge in Del P for a point set $P \subset \mathbb{R}^3$. Show that if pq does not intersect its dual Voronoi facet $g = \text{dual } pq$, the line of pq does not intersect g either.

10. For $\alpha > 0$, a function $f : \Sigma \to \mathbb{R}$ is called α-Lipschitz if $f(x) \leq f(y) + \alpha \|x - y\|$ for any two points x, y in Σ. Given an arbitrary function $f : \Sigma \to \mathbb{R}$, consider the functions

$$f_m(x) = \min_{p \in \Sigma} \{ f(p) + \alpha \|x - p\| \},$$
$$f_M(x) = \max_{p \in \Sigma} \{ f(p) - \alpha \|x - p\| \}.$$

Show that both f_m and f_M are α-Lipschitz.

11. Consider the functions ρ_i and ρ_o as in Section 1.2.2. Show that these functions may be continuous but not 1-Lipschitz.

2

Curve Reconstruction

The simplest class of manifolds that pose nontrivial reconstruction problems are curves in the plane. We will describe two algorithms for curve reconstruction, CRUST and NN-CRUST in this chapter. First, we will develop some general results that will be applied to prove the correctness of the both algorithms.

A single curve in the plane is defined by a map $\xi : [0, 1] \to \mathbb{R}^2$ where $[0, 1]$ is the closed interval between 0 and 1 on the real line. The function ξ is one-to-one everywhere except at the endpoints where $\xi(0) = \xi(1)$. The curve is C^1-*smooth* if ξ has a continuous nonzero first derivative in the interior of $[0, 1]$ and the right derivative at 0 is same as the left derivative at 1 both being nonzero. If ξ has continuous ith derivatives, $i \geq 1$, at each point as well, the curve is called C^i-smooth. When we refer to a curve Σ in the plane, we actually mean the image of one or more such maps. By definition Σ does not self-intersect though it can have multiple components each of which is a closed curve, that is, without any endpoint.

For a finite sample to be a ε-sample for some $\varepsilon > 0$, it is essential that the local feature size f is strictly positive everywhere. While this is true for all C^2-smooth curves, there are C^1-smooth curves with zero local feature size at some point. For example, consider the curve

$$y = |x|^{\frac{4}{3}} \quad \text{for} -1 \leq x \leq 1$$

and join the endpoints $(-1, 1)$ and $(1, 1)$ with a smooth curve. This curve is C^1-smooth at $(0, 0)$ and its medial axis passes through the point $(0, 0)$. Therefore, the local feature size is zero at $(0, 0)$.

We learnt that C^1-smooth curves do not necessarily have positive minimum local feature size while C^2-smooth curves do. Are there curves in between C^1- and C^2-smooth classes with positive local feature size everywhere? Indeed, there is a class called $C^{1,1}$-smooth curves with this property. These curves are C^1-smooth and have normals satisfying a Lipschitz continuity property. To

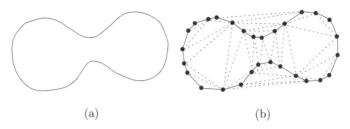

(a)   (b)

Figure 2.1. (a) A smooth curve and (b) its reconstruction from a sample shown with solid edges.

avoid confusions about narrowing down the class, we explicitly assume that Σ has strictly positive local feature size everywhere.

For any two points x, y in Σ define two curve segments, $\gamma(x, y)$ and $\gamma'(x, y)$ between x and y, that is, $\Sigma = \gamma(x, y) \cup \gamma'(x, y)$ and $\gamma(x, y) \cap \gamma'(x, y) = \{x, y\}$. Let P be a set of sample points from Σ. We say a curve segment is *empty* if its interior does not contain any point from P. An edge connecting two sample points, say p and q, is called *correct* if either $\gamma(p, q)$ or $\gamma'(p, q)$ is empty. In other words, p and q are two consecutive sample points on Σ. Any edge that is not correct is called *incorrect*. The goal of *curve reconstruction* is to compute a piecewise linear curve consisting of all and only correct edges. In Figure 2.1(b), all solid edges are correct and dotted edges are incorrect.

We will describe CRUST in Subsection 2.2 and NN-CRUST in Subsection 2.3. Some general results are presented in Subsection 2.1 which are used later to claim the correctness of the algorithms.

2.1 Consequences of ε-Sampling

Let P be a ε-sample of Σ. For sufficiently small $\varepsilon > 0$, several properties can be proved.

Lemma 2.1 (Empty Segment). *Let $p \in P$ and $x \in \Sigma$ so that $\gamma(p, x)$ is empty. Let the perpendicular bisector of px intersect the empty segment $\gamma(p, x)$ at z. If $\varepsilon < 1$ then*

(i) the ball $B_{z, \|p-z\|}$ intersects Σ only in $\gamma(p, x)$,
(ii) the ball $B_{z, \|p-z\|}$ is empty, and
(iii) $\|p - z\| \le \varepsilon f(z)$.

Proof. Let $B = B_{z, \|p-z\|}$ and $\gamma = \gamma(p, x)$. Suppose $B \cap \Sigma \ne \gamma$ (see Figure 2.2). Shrink B continuously centering z until Int $B \cap \Sigma$ becomes a

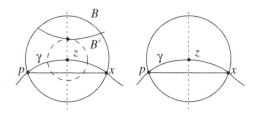

Figure 2.2. Illustration for the Empty Segment Lemma 2.1. The picture on the left is impossible while the one on the right is correct.

1-ball and it is tangent to some other point of Σ. Let B' be the shrunken ball. The ball B' exists as $B_{z,\delta} \cap \Sigma$ is a 1-ball for some sufficiently small $\delta > 0$ and $B \cap \Sigma$ is not a 1-ball. The ball B' is empty of any sample point as Int B' intersects Σ only in a subset of γ which is empty. But, since $B' \cap \Sigma$ is not a 1-ball, it contains a medial axis point by the Feature Ball Lemma 1.1. Thus, its radius is at least $f(z)$. The point z does not have any sample point within $f(z)$ distance as B' is empty. This contradicts that P is a ε-sample of Σ where $\varepsilon < 1$. Therefore, B intersects Σ only in $\gamma(p, x)$ completing the proof of (i).

Property (ii) follows immediately as $\gamma(p, x)$ is empty and B intersects Σ only in $\gamma(p, x)$. By ε-sampling, the nearest sample point p to z is within $\varepsilon f(z)$ distance establishing (iii). ∎

The Empty Segment Lemma 2.1 implies that points in an empty segment are close and any correct edge is Delaunay when ε is small.

Lemma 2.2 (Small Segment). *Let x, y be any two points so that $\gamma(x, y)$ is empty. Then $\|x - y\| \leq \frac{2\varepsilon}{1-\epsilon} f(x)$ for $\varepsilon < 1$.*

Proof. Since $\gamma(x, y)$ is empty, it is a subset of an empty segment $\gamma(p, q)$ for two sample points p and q. Let z be the point where the perpendicular bisector of pq meets $\gamma(p, q)$. Consider the ball $B = B_{z,\|p-z\|}$. Since $\gamma(p, q)$ is empty, the ball B has the properties stated in the Empty Segment Lemma 2.1. Since B contains $\gamma(p, q)$, both x and y are in B. Therefore, $\|z - x\| \leq \varepsilon f(z)$ by the ε-sampling condition. By the Feature Translation Lemma 1.3 $f(z) \leq \frac{f(x)}{1-\varepsilon}$. We have

$$\|x - y\| \leq 2\|p - z\| \leq 2\varepsilon f(z)$$
$$\leq \frac{2\varepsilon}{1 - \varepsilon} f(x).$$

∎

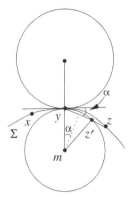

Figure 2.3. Illustration for the Segment Angle Lemma 2.4.

Lemma 2.3 (Small Edge). *Let pq be a correct edge. For $\varepsilon < 1$,*

(i) $\| p - q \| \leq \frac{2\varepsilon}{1-\varepsilon} f(p)$ *and*
(ii) pq is Delaunay.

Proof. Any correct edge pq has the property that either $\gamma(q, p)$ or $\gamma(p, q)$ is empty. Therefore, (i) is immediate from the Small Segment Lemma 2.2. It follows from property (ii) of the Empty Segment Lemma 2.1 that there exists an empty ball circumscribing the correct edge pq proving (ii). ∎

If three points x, y, and z on Σ are sufficiently close, the segments xy and yz make small angles with the tangent at y. This implies that the angle $\angle xyz$ is close to π. As a corollary two adjacent correct edges make an angle close to π.

Lemma 2.4 (Segment Angle). *Let x, y, and z be three points on Σ with $\| x - y \|$ and $\| y - z \|$ being no more than $\frac{2\varepsilon}{1-\varepsilon} f(y)$ for $\varepsilon < \frac{1}{2}$. Let α be the angle between the tangent to Σ at y and the line segment yz. One has*

(i) $\alpha \leq \arcsin \frac{\varepsilon}{1-\varepsilon}$ *and*
(ii) $\angle xyz \geq \pi - 2 \arcsin \frac{\varepsilon}{1-\varepsilon}$.

Proof. Consider the two medial balls sandwiching Σ at y as in Figure 2.3. Let α be the angle between the tangent at y and the segment yz. Since z lies outside the medial balls, the length of the segment yz' is no more than that of yz where z' is the point of intersection of yz and a medial ball as shown.

In that case,

$$\alpha \leq \arcsin\left(\left(\frac{\|y - z'\|}{2}\right) / (\|m - y\|)\right)$$

$$= \arcsin\left(\left(\frac{\|y - z\|}{2}\right) / (\|m - y\|)\right).$$

It is given that $\|y - z\| \leq \frac{2\varepsilon}{1-\varepsilon} f(y)$ where $\varepsilon < \frac{1}{2}$. Also, $\|m - y\| \geq f(y)$ since m is a medial axis point. Plugging in these values we get

$$\alpha \leq \arcsin \frac{\varepsilon}{1 - \varepsilon}$$

completing the proof of (i). We have

$$\angle myz \geq \frac{\pi}{2} - \alpha$$

$$\angle myz \geq \frac{\pi}{2} - \arcsin \frac{\varepsilon}{1 - \varepsilon}.$$

Similarly, it can be shown that $\angle myx \geq \frac{\pi}{2} - \arcsin \frac{\varepsilon}{1-\varepsilon}$. Property (ii) follows immediately as $\angle xyz = \angle myz + \angle myx$. ∎

Since any correct edge pq has a length no more than $\frac{2\varepsilon}{1-\varepsilon} f(p)$ for $\varepsilon < 1$ (Small Edge Lemma 2.3), we have the following result.

Lemma 2.5 (Edge Angle). *Let pq and pr be two correct edges incident to p. We have $\angle qpr \geq \pi - 2 \arcsin \frac{\varepsilon}{1-\varepsilon}$ for $\varepsilon < \frac{1}{2}$.*

2.2 Crust

We have already seen that all correct edges connecting consecutive sample points in a ε-sample are present in the Delaunay triangulation of the sample points if $\varepsilon < 1$. The main algorithmic challenge is to distinguish these edges from the rest of the Delaunay edges. The CRUST algorithm achieves this by observing some properties of the Voronoi vertices.

2.2.1 Algorithm

Consider Figure 2.4. The left picture shows the Voronoi diagram clipped within a box for a dense sample of a curve. The picture on the right shows the Voronoi vertices separately. A careful observation reveals that the Voronoi vertices lie near the medial axis of the curve (Exercise 8). The CRUST algorithm exploits this fact. All empty balls circumscribing incorrect edges in Del P cross the medial axis and hence contain Voronoi vertices inside. Therefore, they cannot appear

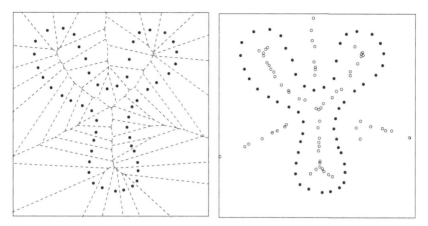

Figure 2.4. Voronoi vertices approximate the medial axis of a curve in the plane. The Voronoi vertices are shown with hollow circles in the right picture.

in the Delaunay triangulation of $P \cup V$ where V is the set of Voronoi vertices in Vor P. On the other hand, all correct edges still survive in Del $(P \cup V)$. So, the algorithm first computes Vor P and then computes the Delaunay triangulation of $P \cup V$ where V is the set of Voronoi vertices of Vor P. The Delaunay edges of Del $(P \cup V)$ that connect two points in P are output. It is proved that an edge is output if and only if it is correct.

CRUST(P)

```
1  compute Vor P;
2  let V be the Voronoi vertices of Vor P;
3  compute Del (P ∪ V);
4  E := ∅;
5  for each edge pq ∈ Del(P ∪ V) do
6      if p ∈ P and q ∈ P
7          E := E ∪ pq;
8      endif
9  output E.
```

The Voronoi and the Delaunay diagrams of a set of n points in the plane can be computed in $O(n \log n)$ time and $O(n)$ space. The second Delaunay triangulation in step 3 deals with $O(n)$ points as the Voronoi diagram of n points can have at most $2n$ Voronoi vertices. Therefore, CRUST runs in $O(n \log n)$ time and takes $O(n)$ space.

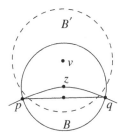

Figure 2.5. Illustration for the Correct Edge Lemma 2.6.

2.2.2 Correctness

The correctness of CRUST is proved in two parts. First, it is shown that each correct edge is present in the output of CRUST (Correct Edge Lemma 2.6). Then, it is shown that no incorrect edge is output (Incorrect Edge Lemma 2.7).

Lemma 2.6 (Correct Edge). *Each correct edge is output by* CRUST *when* $\varepsilon < \frac{1}{5}$.

Proof. Let pq be a correct edge. Let z be the point where the perpendicular bisector of pq intersects the empty segment $\gamma(p, q)$. Consider the ball $B = B_{z, \|p-z\|}$. This ball is empty of any point from P when $\varepsilon < 1$ (Empty Segment Lemma 2.1 (i)). We show that this ball does not contain any Voronoi vertex of Vor$P$ either.

Suppose that B contains a Voronoi vertex, say v, from V (Figure 2.5). Then by simple circle geometry the maximum distance of v from p is $2\|p - z\|$. Thus, $\|p - v\| \leq 2\|p - z\|$. Since $\|p - z\| \leq \varepsilon f(z)$ by the Empty Segment Lemma 2.1(iii), we have

$$\|p - v\| \leq 2\varepsilon f(z) \leq \frac{2\varepsilon}{1 - \varepsilon} f(p).$$

The Delaunay ball B' centering v contains three points from P on its boundary. This means bd$B' \cap \Sigma$ is not a 0-sphere. So, B' contains a medial axis point by the Feature Ball Lemma 1.1. As the Delaunay ball B' is empty, p cannot lie in Int B'. So, the medial axis point in B' lies within $2\|p - v\|$ distance from p. Therefore, $2\|p - v\| \geq f(p)$. But, $\|p - v\| \leq \frac{2\varepsilon}{1-\varepsilon} f(p)$ enabling us to reach a contradiction when $\frac{2\varepsilon}{1-\varepsilon} < \frac{1}{2}$, that is, when $\varepsilon < \frac{1}{5}$.

Therefore, for $\varepsilon < \frac{1}{5}$, there is a circumscribing ball of pq empty of any point from $P \cup V$. So, it appears in Del $(P \cup V)$ and is output by CRUST as it connects two points from P. ∎

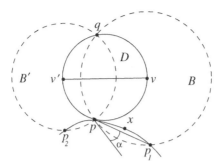

Figure 2.6. Illustration for the Incorrect Edge Lemma 2.7.

Lemma 2.7 (Incorrect Edge). *No incorrect edge is output by* CRUST *when* $\varepsilon < 1/5$.

Proof. We need to show that there is no ball, empty of both sample points and Voronoi vertices, circumscribing an incorrect edge between two sample points, say p and q. For the sake of contradiction, assume that D is such a ball.

Let v and v' be the two points where the perpendicular bisector of pq intersects the boundary of D (see Figure 2.6). Consider the two balls $B = B_{v,r}$ and $B' = B_{v',r'}$ that circumscribe pq.

We claim that both B and B' are empty of any sample points. Suppose on the contrary, any one of them, say B, contains a sample point. Then, one can push D continually toward B by moving its center on the perpendicular bisector of pq and keeping p, q on its boundary. During this motion, the deformed D would hit a sample point s for the first time before its center reaches v. At that moment p, q, and s define a ball empty of any other sample points. The center of this ball is a Voronoi vertex in Vor P which resides inside D. This is a contradiction as D is empty of any Voronoi vertex from V.

The angle $\angle vpv'$ is $\pi/2$ as vv' is a diameter of D. The tangents to the boundary circles of B and B' at p are perpendicular to vp and $v'p$ respectively. Therefore, the tangents make an angle of $\pi/2$. This implies that Σ cannot be tangent to both B and B' at p.

First, consider the case where Σ is tangent neither to B nor to B' at p. Let p_1 and p_2 be the points of intersection of Σ with the boundaries of B and B' respectively that are consecutive to p among all such intersections. Our goal will be to show that either the curve segment pp_1 or the curve segment pp_2 intersects B or B' rather deeply and thereby contributing a long empty segment which is prohibited by the sampling condition.

The curve segment between p and p_1 and the curve segment between p and p_2 do not have any sample point other than p. By the Small Segment Lemma 2.2 both $\|p - p_1\|$ and $\|p - p_2\|$ are no more than $\frac{2\varepsilon}{1-\varepsilon} f(p)$ for $\varepsilon < \frac{1}{5}$. So by the Segment Angle Lemma 2.4, $\angle p_1 p p_2 \leq \pi - 2 \arcsin \frac{2\varepsilon}{1-\varepsilon}$.

Without loss of generality, let the angle between pp_1 and the tangent to B at p be larger than the angle between pp_2 and the tangent to B' at p. Then, pp_1 makes an angle α with the tangent to B at p where

$$
\alpha \geq \frac{1}{2}\left(\left(\pi - 2 \arcsin \frac{\varepsilon}{1-\varepsilon}\right) - \frac{\pi}{2}\right)
$$
$$
= \frac{\pi}{4} - \arcsin \frac{\varepsilon}{1-\varepsilon}.
$$

Consider the other case where Σ is tangent to one of the two balls B and B' at p. Without loss of generality, assume that it is tangent to B' at p. Again the lower bound on the angle α as stated above holds.

Let x be the point where the perpendicular bisector of pp_1 intersects the curve segment between p and p_1. Clearly, x is in B. Since B intersects Σ at p and q which are not consecutive sample points, it cannot contain $\gamma(p, q)$ or $\gamma'(p, q)$ inside completely. This means $B \cap \Sigma$ cannot be a 1-ball. So, by the Feature Ball Lemma 1.1, B has a medial axis point and thus its radius r is at least $f(x)/2$. By simple geometry, one gets that

$$
\|p - x\| \geq \frac{1}{2}\|p - p_1\|
$$
$$
= r \sin \alpha
$$
$$
\geq \frac{1}{2} f(x) \sin \alpha.
$$

By property (iii) of the Empty Segment Lemma 2.1 $\|p - x\| \leq \varepsilon f(x)$. We reach a contradiction if

$$
2\varepsilon < \sin\left(\frac{\pi}{4} - \arcsin \frac{\varepsilon}{1-\varepsilon}\right).
$$

For $\varepsilon < \frac{1}{5}$, this inequality is satisfied. ∎

Combining the Correct Edge Lemma 2.6 and the Incorrect Edge Lemma 2.7 we get the following theorem.

Theorem 2.1. *For $\varepsilon < \frac{1}{5}$,* CRUST *outputs all and only correct edges.*

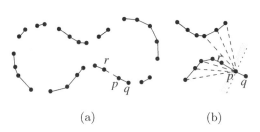

(a)   (b)

Figure 2.7. (a) Only nearest neighbor edges may not reconstruct a curve and (b) half neighbor edges such as pr fill up the gaps.

2.3 NN-Crust

The next algorithm for curve reconstruction is based on the concept of nearest neighbors. A point $p \in P$ is a nearest neighbor of $q \in P$ if there is no other point $s \in P \setminus \{p, q\}$ with $\|q - s\| < \|q - p\|$. Notice that p being a nearest neighbor of q does not necessarily mean that q is a nearest neighbor of p.

We first observe that edges that connect nearest neighbors in P must be correct edges if P is sufficiently dense. But, all correct edges do not connect nearest neighbors. Figure 2.7 shows all edges that connect nearest neighbors. The missing correct edges in this example connect points that are not nearest neighbors. However, these correct edges connect points that are not very far from being nearest neighbors. We capture them in NN-CRUST using the notion of *half neighbors*.

2.3.1 Algorithm

Let pq be an edge connecting p to its nearest neighbor q and $\vec{pq}$ be the vector from p to q. Consider the closed half-plane H bounded by the line passing through p with $\vec{pq}$ as outward normal. Clearly, $q \notin H$. The nearest neighbor to p in the set $H \cap P$ is called its *half neighbor*. In Figure 2.7(b), r is the half neighbor of p. It can be shown that two correct edges incident to a sample point connect it to its nearest and half neighbors.

The above discussion immediately suggests an algorithm for curve reconstruction. But, we need efficient algorithms to compute nearest neighbor and half neighbor for each sample point. The Delaunay triangulation Del P turns out to be useful for this computation as all correct edges are Delaunay if P is sufficiently dense. The Small Edge Lemma 2.3 implies that, for each sample point p, it is sufficient to check only the Delaunay edges to determine correct edges. We check all edges incident to p in Del P and determine the shortest edge connecting it to its nearest neighbor, say q. Next, we check all other edges incident to p which make at least $\frac{\pi}{2}$ angle with pq at p and choose the shortest

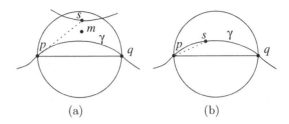

(a)   (b)

Figure 2.8. Diametric ball of pq intersects Σ in (a) two components and (b) single component.

among them. This second edge connects p to its half neighbor. The entire computation can be done in time proportional to the number of edges incident to p. Since the sum of the number of incident edges over all vertices in the Delaunay triangulation is $O(n)$ where $|P| = n$, correct edge computation takes only $O(n)$ time once Del P is computed. The Delaunay triangulation of a set of n points in the plane can be computed in $O(n \log n)$ time which implies that NN-crust takes $O(n \log n)$ time.

NN-CRUST(P)

1   compute Del P;
2    $E = \emptyset$;
3   for each $p \in P$ do
4   compute the shortest edge pq in Del P;
5   compute the shortest edge ps so that $\angle pqs \geq \frac{\pi}{2}$;
6        $E = E \cup \{pq, ps\}$;
7   endfor
8   output E.

2.3.2 Correctness

As we discussed before, NN-CRUST computes edges connecting each sample point to its nearest and half neighbors. The correctness of NN-CRUST follows from the proofs that these edges are correct.

Lemma 2.8 (Neighbor). *Let $p \in P$ be any sample point and q be its nearest neighbor. The edge pq is correct for $\varepsilon < \frac{1}{3}$.*

Proof. Consider the ball B with pq as diameter. If B does not intersect Σ in a 1-ball, it contains a medial axis point by the Feature Ball Lemma 1.1 (see Figure 2.8(a)). This means $\|p - q\| > f(p)$. A correct edge ps satisfies

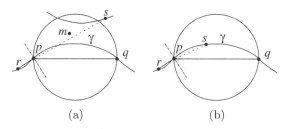

(a)   (b)

Figure 2.9. Diametric ball of pq intersects Σ in (a) more than one component and (b) a single component.

$\|p - s\| \leq \frac{2\varepsilon}{1-\varepsilon} f(p)$ by the Small Edge Lemma 2.3. Thus, for $\varepsilon < \frac{1}{3}$ we have $\|p - s\| < \|p - q\|$, a contradiction to the fact that q is the nearest neighbor to p.

So, B intersects Σ in a 1-ball, namely $\gamma = \gamma(p, q)$ as shown in Figure 2.8(b). If pq is not correct, γ contains a sample point, say s, between p and q inside B. Again, we reach a contradiction as $\|p - s\| < \|p - q\|$. ∎

Next we show that edges connecting a sample point to its half neighbors are also correct.

Lemma 2.9 (Half Neighbor). *An edge pq where q is a half neighbor of p is correct when $\varepsilon < \frac{1}{3}$.*

Proof. Let r be the nearest neighbor of p. According to the definition $\overrightarrow{pq}$ makes at least $\frac{\pi}{2}$ angle with $\overrightarrow{pr}$.

If pq is not correct, consider the correct edge ps incident to p other than pr. By the Edge Angle Lemma 2.5, $\overrightarrow{ps}$ also makes at least $\frac{\pi}{2}$ angle with $\overrightarrow{pr}$ for $\varepsilon < 1/3$. We show that s is closer to p than q. This contradicts that q is the half neighbor of p since both $\overrightarrow{ps}$ and $\overrightarrow{pq}$ make an angle at least $\frac{\pi}{2}$ with $\overrightarrow{pr}$.

Consider the ball B with pq as a diameter. If B does not intersect Σ in a 1-ball (Figure 2.9(a)), it would contain a medial axis point and thus $\|p - q\| \geq f(p)$. On the other hand, for $\varepsilon < \frac{1}{3}$, $\|p - s\| \leq \frac{2\varepsilon}{1-\varepsilon} f(p)$ by the Small Edge Lemma 2.3. We get $\|p - s\| < \|p - q\|$ for $\varepsilon < \frac{1}{3}$ as required for contradiction. Next, assume that B intersects Σ in a 1-ball, namely in $\gamma(p, q)$, as in Figure 2.9(b). Since pq is not a correct edge, s must be on this curve segment. It implies $\|p - s\| < \|p - q\|$ as required for contradiction. ∎

Theorem 2.2. NN-CRUST *computes all and only correct edges when $\varepsilon < \frac{1}{3}$.*

Proof. By the Small Edge Lemma 2.3 all correct edges are Delaunay. Steps 4 and 5 assure that all edges joining sample points to their nearest and half neighbors are computed as output. These edges are correct by the Neighbor Lemma 2.8 and the Half Neighbor Lemma 2.9 when $\varepsilon < \frac{1}{3}$. Also, there is no other correct edges since each sample point can only be incident to exactly two correct edges. ∎

2.4 Notes and Exercises

In its simplest form the curve reconstruction problem appears in applications such as pattern recognition, image boundary detection, and cluster analysis. In the 1980s, several geometric graphs connecting a set of points in the plane were discovered which reveal a pattern among the points. The influence graph of Toussaint [11]; the β-skeleton of Kirkpatrick and Radke [62]; and the α-shapes of Edelsbrunner, Kirkpatrick, and Seidel [46] are such graphs.

Recall that a sample of a curve Σ is called globally δ-*uniform* if each point $x \in \Sigma$ has a sample point within a fixed distance δ. Several algorithms were devised to reconstruct curves from δ-uniform samples with δ being sufficiently small. Attali proposed a Delaunay-based reconstruction for such samples [9] (Exercise 3). de Figueiredo and de Miranda Gomes [27] showed that Euclidean minimum spanning tree (EMST) can reconstruct curves with boundaries from sufficiently dense uniform sample.

For a point set $P \subset \mathbb{R}^2$, let $\mathbb{N}$ denote the space of all points covered by open 2-balls of radius α around each point in P. The α-shape of P defined by Edelsbrunner, Kirkpatrick, and Seidel [46] is the underlying space of the restricted Delaunay triangulation Del $P|_\mathbb{N}$. Bernardini and Bajaj [12] proved that the α-shapes reconstruct curves from globally uniform samples that is sufficiently dense (Exercise 6).

The first breakthrough in reconstructing curves from nonuniform samples was made by Amenta, Bern, and Eppstein [5]. The presented CRUST algorithm is taken from this paper with some modifications in the proofs. Following the development of CRUST, Dey and Kumar devised the NN-CRUST algorithm [36]. The presented NN-CRUST algorithm is taken from this paper again with some modifications in the proofs. This algorithm also can reconstruct curves in three and higher dimensions, albeit with appropriate modifications of the proofs (Exercise 4).

The CRUST and NN-CRUST assume that the sample is derived from a smooth curve without boundaries. The questions of reconstructing nonsmooth curves and curves with boundaries have also been studied.

Giesen [54] showed that a fairly large class of nonsmooth curves can be reconstructed by Traveling Salesman Path (or Tour). A curve Σ is called *benign* if the left tangent and the right tangent exist at each point and make an angle less than π. Giesen proved that, a benign curve Σ can be reconstructed from a sufficiently dense uniform sample by the Traveling Salesman Path (or Tour) in case Σ has a boundary (or no boundary). The uniform sampling condition was later removed by Althaus and Mehlhorn [3], who also gave a polynomial time algorithm to compute the Traveling Salesman Path (or Tour) in the special case of curve reconstruction. The Traveling Salesman approach cannot handle curves with multiple components. Also, the sample points representing the boundaries need to be known a priori to choose between a path or a tour.

Dey, Mehlhorn, and Ramos [38] presented an algorithm named CONSERVA-TIVE CRUST that provably reconstructs smooth curves with boundaries. Any algorithm for handling curves with boundaries faces a dilemma when an input point set samples a curve without boundary densely and simultaneously samples densely another curve with boundary. This dilemma is resolved in CONSERVATIVE CRUST by a justification on the output. For any input point set P, the graph output by the algorithm is guaranteed to be the reconstruction of a smooth curve possibly with boundary for which P is a dense sample. The main idea of the algorithm is that an edge pq is output only if its diametric ball is empty of all Voronoi vertices in Vor P. The rationale behind this choice is that these edges are small enough with respect to local feature size of the sampled curve since the Voronoi vertices approximate the medial axis. With a sampling condition tailored to handle nonsmooth curves, Funke and Ramos [52] and Dey and Wenger [41] proposed algorithms to reconstruct nonsmooth curves. The algorithm of Funke and Ramos can handle boundaries as well.

Exercises

(The exercise numbers with the superscript h and o indicate *hard* and *open* questions respectively.)

1. Give an example of a point set P such that P is a 1-sample of two curves for which the correct reconstructions are different.
2. Given a $\frac{1}{4}$-sample P of a C^2-smooth curve, show that all correct edges are Gabriel in Del $(P \cup V)$ where V is the set of Voronoi vertices in Vor P.
3. Let P be a ε-sample of a C^2-smooth curve without boundary. Let η_{pq} be the sum of the angles opposite to pq in the two (or one if pq is a convex hull edge) triangles incident to pq in Del P. Prove that there is a ε for which pq is correct if and only if $\eta_{pq} < \pi$.
4. Show that the NN-CRUST algorithm can reconstruct curves in three dimensions from sufficiently dense samples.

5. The Correct Edge Lemma 2.6 is proved for $\varepsilon < \frac{1}{5}$. Show that it also holds for $\varepsilon \leq \frac{1}{5}$. Similarly, show that the Neighbor Lemma 2.8 and the Half Neighbor Lemma 2.9 hold for $\varepsilon \leq \frac{1}{3}$.

6[h]. Establish conditions for α and δ to guarantee that an α-shape reconstructs a C^2-smooth curve in the plane from a globally δ-uniform sample.

7[o]. Gold and Snoeyink [58] showed that the CRUST algorithm can be modified to guarantee a reconstruction with $\varepsilon < 0.42$. Althaus [2] showed that the NN-CRUST algorithm can be proved to reconstruct curves from ε-samples for $\varepsilon < 0.5$. Can this bound on ε be improved? What is the largest value of ε for which curves can be reconstructed from ε-samples?

8[h]. Let $v \in V_p$ be a Voronoi vertex in the Voronoi diagram Vor P of a ε-sample P of a C^2-smooth curve Σ. Show that there exists a point m in the medial axis of Σ so that $\|m - v\| = \tilde{O}(\varepsilon)f(p)$ when ε is sufficiently small (see Section 1.2.3 for $\tilde{O}$ definition).

3

Surface Samples

In this chapter we introduce some of the properties of surfaces and their samples in three dimensions. The results developed in this chapter are used in later chapters to design algorithms for surface reconstruction and prove their guarantees. Before we talk about these results, let us explain what we mean by smooth surfaces.

Consider a map $\pi : U \to V$ where U and V are the open sets in $\mathbb{R}^2$ and $\mathbb{R}^3$ respectively. The map π has three components, namely $\pi(x) = (\pi_1(x), \pi_2(x), \pi_3(x))$ where $x = (x_1, x_2)$ is a point in $\mathbb{R}^2$. The three by two matrix of first-order partial derivatives $(\frac{\partial \pi_i(x)}{\partial x_j})_{i,j}$ is called the *Jacobian* of π at x. We say π is *regular* if its Jacobian at each point of U has rank 2. The map π is C^i-continuous if the ith order $(i > 0)$ partial derivatives of π are continuous.

For $i > 0$, a subset $\Sigma \subset \mathbb{R}^3$ is a C^i-*smooth* surface if each point $x \in \Sigma$ satisfies the following condition. There is a neighborhood $W \subset \mathbb{R}^3$ of x and a map $\pi : U \to W \cap \Sigma$ of an open set $U \subset \mathbb{R}^2$ onto $W \cap \Sigma$ so that

(i) π is C^i-continuous,
(ii) π is a homeomorphism, and
(iii) π is regular.

The first condition says that π is continuously differentiable at least up to ith order. The second condition imposes one-to-one property which eliminates self-intersections of Σ. The third condition together with the first actually enforce the smoothness. It makes sure that the tangent plane at each point in Σ is well defined. All of these three conditions together imply that the functions like π defined in the neighborhood of each point of Σ overlap smoothly. There are two extremes of smoothness. If the partial derivatives of π of all orders are continuous, we say Σ is C^∞-smooth. On the other hand,

41

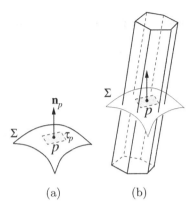

(a)   (b)

Figure 3.1. (a) Tangent plane and the normal at a point on a smooth surface and (b) a long thin Voronoi cell elongated along the normal direction.

if Σ is not C^1-smooth but is at least a 2-manifold, we say it is C^0-smooth or *nonsmooth*.

In this chapter and the chapters to follow, we assume that Σ is a C^2-smooth surface. Notice that, by the definition of smoothness (condition (ii)) Σ is a 2-manifold without boundary. We also assume that Σ is compact since we are interested in approximating Σ with a finite simplicial complex. We need one more assumption. Just like the curves, for a finite point set to be a ε-sample for some $\varepsilon > 0$, we need that $f(x) > 0$ for any point x in Σ. It is known that C^2-smooth surfaces necessarily have positive feature size everywhere. The example in Chapter 2 for curves can be extended to surfaces to claim that a C^1-smooth surface may not have nonzero local feature sizes everywhere.

As a C^2-smooth surface Σ has a tangent plane τ_x and a normal $\mathbf{n}_x$ defined at each point $x \in \Sigma$. We assume that the normals are oriented outward. More precisely, $\mathbf{n}_x$ points locally to the unbounded component of $\mathbb{R}^3 \setminus \Sigma$. If Σ is not connected, $\mathbf{n}_x$ points locally to the unbounded component of $\mathbb{R}^3 \setminus \Sigma'$ where x is in Σ', a connected component of Σ.

An important fact used in surface reconstruction is that, disregarding the orientation, the direction of the surface normals can be approximated from the sample. An illustration in $\mathbb{R}^2$ is helpful here. See Figure 2.4 in Chapter 2 which shows the Voronoi diagram of a dense sample on a smooth curve. This Voronoi diagram has a specific structure. Each Voronoi cell is elongated along the normal direction at the sample points. Fortunately, the same holds in three dimensions. The three-dimensional Voronoi cells are long, thin, and the direction of the elongation matches with the normal direction at the sample points when the sample is dense (see Figure 3.1).

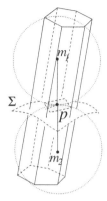

Figure 3.2. Medial axis points m_1 and m_2 are in the Voronoi cell V_p.

3.1 Normals

Let $P \subset \mathbb{R}^3$ be a ε-sample of Σ. If P is all we know about Σ, it is impossible to know the line of direction of $\mathbf{n}_p$ exactly at a point $p \in P$. However, it is conceivable that as P gets denser, we should have more accurate idea about the direction of $\mathbf{n}_p$ by looking at the adjacent points. This is what is done using the Voronoi cells in Vor P.

For further developments we will often need to talk about how one vector approximates another one in terms of the angles between them. We denote the angle between two vectors $\mathbf{u}$ and $\mathbf{v}$ as $\angle(\mathbf{u}, \mathbf{v})$. For vector approximations that disregard the orientation, we use a slightly different notation. This approximation measures the acute angle between the lines containing the vectors. We use $\angle_a(\mathbf{u}, \mathbf{v})$ to denote this acute angle between two vectors $\mathbf{u}$ and $\mathbf{v}$. Since any such angle is acute, we have the triangular inequality $\angle_a(\mathbf{u}, \mathbf{v}) \leq \angle_a(\mathbf{u}, \mathbf{w}) + \angle_a(\mathbf{v}, \mathbf{w})$ for any three vectors $\mathbf{u}$, $\mathbf{v}$, and $\mathbf{w}$.

3.1.1 Approximation of Normals

It turns out that the structure of the Voronoi cells contains information about normals. Indeed, if the sample is sufficiently dense, the Voronoi cells become long and thin along the direction of the normals at the sample points. One reason for this structural property is that a Voronoi cell V_p must contain the medial axis points that are the centers of the medial balls tangent to Σ at p (see Figure 3.2).

Lemma 3.1 (Medial). *Let m_1 and m_2 be the centers of the two medial balls tangent to Σ at p. The Voronoi cell V_p contains m_1 and m_2.*

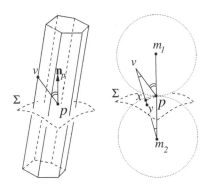

Figure 3.3. Illustration for the Normal Lemma 3.2.

Proof. Denote the medial ball with center m_1 as B. The ball B meets the surface Σ only tangentially at points, one of which is p. Thus, B is empty of any point from Σ and P in particular. Therefore, the center m_1 has p as the nearest point in P. By definition of Voronoi cells, m_1 is in V_p. A similar argument applies to the other medial axis point m_2.   ∎

We have already mentioned that the Voronoi cells are long and thin and they are elongated along the direction of the normals. The next lemma formalizes this statement by asserting that as we go further from p within V_p, the direction to p becomes closer to the normal direction.

Lemma 3.2 (Normal). *For $\mu > 0$ let $v \notin \Sigma$ be a point in V_p with $\|v - p\| > \mu f(p)$. For $\varepsilon < 1$, $\angle_a(\overrightarrow{vp}, \mathbf{n}_p) \le \arcsin \frac{\varepsilon}{\mu(1-\varepsilon)} + \arcsin \frac{\varepsilon}{1-\varepsilon}$.*

Proof. Let m_1 and m_2 be the two centers of the medial balls tangent to Σ at p where m_1 is on the same side of Σ as v is. Both m_1 and m_2 are in V_p by the Medial Lemma 3.1. The line joining m_1 and p is normal to Σ at p by the definition of medial balls. Similarly, the line joining m_2 and p is also normal to Σ at p. Therefore, m_1, m_2, and p are colinear (see Figure 3.3). Consider the triangle pvm_2. We are interested in the angle $\angle m_1 pv$ which is equal to $\angle_a(\overrightarrow{pv}, \mathbf{n}_p)$. From the triangle pvm_2 we have

$$\angle m_1 pv = \angle pvm_2 + \angle vm_2 p.$$

To measure the two angles on the right-hand side, drop the perpendicular px from p onto the segment vm_2. The line segment vm_2 intersects Σ, say at y, since m_1 and m_2 and hence v and m_2 lie on opposite sides of Σ. Furthermore, y must lie inside V_p since any point on the segment joining two points v and m_2 in a convex set V_p must lie within the same convex set. This means y has p

as the nearest sample point and thus

$\|x - p\| \le \|y - p\| \le \varepsilon f(y)$ by the ε-sampling condition.

Using the Feature Translation Lemma 1.3 we get

$$\|x - p\| \le \frac{\varepsilon}{1 - \varepsilon} f(p)$$

when $\varepsilon < 1$. We have

$$\angle pvm_2 = \arcsin \frac{\|x - p\|}{\|v - p\|} \le \arcsin \frac{\varepsilon}{\mu(1 - \varepsilon)} \quad \text{as } \|v - p\| \ge \mu f(p).$$

Similarly,

$$\angle vm_2 p = \arcsin \frac{\|x - p\|}{\|m_2 - p\|} \le \arcsin \frac{\varepsilon}{1 - \varepsilon} \quad \text{as } \|m_2 - p\| \ge f(p).$$

The assertion of the lemma follows immediately. ∎

3.1.2 Normal Variation

The directions of the normals at nearby points on Σ cannot vary too abruptly. In other words, the surface looks flat locally. This fact is used later in many proofs.

Lemma 3.3 (Normal Variation). *If $x, y \in \Sigma$ are any two points with $\|x - y\| \le \rho f(x)$ for $\rho < \frac{1}{3}$, $\angle(\mathbf{n}_x, \mathbf{n}_y) \le \frac{\rho}{1 - 3\rho}$.*

Proof. Let $\ell(t)$ denote any point on the segment xy parameterized by its distance t from x. Let $x(t)$ be the nearest point on Σ from $\ell(t)$. The rate of change of normal $\mathbf{n}_{x(t)}$ at $x(t)$ is $\mathbf{n}'_t = \frac{dx(t)}{dt}$ as t changes. The total variation in normals between x and y is

$$\angle(\mathbf{n}_x, \mathbf{n}_y) \le \int_{xy} |\mathbf{n}'_t| dt \le \|x - y\| \max_t |\mathbf{n}'_t|.$$

The surface Σ is squeezed locally in-between two medial ball that are tangent to Σ at $x(t)$. The radius of the smaller medial ball cannot be larger than the radius of curvature of Σ at $x(t)$. This means Σ cannot turn faster than the smaller of the two medial balls at $x(t)$. Referring to Figure 3.4, we have

$$dt = (\|m_2 - x(t)\| - \|x(t) - \ell(t)\|) \tan d\theta$$
$$\ge (f(x(t)) - \|x(t) - \ell(t)\|) \tan d\theta.$$

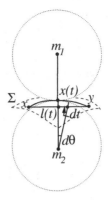

Figure 3.4. Illustration for the Normal Variation Lemma 3.3.

As

$$\lim_{d\theta \to 0} \frac{\tan d\theta}{d\theta} = 1$$

and

$$\|x(t) - \ell(t)\| \leq \|x - \ell(t)\| \leq \|x - y\| \leq \rho f(x)$$

we get

$$|\mathbf{n}'_t| = \lim_{d\theta \to 0} \left| \frac{d\theta}{dt} \right| \leq \frac{1}{(f(x(t)) - \|x(t) - \ell(t)\|)} \leq \frac{1}{(f(x(t)) - \rho f(x))}$$

provided $f(x(t)) - \rho f(x) > 0$. Also,

$$\|x(t) - x\| \leq \|x(t) - \ell(t)\| + \|x - \ell(t)\| \leq 2\rho f(x).$$

By the Lipschitz Continuity Lemma 1.2, $f(x(t)) \geq (1 - 2\rho)f(x)$. Therefore,

$$|\mathbf{n}'_t| \leq \frac{1}{(1 - 3\rho)f(x)} \quad \text{and} \quad \angle(\mathbf{n}_x, \mathbf{n}_y) \leq \frac{\rho}{1 - 3\rho}$$

provided

$$f(x(t)) - \rho f(x) > 0$$
$$\text{or, } (1 - 3\rho)f(x) > 0$$
$$\text{or, } \rho < \frac{1}{3}.$$

■

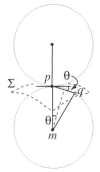

Figure 3.5. Illustration for the Edge Normal Lemma 3.4.

3.1.3 Edge and Triangle Normals

In Section 2.1, we saw that edges joining nearby points on a curve are almost parallel to the tangents at the endpoints of the edge. Similar results also hold for triangles connecting points on surfaces. But, the size is measured by circumradius. In fact, a triangle connecting three nearby points on a surface but with a large circumradius may lie almost perpendicular to the surface. However, if its circumradius is small compared to the local feature sizes at its vertices, it has to lie almost parallel to the surface. For an edge, half of its length is the same as its circumradius. Therefore, a small edge lies almost parallel to the surface. In essence if an edge or a triangle has a small circumradius, it must lie flat to the surface. We quantify these claims in the next two lemmas.

Lemma 3.4 (Edge Normal). *For an edge pq with $\|p - q\| \le 2f(p)$, the angle $\angle_a(\overrightarrow{pq}, \mathbf{n}_p)$ is at least $\frac{\pi}{2} - \arcsin \frac{\|p-q\|}{2f(p)}$.*

Proof. Consider the two medial balls sandwiching the surface Σ at p. The point q cannot lie inside any of these two balls as they are empty of points from Σ. So, the smallest angle pq makes with $\mathbf{n}_p$ cannot be smaller than the angle pq makes with $\mathbf{n}_p$ when q is on the boundary of any of these two balls. In this case let θ be the angle between pq and the tangent plane at p. Clearly, (see Figure 3.5)

$$\sin \theta = \frac{\|p - q\|}{2\|m - p\|}$$

$$\le \frac{\|p - q\|}{2f(p)}.$$

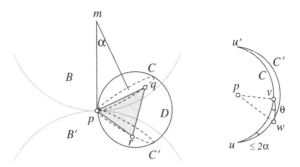

Figure 3.6. Illustration for the Triangle Normal Lemma 3.5. The two great arcs on the right picture are the intersections of the unit sphere with the planes containing C and C'.

Therefore,

$$\angle_a(\overrightarrow{pq}, \mathbf{n}_p) = \frac{\pi}{2} - \theta$$

$$\geq \frac{\pi}{2} - \arcsin \frac{\|p - q\|}{2f(p)}. \qquad \blacksquare$$

It follows immediately from the Edge Normal Lemma 3.4 that small edges make a large angle with the surface normals at the vertices. For example, if pq has a length less than $\rho f(p)$ for $\rho < 2$, the angle $\angle_a(\overrightarrow{pq}, \mathbf{n}_p)$ is more than $\frac{\pi}{2} - \arcsin \frac{\rho}{2}$.

Next consider a triangle $t = pqr$ where p is the vertex subtending a maximal angle in pqr. Let R_{pqr} denote the circumradius of pqr.

Lemma 3.5 (Triangle Normal). *If $R_{pqr} \leq \frac{f(p)}{\sqrt{2}}$,*

$$\angle_a(\mathbf{n}_{pqr}, \mathbf{n}_p) \leq \arcsin \frac{R_{pqr}}{f(p)} + \arcsin \left(\frac{2}{\sqrt{3}} \sin \left(2 \arcsin \frac{R_{pqr}}{f(p)} \right) \right)$$

where $\mathbf{n}_{pqr}$ is the normal of pqr.

Proof. Consider the medial balls $B = B_{m,\ell}$ and $B' = B_{m',\ell'}$ that are tangent to Σ at p. Let D be the diametric ball of t (smallest circumscribing ball); refer to Figure 3.6. The radius of D is R_{pqr}. Let C and C' be the circles in which the boundary of D intersects the boundaries of B and B' respectively. The line normal to Σ at p passes through m, the center of B. Let α be the larger of the two angles this normal line makes with the normals to the planes containing C and C'. Since the radii of C and C' are at most R_{pqr} we have

$$\alpha \leq \arcsin \frac{R_{pqr}}{\|p - m\|} \leq \arcsin \frac{R_{pqr}}{f(p)}.$$

It follows from the definition of α that the planes containing C and C' make a wedge, say W, with an acute dihedral angle no more than 2α.

The other two vertices q, r of t cannot lie inside B or B'. This implies that t lies completely in the wedge W. Let π_t, π, and π' denote the planes containing t, C, and C' respectively. Consider a unit sphere centered at p. This sphere intersects the line $\pi \cap \pi'$ at two points, say u and u'. Within W let the lines $\pi_t \cap \pi$ and $\pi_t \cap \pi'$ intersect the unit sphere at v and w respectively. See the picture on the right in Figure 3.6. Without loss of generality, assume that the angle $\angle uvw \leq \angle uwv$. Consider the spherical triangle uvw. We are interested in the spherical angle $\theta = \angle uvw$ which is also the acute dihedral angle between the planes containing t and C. We have the following facts. The arc length of wv, denoted $|wv|$, is at least $\pi/3$ since p subtends the largest angle in t and t is in the wedge W. The spherical angle $\angle vuw$ is less than or equal to 2α. By standard sine laws in spherical geometry, we have

$$\sin \theta = \sin |uw| \frac{\sin \angle vuw}{\sin |wv|} \leq \sin |uw| \frac{\sin 2\alpha}{\sin |wv|}.$$

If $\pi/3 \leq |wv| \leq 2\pi/3$, we have

$$\sin |wv| \geq \sqrt{3}/2$$

and hence

$$\theta \leq \arcsin \left(\frac{2}{\sqrt{3}} \sin 2\alpha \right).$$

For the range $2\pi/3 < |wv| < \pi$, we use the fact that $|uw| + |wv| \leq \pi$. The arc length $|wv|$ cannot be longer than both $|wu'|$ and $|vu'|$ since $\angle vu'w \leq 2\alpha < \pi/2$ for $R_{pqr} \leq \frac{f(p)}{\sqrt{2}}$. If $|wv| \leq |wu'|$, we have

$$|uw| + |wv| \leq |uu'| = \pi.$$

Otherwise, $|wv| \leq |vu'|$. Then, we use the fact that $|uw| \leq |uv|$ as $\angle uvw \leq \angle uwv$. So, again

$$|uw| + |wv| \leq |uu'| = \pi.$$

Therefore, when $|wv| > \frac{2\pi}{3}$, we get

$$\frac{\sin |uw|}{\sin |wv|} < 1.$$

Thus, $\theta \leq \arcsin \left(\frac{2}{\sqrt{3}} \sin 2\alpha \right)$.

The normals to t and Σ at p make an acute angle at most $\alpha + \theta$ proving the lemma. ∎

3.2 Topology

The sample P as a set of discrete points does not have the topology of Σ. A connection between the topology of Σ and P can be established through the restricted Voronoi and Delaunay diagrams. In particular, one can show that the underlying space of the restricted Delaunay triangulation Del $P|_\Sigma$ is homeomorphic to Σ if the sample P is sufficiently dense. Although we will not be able to compute Del $P|_\Sigma$, the fact that it is homeomorphic to Σ will be useful in the surface reconstruction later.

3.2.1 Topological Ball Property

The underlying space of Del $P|_\Sigma$ becomes homeomorphic to Σ when the Voronoi diagram Vor P intersects Σ nicely. This condition is formalized by the topological ball property which says that the restricted Voronoi cells in each dimension is a ball.

Definition 3.1. *Let F denote any Voronoi face of dimension k, $0 \le k \le 3$, in* Vor$P$ *which intersects Σ and $F|_\Sigma = F \cap \Sigma$ be the corresponding restricted Voronoi face. The face F satisfies the topological ball property if $F|_\Sigma$ is a (i) $(k-1)$-ball and (ii)* Int $F \cap \Sigma =$ Int $F|_\Sigma$. *The pair (P, Σ) satisfies the topological ball property if all Voronoi faces $F \in$ Vor P satisfy the topological ball property.*

Condition (i) means that Σ intersects a Voronoi cell in a single topological disk, a Voronoi facet in a single curve segment, a Voronoi edge in a single point, and does not intersect any Voronoi vertex (see Figure 3.7). Condition (ii) avoids any tangential intersection between a Voronoi face and Σ.

The following theorem is an important result relating the topology of a surface to a point sample.

Theorem 3.1. *The underlying space of* Del$P|_\Sigma$ *is homeomorphic to Σ if the pair (P, Σ) satisfies the topological ball property.*

Our aim is to show that, when P is a dense sample, the topology of Σ can be captured from P. Specifically, we prove that the pair (P, Σ) satisfies the topological ball property when ε is sufficiently small. The proof frequently uses the next two lemmas to reach a contradiction. The first one says that the points in a restricted Voronoi cell, that is, the points of Σ in a Voronoi cell, cannot be far apart. The second one says that any line almost normal to the surface cannot intersect it twice within a small distance.

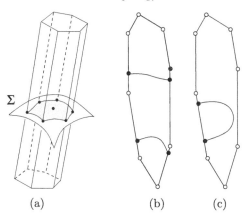

(a)   (b)   (c)

Figure 3.7. (a) A surface Σ intersects a Voronoi cell and its faces with the topological ball property, (b) a surface not intersecting a Voronoi facet in a 1-ball, and (c) a surface not intersecting a Voronoi edge in a 0-ball.

Lemma 3.6 (Short Distance). *Let x and y be any two points in a restricted Voronoi cell $V_p|_\Sigma$. For $\varepsilon < 1$, we have*

(i) $\|x - p\| \le \frac{\varepsilon}{1-\varepsilon} f(p)$ and
(ii) $\|x - y\| \le \frac{2\varepsilon}{1-\varepsilon} f(x)$.

Proof. Since x has p as the nearest sample point, $\|x - p\| \le \varepsilon f(x)$ for $\varepsilon < 1$. Apply the Feature Translation Lemma 1.3 to claim (i). For (ii), observe that

$$\|x - y\| \le \|x - p\| + \|y - p\|$$
$$\le \varepsilon(f(x) + f(y))$$

By the Lipschitz Continuity Lemma 1.2

$$f(y) \le f(x) + \|x - y\|$$
$$\le f(x) + \varepsilon(f(x) + f(y)), \text{ or}$$
$$(1 - \varepsilon)f(y) \le (1 + \varepsilon)f(x).$$

Therefore, for $\varepsilon < 1$,

$$\|x - y\| \le \varepsilon\left(1 + \frac{1+\varepsilon}{1-\varepsilon}\right) f(x) \le \frac{2\varepsilon}{1-\varepsilon} f(x).$$

∎

A restricted Delaunay edge pq is dual to a Voronoi facet that intersects Σ. Any such intersection point, say x, is within $\frac{\varepsilon}{1-\varepsilon} f(p)$ distance from p by the Short

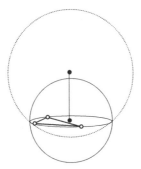

Figure 3.8. The circumradius of a triangle which is also the radius of its diametric ball (shown with solid circle) is no more than the radius of a circumscribing ball (shown with dotted circle).

Distance Lemma 3.6. The length of pq cannot be more than twice the distance between x and p. Hence, $\|p - q\| \leq \frac{2\varepsilon}{1-\varepsilon} f(p)$. We can extend this argument to the restricted Delaunay triangles too. A restricted Delaunay triangle t is dual to a Voronoi edge e that intersects Σ. The intersection point, say x, belongs to the Voronoi cells adjacent to e. Let V_p be any such cell. The point x is the center of a circumscribing ball of the triangle dual to e. By the Short Distance Lemma 3.6, x is within $\frac{\varepsilon}{1-\varepsilon} f(p)$ distance from p. The ball $B_{x,\|x-p\|}$ circumscribes t. The circumradius of t is no more than $\|x - p\|$ as the circumradius of a triangle cannot be more than any of its circumscribing ball (see Figure 3.8). Thus, the following corollary is immediate from the Short Distance Lemma 3.6.

Corollary 3.1. *For $\varepsilon < 1$, we have*

(i) the length of a restricted Delaunay edge e is at most $\frac{2\varepsilon}{1-\varepsilon} f(p)$ where p is any vertex of e and

(ii) the circumradius of any restricted Delaunay triangle t is at most $\frac{\varepsilon}{1-\varepsilon} f(p)$ where p is any vertex of t.

Lemma 3.7 (Long Distance). *Suppose a line intersects Σ in two points x and y and makes an angle no more than ξ with $\mathbf{n}_x$. One has $\|x - y\| \geq 2f(x) \cos \xi$.*

Proof. Consider the two medial balls at x as in Figure 3.9. The line meets the boundaries of these two balls at x and at points that must be at least $2r \cos \xi$ distance away from x where r is the radius of the smaller of the two balls. Since $r \geq f(x)$, the result follows as y cannot lie inside any of the two medial balls. ∎

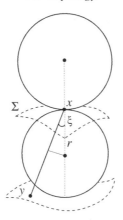

Figure 3.9. Illustration for the Long Distance Lemma 3.7.

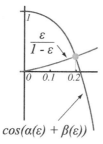

Figure 3.10. The graphs of the two functions on the left and right hand sides of the inequality in Condition A.

3.2.2 Voronoi Faces

Next we consider in turn the Voronoi edges, Voronoi facets, and Voronoi cells and show that they indeed satisfy the topological ball property if ε satisfies Condition A as stated below. For $\varepsilon < \frac{1}{3}$, let

$$\alpha(\varepsilon) = \frac{\varepsilon}{1 - 3\varepsilon}$$

$$\beta(\varepsilon) = \arcsin \frac{\varepsilon}{1 - \varepsilon} + \arcsin \left(\frac{2}{\sqrt{3}} \sin \left(2 \arcsin \frac{\varepsilon}{1 - \varepsilon} \right) \right).$$

Condition A $\varepsilon < \frac{1}{3}$ and $\cos(\alpha(\varepsilon) + \beta(\varepsilon)) > \frac{\varepsilon}{1 - \varepsilon}$.

Figure 3.10 shows that in the range $0 < \varepsilon \leq \frac{1}{3}$, Condition A holds for ε a little less than 0.2. So, for example, $\varepsilon \leq 0.18$ is a safe choice. Since Condition A stipulates $\varepsilon < \frac{1}{3}$, lemmas such as Normal Variation, Long Distance, Short Distance, and Corollary 3.1 can be applied under Condition A.

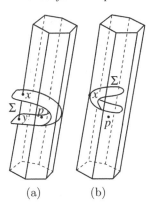

(a)   (b)

Figure 3.11. Illustration for the Voronoi Edge Lemma 3.8. A Voronoi edge intersecting the surface (a) at two points and (b) tangentially in a single point.

Lemma 3.8 (Voronoi Edge). *A Voronoi edge intersects* Σ *transversally in a single point if Condition* A *holds.*

Proof. Suppose for the sake of contradiction there is a Voronoi edge e in a Voronoi cell V_p intersecting Σ at two points x and y, or at a single point tangentially (see Figure 3.11). The dual Delaunay triangle, say pqr, is a restricted Delaunay triangle. By Corollary 3.1, its circumradius is no more than $\frac{\varepsilon}{1-\varepsilon} f(p)$. By the Triangle Normal Lemma 3.5, $\angle_a(\mathbf{n}_{pqr}, \mathbf{n}_p) \leq \beta(\varepsilon)$ if

$$\frac{1}{\sqrt{2}} > \frac{\varepsilon}{1 - \varepsilon}$$

a restriction satisfied by Condition A.

The Normal Variation Lemma 3.3 puts an upper bound of $\alpha(\varepsilon)$ on the angle between the normals at p and x as $\|x - p\| \leq \varepsilon f(x)$. Let ξ denote the angle between $\mathbf{n}_x$ and the Voronoi edge e. We have

$$\xi = \angle_a(\mathbf{n}_x, \mathbf{n}_{pqr}) \leq \angle_a(\mathbf{n}_x, \mathbf{n}_p) + \angle_a(\mathbf{n}_p, \mathbf{n}_{pqr})$$
$$\leq \alpha(\varepsilon) + \beta(\varepsilon). \tag{3.1}$$

If e intersects Σ tangentially at x, we have $\xi = \frac{\pi}{2}$ requiring $\alpha(\varepsilon) + \beta(\varepsilon) \geq \frac{\pi}{2}$. Condition A requires $\varepsilon < 0.2$ which gives $\alpha(\varepsilon) + \beta(\varepsilon) < \frac{\pi}{2}$. Therefore, when Condition A is satisfied, e cannot intersect Σ tangentially. So, assume that e intersects Σ at two points x and y.

By the Short Distance Lemma 3.6, $\|x - y\| \leq \frac{2\varepsilon}{1-\varepsilon} f(x)$ and by the Long Distance Lemma 3.7, $\|x - y\| \geq 2 f(x) \cos \xi$. A contradiction is reached when

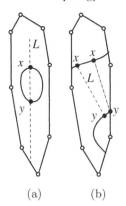

(a)   (b)

Figure 3.12. A Voronoi facet intersecting Σ (a) in a cycle and (b) in two segments.

$2\cos\xi > \frac{2\varepsilon}{1-\varepsilon}$, or

$$\cos(\alpha(\varepsilon) + \beta(\varepsilon)) > \frac{\varepsilon}{1-\varepsilon}. \tag{3.2}$$

Condition A satisfies Inequality 3.2 giving the required contradiction. ∎

Lemma 3.9 (Voronoi Facet). *A Voronoi facet F intersects Σ transversally in a 1-ball if Condition A is satisfied.*

Proof. The intersection of F with Σ may contradict the assertion of the lemma if (i) Σ touches F tangentially at a point, (ii) Σ intersects F in a 1-sphere, that is, a cycle, or (iii) Σ intersects F in more than one component.

The dual Delaunay edge, say pq, of F is in the restricted Delaunay triangulation. Let $\mathbf{n}_F$ denote the normal to F. Its direction is the same as that of pq up to orientation. We have $\|p - q\| \leq \frac{2\varepsilon}{1-\varepsilon} f(p)$ by Corollary 3.1. Therefore, the Edge Normal Lemma 3.4 gives

$$\angle_a(\mathbf{n}_p, \mathbf{n}_F) \geq \frac{\pi}{2} - \arcsin\frac{\varepsilon}{1-\varepsilon}$$

as long as $\varepsilon < 1$.

If Σ meets F tangentially at a point x, we have $\angle_a(\mathbf{n}_x, \mathbf{n}_F) = 0$ and by the Normal Variation Lemma 3.3 $\angle\mathbf{n}_p, \mathbf{n}_x \leq \frac{\varepsilon}{1-3\varepsilon}$ when $\varepsilon < \frac{1}{3}$. This means, for $\varepsilon < \frac{1}{3}$, we have

$$\frac{\pi}{2} - \arcsin\frac{\varepsilon}{1-\varepsilon} \leq \angle_a(\mathbf{n}_p, \mathbf{n}_F) \leq \frac{\varepsilon}{1-3\varepsilon} = \alpha(\varepsilon).$$

The above inequality contradicts the upper bound for ε given by Condition A.

If Σ meets F in a cycle, let x be any point on it and L be the line on F intersecting the cycle at x orthogonally (see Figure 3.12(a)). This line must meet the cycle in another point, say y. The angle between L and $\mathbf{n}_x$ satisfies $\angle_a(L, \mathbf{n}_x) \leq \angle_a(L', \mathbf{n}_x)$ for any other line L' on F passing through x. Choose L' that minimizes the angle with $\mathbf{n}_p$. The line L' being on the Voronoi facet F makes exactly $\frac{\pi}{2}$ angle with the dual restricted Delaunay edge, say pq. We know by the Edge Normal Lemma 3.4

$$\angle_a(\overrightarrow{pq}, \mathbf{n}_p) \geq \frac{\pi}{2} - \arcsin \frac{\varepsilon}{1 - \varepsilon}.$$

Therefore, for $\varepsilon < 1$,

$$\angle_a(L', \mathbf{n}_p) = \frac{\pi}{2} - \angle_a(\overrightarrow{pq}, \mathbf{n}_p) \leq \arcsin \frac{\varepsilon}{1 - \varepsilon}.$$

These facts with the Normal Variation Lemma 3.3 give

$$\angle_a(L', \mathbf{n}_x) \leq \angle_a(L', \mathbf{n}_p) + \angle(\mathbf{n}_p, \mathbf{n}_x) \leq \arcsin \frac{\varepsilon}{1 - \varepsilon} + \alpha(\varepsilon) \qquad (3.3)$$

for $\varepsilon < \frac{1}{3}$.

The right-hand side of Inequality 3.3 is less than the upper bound for ξ in the proof of the Voronoi Edge Lemma 3.8. Thus, we reach a contradiction between distances implied by the Short Distance Lemma 3.6 and the Long Distance Lemma 3.7 when Condition A holds.

In the case Σ meets F in two or more components as in Figure 3.12(b), consider any point x in one of the components. Let y be the closest point to x on any other component, say C. If the line L joining x and y meets C orthogonally at y we have the situation as in the previous case with only x and y interchanged. In the other case, y lies on the boundary of C on a Voronoi edge. The angle between L and $\mathbf{n}_y$ is less than the angle between the Voronoi edge and $\mathbf{n}_y$ which is no more than $\alpha(\varepsilon) + \beta(\varepsilon)$ as proved in the Voronoi Edge Lemma 3.8 (Inequality 3.1). We reach a contradiction again between two distances using the same argument.   ∎

Lemma 3.10 (Voronoi Cell). *A Voronoi cell V_p intersects Σ in a 2-ball if Condition A holds.*

Proof. We have $W = V_p \cap \Sigma$ contained in a ball B of radius $\frac{\varepsilon}{1-\varepsilon} f(p)$ by the Short Distance Lemma 3.6. If W is a manifold without boundary, B contains a medial axis point m by the Feature Ball Lemma 1.1. Then the radius of B is at least

$$\frac{\|m - p\|}{2} \geq \frac{f(p)}{2}.$$

We reach a contradiction if $\varepsilon < \frac{1}{3}$ which is satisfied by Condition A. So, assume that W is a manifold with boundary. It may not be a 2-ball only if it is nonorientable, has a handle, or has more than one boundary cycle. If W were nonorientable, so would be Σ, which is impossible. In case W has a handle, $B \cap \Sigma$ is not a 2-ball. By the Feature Ball Lemma 1.1, it contains a medial axis point reaching a contradiction again for $\varepsilon < \frac{1}{3}$ which is satisfied by Condition A.

The only possibility left is that W has more than one boundary cycles. Let L be the line of the normal at p. Consider a plane that contains L and intersects at least two boundary cycles. Such a plane exists since otherwise L must intersect W at a point other than p and we reach a contradiction between two distance lemmas. The plane intersects V_p in a convex polygon and W in at least two curves. We can argue as in the proof of the Voronoi Facet Lemma 3.9 to reach a contradiction between two distance lemmas. ∎

Condition A holds for $\varepsilon \leq 0.18$. Therefore, the Voronoi Edge Lemma, Facet Lemma, and Cell Lemma hold for $\varepsilon \leq 0.18$. Then, Theorem 3.1 leads to the following result.

Theorem 3.2 (Topological Ball.). *Let P be an ε-sample of a smooth surface Σ. For $\varepsilon \leq 0.18$, (P, Σ) satisfies the topological ball property and hence the underlying space of* $\mathrm{Del}P|_\Sigma$ *is homeomorphic to Σ.*

3.3 Notes and exercises

The remarkable connection between ε-samples of a smooth surface and the Voronoi diagram of the sample points was first discovered by Amenta and Bern [4]. The Normal Lemma 3.2 and the Normal Variation Lemma 3.3 are two key observations made in this paper. The topological ball property that ensures the homeomorphism between the restricted Delaunay triangulation and the surface was discovered by Edelsbrunner and Shah [48]. Amenta and Bern observed that the Voronoi diagram of a sufficiently dense sample satisfies the topological ball property though the proof was not as rigorous as presented here. The proof presented here is adapted from Cheng, Dey, Edelsbrunner, and Sullivan [23].

Exercises

1. Let the restricted Voronoi cell $V_p|\Sigma$ be adjacent to the restricted Voronoi cell $V_q|\Sigma$ in the restricted Voronoi diagram $\mathrm{Vor}P|\Sigma$. Show that the distance between any two points x and y from the union of $Vp|\Sigma$ and $Vq|\Sigma$ is $\tilde{O}(\varepsilon)f(x)$ when ε is sufficiently small.

2. A version of the Edge Normal Lemma 3.4 can be derived from the Triangle Normal Lemma 3.5, albeit with a slightly worse angle bound. Derive this angle bound and carry out the proof of the topological ball property with this bound. Find out an upper bound on ε for the proof.

3. The topological ball property is a sufficient but not a necessary condition for the homeomorphism between a sampled surface and a restricted Delaunay triangulation of it. Establish this fact by an example.

4. Show an example where
   (i) all Voronoi edges satisfy the topological ball property, but the Voronoi cell does not,
   (ii) all Voronoi facets satisfy the topological ball property, but the Voronoi cell does not.

5. Show that for any $n > 0$, there exists a C^2-smooth surface for which a sample with n points has the Voronoi diagram where no Voronoi edge intersects the surface.

6^h. Let F be a Voronoi facet in the Voronoi diagram Vor P where P is an ε-sample of a C^2-smooth surface Σ. Let Σ intersect F in a single interval and the intersection points with the Voronoi edges lie within $\varepsilon f(p)$ away from p where $F \subset V_p$. Show that all points of $F \cap \Sigma$ lie within $\varepsilon f(p)$ distance when ε is sufficiently small.

7. Let F and Σ be as described in Exercise 6, but $F \cap \Sigma$ contains two or more topological intervals. Show that there exists a Voronoi edge $e \in F$ so that $e \cap \Sigma$ is at least $\lambda f(p)$ away from p where $\lambda > 0$ is an appropriate constant.

8°. Let the pair (P, Σ) satisfy the topological ball property. We know that the underlying space of Del $P|_\Sigma$ and Σ are homeomorphic. Prove or disprove that they are isotopic.

4

Surface Reconstruction

In the previous chapter we learned that the restricted Delaunay triangulation is a good approximation of a densely sampled surface Σ from both topological and geometric view point. Unfortunately, we cannot compute this triangulation because the restricted Voronoi diagram Vor $P|_\Sigma$ cannot be computed without knowing Σ. As a remedy we approximate the restricted Voronoi diagram and compute a set of triangles that is a superset of all restricted Delaunay triangles. This set is pruned to extract a manifold surface which is output as an approximation to the sampled surface Σ.

4.1 Algorithm

First, we observe that each restricted Voronoi cell $V_p|_\Sigma = V_p \cap \Sigma$ is almost flat if the sample is sufficiently dense. This follows from the Normal Variation Lemma 3.3 as the points in $V_p|_\Sigma$ cannot be far apart if ε is small. In particular, $V_p|_\Sigma$ lies within a thin neighborhood of the tangent plane τ_p at p. So, we need two approximations: (i) an approximation to τ_p or equivalently to $\mathbf{n}_p$ and (ii) an approximation to $V_p|_\Sigma$ based on the approximation to $\mathbf{n}_p$. The following definitions of *poles* and *cocones* are used for these two approximations.

4.1.1 Poles and Cocones

Definition 4.1 (Poles). *The farthest Voronoi vertex, denoted p^+, in V_p is called the* positive pole *of p. The* negative pole *of p is the farthest point $p^- \in V_p$ from p so that the two vectors from p to p^+ and p^- make an angle more than $\frac{\pi}{2}$. We call $\mathbf{v}_p = p^+ - p$, the* pole vector *for p. If V_p is unbounded, p^+ is taken at infinity and the direction of $\mathbf{v}_p$ is taken as the average of all directions given by the unbounded Voronoi edges.*

The following lemma is a direct consequence of the Normal Lemma 3.2. It says that the pole vectors approximate the true normals at the sample points.

Lemma 4.1 (Pole). *For $\varepsilon < 1$, the angle between the normal $\mathbf{n}_p$ at p and the pole vector $\mathbf{v}_p$ satisfies the inequality*

$$\angle_a(\mathbf{n}_p, \mathbf{v}_p) \leq 2 \arcsin \frac{\varepsilon}{1 - \varepsilon}.$$

Proof. First, consider the case where V_p is bounded. Since the Voronoi cell V_p contains the centers of the medial balls at p, we have $\|p^+ - p\| \geq f(p)$. Thus, plugging $\mu = 1$ in the Normal Lemma 3.2 we obtain the result immediately.

Next, consider the case where V_p is unbounded. In this case $\mathbf{v}_p$ is computed as the average of the directions of the infinite Voronoi edges. The angle $\angle_a(\mathbf{v}_p, \mathbf{n}_p)$ in this case cannot be more than the worst angle made by an infinite Voronoi edge with $\mathbf{n}_p$. An infinite Voronoi edge e makes the same angle with $\mathbf{n}_p$ as the vector $\overrightarrow{pp_\infty}$ does, where the infinite endpoint of e is taken at p_∞. Again we have $\|p - p_\infty\| \geq f(p)$ and the Normal Lemma 3.2 can be applied with $\mu = 1$ to give the result. ∎

The Pole Lemma 4.1 says that the pole vector approximates the normal $\mathbf{n}_p$. Thus, the plane $\tilde{\tau}_p$ passing through p with the pole vector as normal approximates the tangent plane τ_p. The following definition of *cocone* accommodates a thin neighborhood around $\tilde{\tau}_p$ to account for the small uncertainty in the estimation of $\mathbf{n}_p$.

Definition 4.2 (Cocone). *The set $C_p = \{y \in V_p : \angle_a(\overrightarrow{py}, \mathbf{v_p}) \geq \frac{3\pi}{8}\}$ is called the cocone of p. In words, C_p is the complement of a double cone that is clipped within V_p. This double cone has p as the apex, the pole vector $\mathbf{v}_p$ as the axis, and an opening angle of $\frac{3\pi}{8}$ with the axis. See Figure 4.1 for an example of a cocone.*

As an approximation to $V_p|_\Sigma$, cocones meet all Voronoi edges that are intersected by Σ. So, if we compute all triangles dual to the Voronoi edges intersected by cocones, we obtain all restricted Delaunay triangles and possibly a few others. We call this set of triangles *cocone triangles*. We will see later that all cocone triangles lie very close to Σ. A cleaning step is necessary to weed out some triangles from the set of cocone triangles so that a 2-manifold is computed as output. This is accomplished by a *manifold extraction* step.

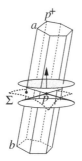

Figure 4.1. The positive pole p^+ helps estimating the normal. The double cone forming the cocone has the apex at p and axis pp^+. The Voronoi edge ab intersects the cocone. Its dual Delaunay triangle is a cocone triangle.

COCONE(P)

1   compute Vor P;

2   $T = \emptyset$;

3   for each Voronoi edge $e \in \text{Vor} P$ do

4   if COCONETRIANGLES(e)

5         $T := T \cup \text{dual } e$;

6   endfor

7   $E :=$EXTRACTMANIFOLD(T);

8   output E.

Let us now look into the details of the two steps COCONETRIANGLES and EXTRACTMANIFOLD.

To check if a Voronoi edge $e = (a, b)$ intersects C_p we consider the three vectors $\mathbf{v}_p$, $\mathbf{a} = \overrightarrow{pa}$, $\mathbf{b} = \overrightarrow{pb}$, and three conditions I, II, and III:

$$\text{I.} \quad \frac{|\mathbf{v}_p^T \mathbf{a}|}{\|\mathbf{v}_p\| \|\mathbf{a}\|} \leq \cos \frac{3\pi}{8} \quad \text{or} \quad \frac{|\mathbf{v}_p^T \mathbf{b}|}{\|\mathbf{v}_p\| \|\mathbf{b}\|} \leq \cos \frac{3\pi}{8},$$

$$\text{II.} \quad \frac{\mathbf{v}_p^T \mathbf{a}}{\|\mathbf{v}_p\| \|\mathbf{a}\|} < 0 \quad \text{and} \quad \frac{-\mathbf{v}_p^T \mathbf{b}}{\|\mathbf{v}_p\| \|\mathbf{b}\|} < 0,$$

$$\text{III.} \quad \frac{\mathbf{v}_p^T \mathbf{a}}{\|\mathbf{v}_p\| \|\mathbf{a}\|} > 0 \quad \text{and} \quad \frac{-\mathbf{v}_p^T \mathbf{b}}{\|\mathbf{v}_p\| \|\mathbf{b}\|} > 0.$$

Condition I checks if any of the vertices a and b of the Voronoi edge e lies inside C_p. Conditions II and III check if both a and b lie outside C_p, but the edge e crosses it. The triangle $t = \text{dual } e$ is marked as a cocone triangle only if e intersects cocones of *all* three vertices of t.

CocoNeTriangles(*e*)

```
1  t := dual e;
2  flag := TRUE;
3  for each vertex p of t do
4      if none of Conditions I, II, and III holds
5          flag:= FALSE;
6  endfor
7  return flag.
```

The set T of cocone triangles enjoys some interesting geometric properties which we exploit in the manifold extraction step as well as in the proofs of geometric and topological guarantees of Cocone. Of course, the sample has to be sufficiently dense for these properties to hold. In the rest of the chapter we assume that $\varepsilon \leq 0.05$ which satisfies Condition A stated in Chapter 3, enabling us to apply the results therein.

4.1.2 Cocone Triangles

First, we show that each triangle in T has a small empty ball circumscribing it, that is, the radius of this ball is small compared to the local feature sizes at their vertices. Notice that the diametric ball of a triangle may not be empty. Hence, the smallest *empty* ball circumscribing a triangle may not be its diametric ball. Nevertheless, a small empty circumscribing ball also means that the circumradius of the triangle is small. This fact together with the Triangle Normal Lemma 3.5 implies that all cocone triangles lie almost flat to the surface.

Lemma 4.2 (Small Triangle). *Let t be any cocone triangle and r denote the radius of the smallest empty ball circumscribing t. For each vertex p of t and $\varepsilon \leq 0.05$, one has*

(i) $r \leq \frac{1.18\varepsilon}{1-\varepsilon} f(p)$ and
(ii) circumradius of t is at most $\frac{1.18\varepsilon}{1-\varepsilon} f(p)$.

Proof. Let z be any point in V_p so that

$$\angle_a(n_p, \overrightarrow{pz}) \geq \frac{3\pi}{8} - 2\arcsin\frac{\varepsilon}{1-\varepsilon}. \tag{4.1}$$

First, we claim that for any such point z, we have $\|z - p\| \leq \frac{1.18\,\varepsilon}{1-\varepsilon} f(p)$ if $\varepsilon \leq 0.05$.

If $\angle_a(\mathbf{n}_p, \overrightarrow{pz}) > \theta = \arcsin \frac{\varepsilon}{\mu(1-\varepsilon)} + \arcsin \frac{\varepsilon}{1-\varepsilon}$, then $\|z - p\| \le \mu f(p)$ according to the Normal Lemma 3.2. With $\mu = \frac{1.18\varepsilon}{1-\varepsilon}$ and $\varepsilon \le 0.05$ we have

$$\theta = \arcsin \frac{1}{1.18} + \arcsin \frac{\varepsilon}{1 - \varepsilon} < \frac{3\pi}{8} - 2\arcsin \frac{\varepsilon}{1 - \varepsilon}. \qquad (4.2)$$

Thus, from Inequalities 4.1 and 4.2 we have

$$\angle_a(\mathbf{n}_p, \overrightarrow{pz}) \ge \frac{3\pi}{8} - 2\arcsin \frac{\varepsilon}{1 - \varepsilon} > \theta. \qquad (4.3)$$

Therefore, any point $z \in V_p$ satisfying Inequality 4.1 also satisfies

$$\|z - p\| \le \frac{1.18\varepsilon}{1 - \varepsilon} f(p).$$

Now let t be any cocone triangle with p being any of its vertices and $e = $ dual t being its dual Voronoi edge. For t to be a cocone triangle, it is necessary that there is a point $y \in e$ so that $\angle_a(\mathbf{v}_p, \overrightarrow{py}) \ge \frac{3\pi}{8}$. Taking into account the angle $\angle_a(\mathbf{v}_p, \mathbf{n}_p)$, this necessary condition implies

$$\angle_a(\mathbf{n}_p, \overrightarrow{py}) \ge \frac{3\pi}{8} - 2\arcsin \frac{\varepsilon}{1 - \varepsilon}$$

which satisfies Inequality 4.1. Hence, we have

$$\|y - p\| \le \frac{1.18\,\varepsilon}{1 - \varepsilon} f(p) \text{ for } \varepsilon \le 0.05.$$

The ball $B_{y,\|y-p\|}$ is empty and circumscribes t proving (i). The claim in (ii) follows immediately from (i) as the circumradius of t cannot be larger than the radius of any ball circumscribing it. ∎

The next lemma proves that all cocone triangles lie almost parallel to the surface. The angle bounds are expressed in terms of $\alpha(\varepsilon)$ and $\beta(\varepsilon)$ that are defined in Chapter 3.

Lemma 4.3 (Cocone Triangle Normal). *Let t be any cocone triangle and $\mathbf{n}_t$ be its normal. For any vertex p of t one has $\angle_a(\mathbf{n}_p, \mathbf{n}_t) \le \alpha(\frac{2.36\varepsilon}{1-\varepsilon}) + \beta(1.18\varepsilon)$ when $\varepsilon \le 0.05$.*

Proof. Let q be a vertex of t with a maximal angle of t. The circumradius of t is at most $\frac{1.18\varepsilon}{1-\varepsilon} f(q)$ by the Small Triangle Lemma 4.2. Then, by the Triangle

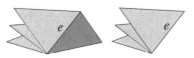

Figure 4.2. The edge e is not sharp in the left picture; it is sharp in the right picture.

Normal Lemma 3.5,

$$\angle_a(\mathbf{n}_q, \mathbf{n}_t) \leq \arcsin \frac{1.18\varepsilon}{1-\varepsilon} + \arcsin \left(\frac{2}{\sqrt{3}} \sin \left(2 \arcsin \frac{1.18\varepsilon}{1-\varepsilon} \right) \right)$$

$$\leq \arcsin \frac{1.18\varepsilon}{1-1.18\varepsilon} + \arcsin \left(\frac{2}{\sqrt{3}} \sin \left(2 \arcsin \frac{1.18\varepsilon}{1-1.18\varepsilon} \right) \right)$$

$$= \beta\,(1.18\varepsilon) \text{ for } \varepsilon \leq 0.05.$$

The distance between p and q is no more than the diameter of the circle circumscribing t, that is, $\|p - q\| \leq \frac{2.36\varepsilon}{1-\varepsilon} f(p)$ (Small Triangle Lemma 4.2). By the Normal Variation Lemma 3.3, $\angle(\mathbf{n}_p, \mathbf{n}_q) \leq \alpha(\frac{2.36\varepsilon}{1-\varepsilon})$. The desired bound for $\angle_a(\mathbf{n}_p, \mathbf{n}_t)$ follows since it is no more than the sum $\angle(\mathbf{n}_p, \mathbf{n}_q) + \angle_a(\mathbf{n}_q, \mathbf{n}_t)$. ∎

4.1.3 Pruning

Prior to the extraction of a 2-manifold from the set of cocone triangles, some of them are pruned. An edge e is *sharp* if any two consecutive cocone triangles around it form an angle more than $\frac{3\pi}{2}$ (see Figure 4.2). Edges with a single triangle incident to them are also sharp by default. We will show later that the cocone triangles include all restricted Delaunay triangles when a sample is sufficiently dense. The set of restricted Delaunay triangles cannot be incident to sharp edges. This implies that we can prune triangles incident to sharp edges and still retain the set of restricted Delaunay triangles. In fact, we can carry out this pruning in a cascaded manner. By deleting one triangle incident to a sharp edge, we may create other sharp edges. Since no restricted Delaunay triangle is pruned, none of their edges become sharp. Therefore, it is safe to delete the new sharp edges with all of their incident triangles.

This pruning step weeds out all triangles incident to sharp edges, but the remaining triangles still may not form a surface. They may form layers of thin pockets creating a nonmanifold. A manifold surface is extracted from this possibly layered set by *walking* outside the space covered by them (see Figure 4.3). The manifold extraction step depends on the fact that cocone triangles contain all restricted Delaunay triangles none of whose edges is sharp. We prove this fact below.

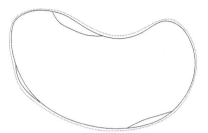

Figure 4.3. Thin pockets left after pruning, a manifold is obtained by walking on the outside indicated by the dotted curve.

Theorem 4.1 (Restricted Delaunay). *For $\varepsilon \leq 0.05$, the following conditions hold:*

(i) cocone triangles contain all restricted Delaunay triangles and
(ii) no restricted Delaunay triangle has a sharp edge.

Proof. Consider (i). Let y be any point in any restricted Voronoi cell $V_p|_\Sigma$. We claim that $\angle_a(\mathbf{n}_p, \overrightarrow{py})$ is larger than $\frac{\pi}{2} - \arcsin \frac{\varepsilon}{2(1-\varepsilon)}$. We have $\|y - p\| \leq \varepsilon f(y)$ since $y \in V_p|_\Sigma$ and P is an ε-sample of Σ. By the Feature Translation Lemma 1.3, $\|y - p\| \leq \frac{\varepsilon}{1-\varepsilon} f(p)$. We can therefore apply the proof of the Edge Normal Lemma 3.4 to establish that

$$\angle_a(\mathbf{n}_p, \overrightarrow{py}) \geq \frac{\pi}{2} - \arcsin \frac{\varepsilon}{2(1 - \varepsilon)}.$$

Let t be any restricted Delaunay triangle and $e = $ dual t be the dual Voronoi edge. Consider the point $y = e \cap \Sigma$. We have $y \in V_p|_\Sigma$ for each of the three points $p \in P$ determining e. For each such p, the angle $\angle_a(\mathbf{n}_p, \overrightarrow{py})$ is larger than $\pi/2 - \arcsin \frac{\varepsilon}{2(1-\varepsilon)}$. Therefore,

$$\begin{aligned}
\angle_a(\overrightarrow{py}, \mathbf{v}_p) &\geq \angle_a(\overrightarrow{py}, \mathbf{n}_p) - \angle_a(\mathbf{n}_p, \mathbf{v}_p) \\
&\geq \frac{\pi}{2} - \arcsin \frac{\varepsilon}{2(1 - \varepsilon)} - \angle_a(\mathbf{n}_p, \mathbf{v}_p).
\end{aligned} \tag{4.4}$$

By the Pole Lemma 4.1 we have

$$\begin{aligned}
\angle_a(\mathbf{n}_p, \mathbf{v}_p) + \arcsin \frac{\varepsilon}{2(1 - \varepsilon)} &\leq 2 \arcsin \frac{\varepsilon}{1 - \varepsilon} + \arcsin \frac{\varepsilon}{2(1 - \varepsilon)} \\
&< \frac{\pi}{8} \text{ for } \varepsilon \leq 0.05.
\end{aligned}$$

So, by Inequality 4.4, $\angle_a(\overrightarrow{py}, \mathbf{v}_p) > \frac{3\pi}{8}$. Therefore, the point y is in the cocone C_p by definition. Hence, t is a cocone triangle.

Consider (ii). Let t_1 and t_2 be adjacent triangles in the restricted Delaunay triangulation with e as their shared edge and let $p \in e$ be any of their shared

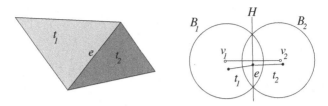

Figure 4.4. Illustration for the Restricted Delaunay Theorem 4.1.

vertices. Since t_1 and t_2 belong to the restricted Delaunay triangulation, they have circumscribing empty balls B_1 and B_2, respectively, centered at points, say v_1 and v_2 of Σ.

The boundaries of B_1 and B_2 intersect in a circle C contained in a plane H, with $e \subset H$. The plane H separates t_1 and t_2, since the third vertex of each triangle lies on the boundary of its circumscribing ball, and $B_1 \subseteq B_2$ on one side of H, while $B_2 \subseteq B_1$ on the other (see Figure 4.4). The line through v_1, v_2 is perpendicular to H. Both v_1 and v_2 belong to the Voronoi facet dual to e. This means v_1 and v_2 belong to a restricted Voronoi cell and the distance $\|v_1 - v_2\| \leq \frac{2\varepsilon}{(1-\varepsilon)} f(v_1)$ by the Short Distance Lemma 3.6. So, the segment $v_1 v_2$ forms an angle of at least $\pi/2 - \arcsin \frac{\varepsilon}{1-\varepsilon}$ with $\mathbf{n}_{v_1}$ (Edge Normal Lemma 3.4). This normal differs, in turn, from $\mathbf{n}_p$ by an angle of at most $\frac{\varepsilon}{1-3\varepsilon}$ (Normal Variation Lemma 3.3). So, the angle between H and $\mathbf{n}_p$ is at most $\frac{\varepsilon}{1-3\varepsilon} + \arcsin \frac{\varepsilon}{1-\varepsilon}$. For small ε, they are nearly parallel. In particular, if $\varepsilon \leq 0.05$, H makes at most $7°$ with $\mathbf{n}_p$. Similarly, plugging $\varepsilon \leq 0.05$ in the angle upper bound of the Cocone Triangle Normal Lemma 4.3, one gets that the normals of both t_1 and t_2 differ from the surface normal at p by at most $24°$.

Thus, we have t_1 on one side of H, t_2 on the other and the smaller angle between H and either triangle is at least $59°$. Hence, the smaller angle between t_1 and t_2 is at least $118°$ and e is not sharp. ∎

4.1.4 Manifold Extraction

A simplicial complex with an underlying space of a 2-manifold is extracted out of the pruned set of cocone triangles. Let $\Sigma' \subseteq \Sigma$ be any connected component of the sampled surface. Since cocone triangles are small (Small Triangle Lemma 4.2), they cannot join points from different components of Σ. Let T' be the pruned set of cocone triangles with vertices in Σ'. Consider the medial axis of Σ'. The triangles of T' lie much closer to Σ' than to its medial axis. Furthermore, T' includes the restricted Delaunay triangulation Del $P|_{\Sigma'}$ (Restricted Delaunay Theorem 4.1). Therefore, if $|T'|$ denotes the underlying space of T', the space $\mathbb{R}^3 \setminus |T'|$ has precisely two disjoint open sets O_{in} and O_{out} containing the inner and outer medial axis of Σ' respectively. The manifold extraction step computes the boundary of the closure of O_{out}, which we simply refer to as the boundary of O_{out}.

Let E' be the boundary of O_{out}. We claim that E' is a 2-manifold. Let p be any vertex of E'. Orient the normal $\mathbf{n}_p$ so that it points toward O_{out}. Consider a sufficiently small ball B centering p. Call the point where the ray of $\mathbf{n}_p$ intersects the boundary of B the *north pole*. Obviously, the north pole is in O_{out}. Let T_p denote the set of triangles in T' which are visible from the north pole within B. The triangles of T_p are in the boundary of O_{out}. Since there is no sharp edge in T', the set of triangles T_p makes a topological disk. We argue that T_p is the only set of triangles in the boundary of O_{out} which are incident to p.

Let $q \neq p$ be a vertex of a triangle $t \in T_p$. The triangle t is in T_q. If not, the line of the normal $\mathbf{n}_p$, when moved parallelly through the edge pq toward q, must hit an edge in T' that is sharp. The assumption to this claim is that the normals $\mathbf{n}_p$ and $\mathbf{n}_q$ are almost parallel and hence the visibility directions at p and q are almost parallel. Since T' does not have any sharp edge, t is in T_q. This means that all topological disks at the vertices of E' are compatible and they form a 2-manifold. This 2-manifold separates O_{out} from T' implying that E' cannot have any other triangles from T' other than the ones in the topological disks described above.

We compute E' from T' as a collection of triangles by a depth first walk in the Delaunay triangulation Del P. Recall that T' is disjoint from any other triangles on a component of Σ different from Σ'. The walk starts with a seed triangle in T'. The routine SEED computes this seed triangle for each component T' of the pruned set by another depth first walk in the Delaunay triangulation. At any generic step, SEED comes to a triangle t via a tetrahedron σ and performs the following steps. First, it checks if t is a cocone triangle. If so, it checks if it belongs to a component T' for which a seed has not yet been picked. If so, the pair (σ, t), also called the *seed pair*, is put into the seed set. Then, it marks all triangles of T' so that any subsequent check can identify that a seed for T' has been picked. The walk continues through the triangles and their adjacent tetrahedra in a depth first manner till a seed pair for each component such as T' of T is found. In a seed pair (σ, t) for a component T', the tetrahedron σ and the triangle t should be in O_{out} and on its boundary E' respectively. To ensure it SEED starts the walk from any convex hull triangle in Del P and continues till it hits a cocone triangle. The initiation of the walk from a convex hull triangle ensures that the first triangle encountered in a component is on the outside of that component or equivalently on the boundary of O_{out} defined for that component. Assuming the function SEED, a high-level description of EXTRACTMANIFOLD is given.

EXTRACTMANIFOLD(T)

1   $T :=$ pruned T;
2   $SD :=$ SEED(T);
3   for each tuple $(\sigma, t) \in SD$ do
4       $E' :=$ SURFTRIANGLES(σ,t);
5       $E := E \cup E'$;
6   endfor
7   return the simplicial complex of E.

The main task in EXTRACTMANIFOLD is done by SURFTRIANGLES which takes a seed pair (σ, t) as input. First, we initialize the surface E' with the seed triangle t which is definitely in E' (line 1). Next, we initialize a stack *Pending* with the triple (σ, t, e) where e is an edge of t (lines 3 and 4). As long as the stack *Pending* is not empty, we pop its top element (σ, t, e). If the edge e is not already processed we call the function SURFACENEIGHBOR to compute a tetrahedron–triangle pair (σ', t') (line 9). The tetrahedron σ' is adjacent to t' and intersects O_{out} where t' is in E' and is adjacent to t via e. The triangle t' is inserted in E'. Then two new triples (σ', t', e') are pushed on the stack *pending* for each edge $e' \neq e$ of t' (lines 11–13). Finally, we return E' (line 16).

SURFTRIANGLES (σ,t)

1   $E' := \{t\}$;
2   *Pending* $:= \emptyset$;
3   pick any edge e of t;
4   push (σ, t, e) on *Pending*;
5   while *Pending* $\neq \emptyset$ do
6   pop (σ, t, e) from *Pending*;
7   if e is not marked processed
8   mark e processed;
9           $(\sigma', t') :=$ SURFACENEIGHBOR (σ, t, e);
10          $E' := E' \cup \{t'\}$;
11   for each edge $e' \neq e$ of t' do
12   push (σ', t', e) on *Pending*;
13   endfor
14   endif
15 endwhile
16 return E'.

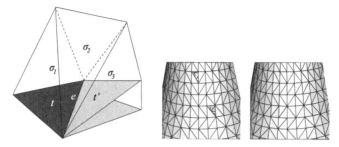

Figure 4.5. A stable computation of SURFACENEIGHBOR (left), a zoom on a reconstruction after an unstable computation with numerical errors (middle), and a stable computation without any numerical error (right).

The question is how to implement the function SURFACENEIGHBOR. It has to output a tuple (σ', t') where t' is the neighbor of t on the surface given by E' and σ' is an adjacent tetrahedron intersecting O_{out}. One can compute the surface neighbor t' of t using some numerical computations involving some dot product computations of vectors. However, these computations often run into trouble due to numerical errors with finite precision arithmetics. In particular, triangles of certain types of flat tetrahedra called *slivers* tend to contribute to these numerical errors and slivers are not uncommon in the Delaunay triangulation of a sample from a surface.

A robust and faster implementation of the function SURFACENEIGHBOR avoids numerical computations by exploiting the combinatorial structure of the Delaunay triangulation. Every triangle in the Delaunay triangulation has two incident tetrahedra if we account for the infinite ones incident to the convex hull triangles. SURFACENEIGHBOR is called with a triple (σ, t, e). It circles over the tetrahedra and triangles incident to the edge e starting from t and going toward the other triangle of σ incident to e. This circular walk stops when another cocone triangle t' is reached. If t' is reached via the tetrahedron σ', we output the pair (σ', t'). Assuming inductively that σ intersects O_{out}, the tetrahedron σ' also intersects O_{out}. For example, in Figure 4.5, SURFACENEIGHBOR is passed on the triple (σ_1, t, e) and then it circles through the tetrahedra $\sigma_1, \sigma_2, \sigma_3$, and their triangles till it reaches t'. At this point it returns (σ_3, t') where both σ_1 and σ_3 lie outside, that is, in O_{out}. SURFTRIANGLES with this implementation of SURFACENEIGHBOR is robust since no numerical decisions are involved (see Figure 4.5). Combinatorial computations instead of numerical ones make SURFTRIANGLES fast provided the Delaunay triangulation is given in a form which allows to answer queries for neighboring tetrahedra quickly.

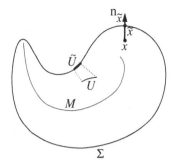

Figure 4.6. Illustration for the map v.

4.2 Geometric Guarantees

In this section we establish more properties of the cocone triangles which are eventually used to prove the geometric and topological guarantees of the output of COCONE. We introduce a map v that takes each point $x \in \mathbb{R}^3$ to its closest point in Σ. Notice that v is well defined everywhere in $\mathbb{R}^3$ except at the medial axis M of Σ. Mathematically, $v : \mathbb{R}^3 \setminus M \to \Sigma$ where $v(x) \in \Sigma$ is closest to x. Observe that the line containing x and $v(x)$ is normal to Σ at x. The map v will be used at many places in this chapter and the chapters to follow. Let

$$\tilde{x} = v(x) \text{ for any point } x \in \mathbb{R}^3 \setminus M \text{ and}$$

$$\tilde{U} = \{\tilde{x} : x \in U\} \text{ for any set } U \subset \mathbb{R}^3 \setminus M.$$

See Figure 4.6 for an illustration.

First, we show that all points of the cocone triangles lie close to the surface. This, in turn, allows us to extend the Cocone Triangle Normal Lemma 4.3 to the interior points of the cocone triangles. The restriction of v to the underlying space $|T|$ of the set of cocone triangles T is a well-defined function; refer to Figure 4.7. For if some point x had more than one closest point on the surface when $\varepsilon \leq 0.05$, x would be a point of the medial axis giving $\|p - x\| \geq f(p)$ for any vertex p of a triangle in T; but by the Small Triangle Lemma 4.2 every point $q \in |T|$ is within $\frac{1.18\,\varepsilon}{1-\varepsilon} f(p)$ distance of a triangle vertex $p \in \Sigma$ for $\varepsilon \leq 0.05$.

In the next two lemmas and also later we use the notation $\tilde{O}(\varepsilon)$ defined in Section 1.2.3.

Lemma 4.4. *Let q be any point in a cocone triangle $t \in T$. The distance between q and the point $\tilde{q}$ is $\tilde{O}(\varepsilon) f(\tilde{q})$ and is at most $0.08 f(\tilde{q})$ for $\varepsilon \leq 0.05$.*

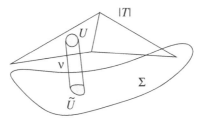

Figure 4.7. The map v restricted to $|T|$.

Proof. By the Small Triangle Lemma 4.2 the circumradius of t is at most $\mu f(p)$ where $\mu = \frac{1.18\,\varepsilon}{1-\varepsilon} \leq .07$ and p is any of its vertices. Let p be a vertex of t subtending a maximal angle of t. Since there is a sample point, namely a vertex of t, within $\mu f(p)$ distance from q, we have $\|q - \tilde{q}\| \leq \mu f(p)$. We are interested in expressing this bound in terms of $f(\tilde{q})$, so we need an upper bound on $\|p - \tilde{q}\|$.

The triangle vertex p has to lie outside the medial balls at $\tilde{q}$, while, since $\tilde{q}$ is the nearest surface point to q, q must lie on the segment between $\tilde{q}$ and the center of one of these medial balls. For any fixed $\|p - q\|$, these facts imply that $\|p - \tilde{q}\|$ is maximized when the angle $\angle pq\tilde{q}$ is a right angle. Thus, $\|p - \tilde{q}\| \leq \sqrt{5}\mu f(p) \leq 0.14 f(p)$ for $\varepsilon \leq 0.05$. This implies that $f(p) = \tilde{O}(\varepsilon)f(\tilde{q})$ and in particular $f(p) \leq 1.17 f(\tilde{q})$ by Lipschitz property of f. We have $\|q - \tilde{q}\| \leq \mu f(p) = \tilde{O}(\varepsilon)f(\tilde{q})$ and $\|q - \tilde{q}\| \leq 0.08 f(\tilde{q})$ in particular. ∎

With a little more work, we can also show that the triangle normal agrees with the surface normal at $\tilde{q}$.

Lemma 4.5. *Let q be a point on triangle $t \in T$. The angle $\angle(\mathbf{n}_{\tilde{q}}, \mathbf{n}_p)$ is at most $14°$ where p is a vertex of t with a maximal angle. Also, the angle $\angle_a(\mathbf{n}_{\tilde{q}}, \mathbf{n}_t)$ is $\tilde{O}(\varepsilon)$ and is at most $38°$ for $\varepsilon \leq 0.05$.*

Proof. We have already seen in the proof of Lemma 4.4 that $\|p - \tilde{q}\| = \tilde{O}(\varepsilon)f(p)$. In particular, $\|p - \tilde{q}\| \leq 0.14 f(p)$ when $\varepsilon \leq 0.05$. Applying the Normal Variation Lemma 3.3, and taking $\rho = \tilde{O}(\varepsilon)$ ($\rho = 0.14$ in particular), shows that the angle between $\mathbf{n}_{\tilde{q}}$ and $\mathbf{n}_p$ is $\tilde{O}(\varepsilon)$ and is less than $14°$. The angle between $\mathbf{n}_t$ and $\mathbf{n}_p$ is $\tilde{O}(\varepsilon)$ and is less than $24°$ for $\varepsilon \leq 0.05$ by the Cocone Triangle Normal Lemma 4.3. Thus, the triangle normal and $\mathbf{n}_{\tilde{q}}$ make $\tilde{O}(\varepsilon)$ angle which is at most $38°$ for $\varepsilon \leq 0.05$. ∎

Lemma 4.2, Lemma 4.4, and Lemma 4.5 imply that the output surface $|E|$ of Cocone is close to Σ both point-wise and normal-wise. The following theorem states this precisely.

Theorem 4.2. *The surface* $|E|$ *output by* COCONE *satisfies the following geometric properties for* $\varepsilon \leq 0.05$.

(i) Each point $p \in |E|$ *is within* $\tilde{O}(\varepsilon)f(x)$ *distance of a point* $x \in \Sigma$. *Conversely, each point* $x \in \Sigma$ *is within* $\tilde{O}(\varepsilon)f(x)$ *distance of a point in* $|E|$.

(ii) Each point p *in a triangle* $t \in E$ *satisfies* $\angle_a(\mathbf{n}_{\tilde{p}}, \mathbf{n}_t) = \tilde{O}(\varepsilon)$.

4.2.1 Additional Properties

We argued in Section 4.1.4 that the underlying space of the simplicial complex output by COCONE is a 2-manifold. Let E be this simplicial complex output by COCONE. A pair of triangles $t_1, t_2 \in E$ are *adjacent* if they share at least one common vertex p. Since the normals to all triangles sharing p differ from the surface normal at p by at most 24° (apply the Cocone Triangle Normal Lemma 4.3), and that normal in turn differs from the pole vector at p by less than 7° (apply the Pole Lemma 4.1), we can orient the triangles sharing p, arbitrarily but consistently. We call the normal facing the positive pole the *inside* normal and the normal facing away from it the *outside* normal. Let θ be the angle between the two inside normals of t_1, t_2. We define the angle at which the two triangles meet at p to be $\pi - \theta$.

PROPERTY I: Every two adjacent triangles in E meet at their common vertex at an angle greater than $\pi/2$.

Requiring this property excludes manifolds which contain sharp folds and, for instance, flat tunnels. Since the cocone triangles are all nearly perpendicular to the surface normals at their vertices (Cocone Triangle Normal Lemma 4.3) and the manifold extraction step eliminates triangles adjacent to sharp edges, E has this property.

PROPERTY II: Every point in P is a vertex of E.

The Restricted Delaunay Theorem 4.1 ensures that the set T of cocone triangles contains all restricted Delaunay triangles even after the pruning. Therefore at this point T contains a triangle adjacent to every sample point in P. Lemma 4.6 below says that each sample point is exposed to the outside for the component of T to which it belongs. This ensures that at least one triangle is selected for each sample point by the manifold extraction step. This implies that E has the second property as well.

Lemma 4.6 (Exposed). *Let* p *be a sample point and let* m *be the center of a medial ball* B *tangent to* Σ *at* p. *No cocone triangle intersects the interior of the segment* pm *for* $\varepsilon \leq 0.05$.

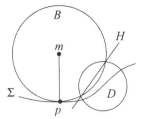

Figure 4.8. Illustration for the exposed lemma.

Proof. To intersect the segment pm, a cocone triangle t would have to intersect B and so would the smallest empty ball circumscribing t. Call it D. Let H be the plane of the circle where the boundaries of B and D intersect (see Figure 4.8). We argue that H separates the interior of pm and t.

On one side of H, B is contained in D and on the other, D is contained in B. Since the vertices of t lie on Σ and hence not in the interior of B, t has to lie in the open halfspace, call it H^+, in which D is outside B. Since D is empty, p cannot lie in the interior of D; but since p lies on the boundary of B, it therefore cannot lie in H^+. We claim that $m \notin H^+$ either.

Since $m \in B$, if it lay in H^+, m would be contained in D. Since m is a point of the medial axis, the radius of D would be at least $\frac{f(p')}{2}$ for any vertex p' of t. For $\varepsilon \leq 0.05$, this contradicts the Small Triangle Lemma 4.2. Therefore p, m, and hence the segment pm cannot lie in H^+ and H separates t and pm. ∎

4.3 Topological Guarantee

Recall that a function $h : \mathbb{X} \to \mathbb{Y}$ defines a homeomorphism between two compact Euclidean subspaces $\mathbb{X}$ and $\mathbb{Y}$ if h is continuous, one-to-one, and onto. In this section, we will show a homeomorphism between Σ and any piecewise-linear 2-manifold made up of cocone triangles from T. The piecewise-linear manifold E selected by the manifold extraction step is such a space thus completing the proof of homeomorphism.

4.3.1 The Map ν

We define the homeomorphism explicitly, using the function $\nu : \mathbb{R}^3 \setminus M \to \Sigma$, as defined earlier. We will consider the restriction ν' of ν to the underlying space $|E|$ of E, that is, $\nu' : |E| \to \Sigma$. Our approach will be first to show that ν' is well-behaved on the sample points themselves and then show that this property extends in the interior of each triangle in E.

Lemma 4.7. *For $\varepsilon \leq 0.05$, $\nu' : |E| \to \Sigma$ is a well-defined continuous function.*

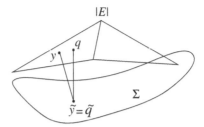

Figure 4.9. ν' maps y and q to the same point which is impossible.

Proof. By the Small Triangle Lemma 4.2, every point $q \in |E|$ is within $\frac{1.18\varepsilon}{1-\varepsilon} f(p)$ of a triangle vertex $p \in \Sigma$ when $\varepsilon \le 0.05$. Therefore, $|E| \subset \mathbb{R}^3 \setminus M$ for $\varepsilon \le 0.05$. It follows that ν' is well defined. It is continuous since it is a restriction of a continuous function.   ∎

Let q be any point such that $\tilde{q}$ is a sample point p. By the Exposed Lemma 4.6, q lies on the segment pm where m is the center of a medial ball touching Σ at p. We have the following.

Corollary 4.1. *For $\varepsilon \le 0.05$, the function ν' is one-to-one from $|E|$ to every sample point p.*

In what follows, we will show that ν' is indeed one-to-one on all of $|E|$. The proof proceeds in three short steps. We show that ν' induces a homeomorphism on each triangle, then on each pair of adjacent triangles and finally on $|E|$ as a whole.

Lemma 4.8. *Let U be a region contained within one triangle $t \in E$ or in adjacent triangles of E. For $\varepsilon \le 0.05$, the function ν' defines a homeomorphism between U and $\tilde{U} \subset \Sigma$.*

Proof. We know that ν' is well defined and continuous on U, so it only remains to show that it is one-to-one. First, we prove that if U is in one triangle t, ν' is one-to-one. For a point $q \in t$, the vector $\mathbf{n}_q$ from $\tilde{q}$ to q is perpendicular to the surface at $\tilde{q}$; since Σ is smooth, the direction of $\mathbf{n}_q$ is unique and well defined. If there were some $y \in t$ with $\tilde{y} = \tilde{q}$, then $q, \tilde{q}$, and y would all be collinear and t itself would have to contain the line segment between q and y (see Figure 4.9). This implies that the normal $\mathbf{n}_q$ is parallel to the plane of t. In other words, $\mathbf{n}_q$ is orthogonal to the normal of t, contradicting the Cocone Triangle Normal Lemma 4.3 which says that the normal of t is nearly parallel to $\mathbf{n}_q$.

Now, we consider the case in which U is contained in more than one triangle. Let q and y be two points in U such that $\tilde{q} = \tilde{y} = x$ and let v be a common vertex of the triangles that contain U. Since v' is one-to-one in one triangle, q and y must lie in the two distinct triangles t_q and t_y. The line l through x with direction $\mathbf{n}_x$ pierces the patch U at least twice; if y and q are not adjacent intersections along l, redefine q so that this is true ($\tilde{q} = x$ for any intersection q of l with U). Now consider the orientation of the patch U according to the direction to the positive pole at v. Either l passes from inside to outside and back to inside when crossing y and q, or from outside to inside and back to outside.

The acute angles between the triangle normals of t_q, t_y, and $\mathbf{n}_x$ are less than $38°$ (Lemma 4.5), that is, the triangles are stabbed nearly perpendicularly by $\mathbf{n}_x$. But since the orientation of U is opposite at the two intersections, the angle between the two *oriented* triangle normals is greater than $104°$, meaning that t_q and t_y must meet at v at an acute angle. This would contradict PROPERTY I, which is that t_q and t_y meet at v at an obtuse angle. Hence, there are no two points y, q in U with $\tilde{q} = \tilde{y}$. ∎

4.3.2 Homeomorphism Proof

We finish the proof for homeomorphism guarantee using a theorem from topology.

Theorem 4.3 (Homeomorphism). *The map v' defines a homeomorphism from the surface $|E|$ computed by* COCONE *to the surface Σ for $\varepsilon \leq 0.05$.*

Proof. Let $\Sigma' \subset \Sigma$ be $v'(|E|)$. We first show that $(|E|, v')$ is a *covering space* of Σ'. Informally, $(|E|, v')$ is a covering space for Σ' if v' maps $|E|$ onto Σ', with no folds or other singularities. Showing that $(|E|, v')$ is a covering space is weaker than showing that v' defines a homeomorphism, since, for instance, it does not preclude several connected components of $|E|$ mapping onto the same component of Σ', or more interesting behavior, such as a torus wrapping twice around another torus to form a *double covering*.

For a set $X \subseteq \Sigma'$, let $\tau(X)$ denote the set in $|E|$ so that $v'(\tau(X)) = X$. Formally, the $(|E|, v')$ is a covering space of Σ' if, for every $x \in \Sigma'$, there is a path-connected *elementary neighborhood* V_x around x such that each path-connected component of $\tau(V_x)$ is mapped homeomorphically onto V_x by v'.

To construct such an elementary neighborhood, note that the set of points $\tau(x)$ corresponding to a point $x \in \Sigma'$ is nonzero and finite, since v' is one-to-one on each triangle of E and there are only a finite number of triangles. For each point $q \in \tau(x)$, we choose an open neighborhood U_q of q, homeomorphic to a

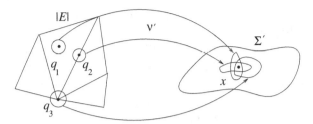

Figure 4.10. Proof of the Homeomorphism Theorem 4.3; $\tau(x) = \{q_1, q_2, q_3\}$.

disk and small enough so that U_q is contained only in triangles that contain q. (see Figure 4.10).

We claim that ν' maps each U_q homeomorphically onto $\tilde{U}_q$. This is because it is continuous, it is onto $\tilde{U}_q$ by definition, and, since any two points x and y in U_q are in adjacent triangles, it is one-to-one by Lemma 4.8.

Let $U'(x) = \bigcap_{q \in \tau(x)} \nu'(U_q)$, the intersection of the maps of each of the U_q. $U'(x)$ is the intersection of a finite number of open neighborhoods, each containing x, so we can find an open disk V_x around x. V_x is path connected and each component of $\tau(V_x)$ is a subset of some U_q and hence is mapped homeomorphically onto V_x by ν'. Thus, $(|E|, \nu')$ is a covering space for Σ'.

We now show that ν' defines a homeomorphism between $|E|$ and Σ'. Since $\nu' : |E| \to \Sigma'$ is onto by definition, we need only that ν' is one-to-one. Consider one connected component G of Σ'. A theorem of algebraic topology says that when $(|E|, \nu')$ is a covering space of Σ', the sets $\tau(x)$ for all $x \in G$ have the same cardinality. We now use Corollary 4.1, that ν' is one-to-one at every sample point. Since each connected component of Σ contains some sample points, it must be the case that ν' is everywhere one-to-one and $|E|$ and Σ' are homeomorphic.

Finally, we show that $\Sigma' = \Sigma$. Since $|E|$ is a 2-manifold without boundary and is compact, Σ' must be as well. So, Σ' cannot include part of a connected component of Σ, and hence Σ' must consist of a subset of the connected components of Σ. Since every connected component of Σ contains a sample p (actually many sample points) and $\nu'(p) = p$, all components of Σ belong to Σ'. Therefore, $\Sigma' = \Sigma$ and $|E|$ and Σ are homeomorphic. ∎

It can also be shown that $|E|$ and Σ are isotopic (Exercise 7). We will show a technique to prove isotopy in Section 6.1.3.

4.4 Notes and Exercises

The problem of reconstructing surfaces from samples dates back to the early 1980s. First, the problem appeared in the form of contour surface reconstruction in medical imaging. A set of cross sections obtained via CAT scan or MRI need to be joined with a surface in this application. The points on the boundary of the cross sections are already joined by a polygonal curve. The problem is to connect these curves in consecutive cross sections. A dynamic programming-based solution for two such consecutive curves was first proposed by Fuchs, Kedem, and Uselton [51]. A result by Gitlin, O'Rourke, and Subramanian [57] shows that, in general, two polygonal curves cannot be joined by nonself intersecting surface with only those vertices; even deciding its possibility is NP-hard. Several solutions with the addition of Steiner points have been proposed to overcome the problem, see Meyers, Skinner, and Sloan [68]. A Delaunay-based solution for the problem was proposed by Boissonnat [15] which is the first Delaunay-based algorithm proposed for a surface reconstruction problem. Later the Delaunay-based method was refined by Boissonnat and Geiger [17] and Cheng and Dey [22].

The most general version of surface reconstruction where no input information other than the point coordinates is used became popular to handle the data from range and laser scanners. In the context of computer graphics and vision, this problem has been investigated intensely in the past decade with emphasis on practical performance. The early work by Hoppe et al. [61], Curless and Levoy [26] and the recent works by Alexa et al. [1], Carr et al. [18], and Ohtake et al. [73] are a few such examples. The α-shape by Edelsbrunner and Mücke [47] is the first popular Delaunay-based surface reconstruction method. It is the generalization of the α-shape concept described in Section 2.4 of Chapter 2. Depending on an input parameter α, Delaunay simplices are filtered based on their circumscribing Delaunay ball sizes. The main drawback of this method is that it is not suitable for nonuniform samples. Also, with the uniform samples, the user is burdened with the selection of an appropriate α.

The first algorithm for surface reconstruction with proved guarantees was devised by Amenta and Bern [4]. They generalized the CRUST algorithm for curve reconstruction to the surface reconstruction problem. The idea of poles and approximating the normals with the pole vector was a significant breakthrough. The crust triangles (Exercise 2) enjoy some nice properties that help the reconstruction. The COCONE algorithm as described here is a successor of CRUST. Devised by Amenta, Choi, Dey, and Leekha [6], this algorithm simplified the CRUST algorithm and its proof of correctness. COCONE eliminated one of the two Voronoi diagram computations of CRUST and also a normal filtering step. The homeomorphism between the reconstructed surface and the original sampled surface was first established by Amenta et al. [6]. Boissonnat and Cazals [16] devised another algorithm for surface reconstruction using the natural neighbor coordinates (see Section 9.7) and proved its correctness using the framework of CRUST. Since the Deluanay triangulations of n points in three dimensions take $O(n^2)$ time and space in the worst case, the complexity of all these algorithms is $O(n^2)$. Funke and Ramos [53] showed how the COCONE algorithm can be adapted to run in $O(n \log n)$ time. Unfortunately, the modified algorithm is not very practical.

Although the Delaunay triangulation of n points in three dimensions may produce $\Omega(n^2)$ simplices in the worst case, such complexities are rarely observed for point samples of surfaces in practice. Erickson [49] started the investigation of determining the complexity of the Delaunay triangulations for points on surfaces. Attali, Boissonnat, and Lieutier [10] proved that indeed the Delaunay triangulation has $O(n \log n)$ complexity if the point sample is locally uniform for a certain class of smooth surfaces.

Exercises

1. We know that Voronoi vertices for a dense sample from a curve in the plane lie near the medial axis. The same is not true for surfaces in three dimensions. Show an example where a Voronoi vertex for an arbitrarily dense sample lies arbitrarily close to the surface.

2^h. Let P be a sample from a C^2-smooth surface Σ and V be the set of poles in Vor P. Consider the following generalization of the CRUST. A triangle in the Del $(P \cup V)$ is a *crust* triangle if all of its vertices are in P. Show the following when P is an ε-sample for a sufficiently small ε.

   (i) All restricted Delaunay triangles in Del $(P \cup V)|_\Sigma$ are crust triangles.

   (ii) All crust triangles have circumradius $\tilde{O}(\varepsilon) f(p)$ where p is a vertex of the triangle.

3. Let t be a triangle in Del P where $B = B_{v,r}$ and $B' = B'_{v',r'}$ are two Delaunay balls circumscribing t. Let x be any point on the circle where the boundaries of B and B' intersect. Show that, if $\angle vxv' > \frac{\pi}{2}$, the triangle normal of t makes an angle of $\tilde{O}(\varepsilon)$ with the normals to Σ at its vertices when P is an ε-sample of Σ for a sufficiently small ε.

4. Recall that P is a locally (ε, δ)-uniform sample of a smooth surface Σ if P is an ε-sample of Σ and each sample point $p \in P$ is at least $\frac{\varepsilon}{\delta} f(p)$ distance away from all other points in P where $\delta > 1$ is a constant. Show that each triangle in the surface output by COCONE for such a sample has a bounded aspect ratio (circumradius to edge length ratio). Also, prove that each vertex has no more than a constant number (determined by ε and δ) of triangles on the surface.

5^h. Let t be a cocone triangle. We showed that any point $x \in t$ is $\tilde{O}(\varepsilon) f(\tilde{x})$ away from its closest point $\tilde{x}$ in Σ. Prove that the bound can be improved to $\tilde{O}(\varepsilon^2) f(\tilde{x})$.

6. We defined a Delaunay triangle t as a cocone triangle if dual t intersects cocones of *all* of its three vertices. Relax the condition by defining t as a cocone triangle if dual t intersects the cocone of *any* of its vertices. Carry out the proofs of different properties of cocone triangles with this modified definition.

7. We showed that the surface $|E|$ computed by Cocone is homeomorphic to Σ when ε is sufficiently small. Prove that $|E|$ is indeed isotopic to Σ.

5

Undersampling

The surface reconstruction algorithm in the previous chapter assumes that the sample is sufficiently dense, that is, ε is sufficiently small. However, the cases of undersampling where this density condition is not met are prevalent in practice. The input data may be dense only in parts of the sampled surface. Regions with small features such as high curvatures are often not well sampled. When sampled with scanners, occluded regions are not sampled at all. Nonsmooth surfaces such as the ones considered in CAD are bound to have undersampling since no finite point set can sample nonsmooth regions to satisfy the ε-sampling condition for a strictly positive ε. Even some surfaces with boundaries can be viewed as a case of undersampling. If Σ is a surface without boundary and $\Sigma' \subset \Sigma$ is a surface with boundary, a sample of Σ' is also a sample of Σ. This sample may be dense for Σ' and not for Σ.

In this chapter we describe an algorithm that detects the regions of undersampling. This detection helps in reconstructing surfaces with boundaries. Later, we will see that this detection also helps in repairing the unwanted holes created in the reconstructed surface due to undersampling.

5.1 Samples and Boundaries

Let P be an input point set that samples a surface Σ where Σ does not have any boundary. The set P does not necessarily sample Σ equally well everywhere, but it does so for a subset (patches) of Σ which we call Σ^ε. The complement $\Sigma \setminus \Sigma^\varepsilon$ are undersampled regions. The boundaries of Σ^ε coincide with those of the undersampled regions. The goal is to reconstruct these boundaries from the input sample P. Since only P is known, we have to define the notion of boundary also with respect to P.

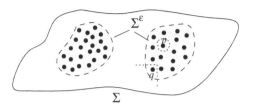

Figure 5.1. ε-sampled patches are shaded darker.

5.1.1 Boundary Sample Points

Definition 5.1. *For any $\varepsilon > 0$, an ε-sampled patch $\Sigma^\varepsilon \subseteq \Sigma$ is the closure of the set $\{x \mid B_{x,\varepsilon f(x)} \cap P \neq \emptyset\}$.*

In the above definition $f : \Sigma \to \mathbb{R}$ is the local feature size function of Σ and not of Σ^ε. Figure 5.1 illustrates the notion of ε-sampled patches for a small ε. Notice that Σ^ε is orientable as it is a subset of a surface $\Sigma \subset \mathbb{R}^3$ without boundary which must be orientable. Also, by definition, Σ^ε is compact.

In any compact surface, interior points are distinguished from boundary points by their neighborhoods. An interior point has a neighborhood homeomorphic to the plane $\mathbb{R}^2$. A boundary point, on the other hand, has a neighborhood homeomorphic to the half plane $\mathbb{H}_+^2 = \{(x_1, x_2) \in \mathbb{R}^2 \mid x_1 \geq 0\}$. Even though all sample points in P may be interior points of the well-sampled patch Σ^ε, the existence of the nonempty boundary should be evident from the arrangement of points in P. We aim for a classification of *interior* and *boundary* sample points that capture the intuitive difference between interior and boundary points. We use the intersection of Σ^ε with the Voronoi diagrams to make this distinction. Let $F_p^\varepsilon = (\mathrm{Int} V_p) \cap \Sigma^\varepsilon$. The set F_p^ε consists of all points in Σ^ε that have p as their nearest sample point. In other words, p is a discrete representative of the surface patch F_p^ε. Or, conversely, F_p^ε can be taken as the neighborhood of p. Using this notion of neighborhood, we define the *interior* and *boundary* sample points.

Definition 5.2. *A sample point p from a sample P of Σ^ε is called* interior *if F_p^ε does not have a boundary point of Σ^ε. Points in P that are not interior are called* boundary *sample points.*

Observe that if p is a boundary sample point, the boundary of Σ^ε intersects the interior of V_p. In Figure 5.1, p is an interior sample point whereas q is a boundary sample point.

5.1.2 Flat Sample Points

The definitions of interior and boundary sample points are useless for computations since the restricted Voronoi diagram Vor $P|\Sigma^\varepsilon$ cannot be computed using only P. Therefore, we need a characterization of the sample points so that they can be distinguished algorithmically. To this end we define a *flatness* condition that can be checked with P while Σ^ε being unknown. It is shown that, under some mild assumptions, the boundary sample points cannot be flat whereas most of the interior sample points are flat.

The definition of flatness is motivated by the observation that the interior sample points have their Voronoi cells skinny and elongated along the normal, a property not satisfied by the boundary sample points. So, we need a measure to determine the "skinnyness" of the Voronoi cells. This motivates the following definitions of *radius* and *height*.

Definition 5.3. *The radius r_p of a Voronoi cell V_p is the radius of the cocone C_p, that is, $r_p = \max\{\|y - p\| \mid y \in C_p\}$. The height h_p is the distance $\|p - p^-\|$ where p^- is the negative pole defined in Section 4.1.*

The radius captures how "fat" the Voronoi cell is, whereas the height captures how "long" it is. The ratio of the radius over the height gives a measure how "skinny" the Voronoi cell is. It is important that the height be defined as the distance to the negative pole rather than to the positive one. Otherwise, a Voronoi cell only stretched toward the positive pole may qualify for a skinny cell, a structure not supported by interior sample points.

Not only do we want to capture the "skinnyness" of the Voronoi cells, but also the direction of their elongation. In case of an interior sample point p, the direction of elongation direction follows the direction of $\mathbf{n}_p$. This means that the pole vector $\mathbf{v}_p$ or its opposite vector match with those at the neighboring sample points in directions. We take the *cocone neighbors* for this check. The set of points in P whose Voronoi cells intersect the cocone of p are called the cocone neighbors of p. Formally, the set

$$N_p = \{q \in P : C_p \cap V_q \neq \emptyset\}$$

is the *cocone neighbors* of p.

The flatness condition is defined relative to two parameters ρ and α.

Definition 5.4. *A sample point $p \in P$ is called (ρ, α)-flat if the following two conditions hold:*

(i) Ratio condition: $r_p \leq \rho h_p$,
(ii) Normal condition: $\forall q$ with $p \in N_q$, $\angle_a(\mathbf{v}_p, \mathbf{v}_q) \leq \alpha$.

Ratio condition imposes that the Voronoi cell is long and thin in the direction of $\mathbf{v}_p$. The normal condition stipulates that the direction of elongation of V_p matches that of the Voronoi cell of any sample point whose cocone neighbor is p. For the theoretical guarantees, we use $\rho = 1.3\varepsilon$ and $\alpha = 0.14$.

We will need the Normal Lemma 3.2 for further analysis. Since we proved this lemma for surfaces without boundary, we cannot apply it to each sample point in P since P only samples Σ^ε well which may have boundaries. However, we can adopt the result for interior sample points as stated below. We can copy the entire proof for the Normal Lemma 3.2 since each point x of Σ^ε in V_p is within $\varepsilon f(x)$ distance from p.

Lemma 5.1 (Interior Normal). *Let p be an interior sample point in an ε-sampled patch Σ^ε with the surface normal $\mathbf{n}_p$ at p. Let y be any point in the Voronoi cell V_p such that $||y - p|| > \mu f(p)$ for some $\mu > 0$. For $\varepsilon < 1$, one has*

$$\angle_a(\overrightarrow{py}, \mathbf{n}_p) \leq \arcsin\left(\frac{\varepsilon}{\mu(1-\varepsilon)}\right) + \arcsin\left(\frac{\varepsilon}{1-\varepsilon}\right).$$

5.2 Flatness Analysis

Our goal is to exploit the definition of flat sample points in a boundary detection algorithm. We prove two theorems that form the basis of this algorithm. The Interior Sample Theorem 5.1 says that the interior sample points with well-sampled neighborhoods are flat and the Boundary Sample Theorem 5.2 says that the boundary sample points cannot be flat.

Lemma 5.2 (Ratio). *Interior sample points satisfy the ratio condition for $\rho = 1.3\varepsilon$ and $\varepsilon \leq 0.01$.*

Proof. Let p be any interior sample point. Letting $\mu = 1$ and y equal a pole of p in the Interior Normal Lemma 5.1 we get, for $\varepsilon \leq 0.01$,

$$\phi = \angle_a(\mathbf{v}_p, \mathbf{n}_p)$$
$$\leq 2\arcsin\left(\frac{\varepsilon}{1-\varepsilon}\right).$$

Let y be any point in C_p. By definition $\angle_a(\mathbf{v}_p, \overrightarrow{yp}) \geq \frac{3\pi}{8}$. From the Interior Normal Lemma 5.1 (applying the contrapositive of the implication stated there) we get $||y - p|| \leq \mu f(p)$ where μ fulfills the inequality

$$\arcsin\left(\frac{\varepsilon}{\mu(1-\varepsilon)}\right) + \arcsin\left(\frac{\varepsilon}{1-\varepsilon}\right) + \phi \leq \frac{3\pi}{8}. \tag{5.1}$$

One can deduce that $\mu \leq 1.3\varepsilon$ satisfies Inequality 5.1 for $\varepsilon \leq 0.01$. That is, the radius of the Voronoi cell V_p is at most $1.3\varepsilon f(p)$, that is, $r_p \leq 1.3\varepsilon f(p)$.

Next, we show that the height $h_p = \|p^- - p\|$ is at least $f(p)$. Recall that p^- is the farthest point in V_p from p so that $(p^- - p)^T \mathbf{v}_p < 0$. Since $\mathbf{n}_p$ makes a small angle up to orientation with $\mathbf{v}_p$, one of the two medial balls going through p has its center m such that the vector $\overrightarrow{mp}$ does not point in the same direction as $\mathbf{v}_p$, that is, $(m - p)^T \mathbf{v}_p < 0$. We know that $\|m - p\| \geq f(p)$ and $m \in V_p$. This means that there is a Voronoi vertex $v \in V_p$ with $\|v - p\| \geq \|m - p\|$ and $(v - p)^T \mathbf{v}_p < 0$. This immediately implies that such a Voronoi vertex p^-, which is furthest from p, is at least $f(p)$ away from p. Therefore, $h_p \geq f(p) \geq \frac{r_p}{1.3\varepsilon}$. Thus, the ratio condition is fulfilled for $\rho = 1.3\varepsilon$ where $\varepsilon \leq 0.01$. ∎

Although the ratio condition holds for all interior sample points, the normal condition may not hold for all of them. Nevertheless, interior sample points with well-sampled neighborhoods satisfy the normal condition. To be precise we introduce the following definition.

Definition 5.5. *An interior sample point p is* deep *if there is no boundary sample point with p as its cocone neighbor.*

Theorem 5.1 (Interior Sample). *All deep interior sample points are (ρ, α)-flat for $\rho = 1.3\varepsilon$, $\alpha = 0.14$, and $\varepsilon \leq 0.01$.*

Proof. It follows from the Ratio Lemma 5.2 that for $\varepsilon \leq 0.01$, deep interior sample points satisfy the ratio condition. We show that they satisfy the normal condition as well. Let q be any Voronoi neighbor of p so that $p \in N_q$. The sample point q is interior by definition. Therefore, we can apply the Interior Normal Lemma 5.1 to assert that $\angle_a(\mathbf{v}_q, \mathbf{n}_q) \leq 2 \arcsin \frac{\varepsilon}{1-\varepsilon}$. Also, by the Ratio Lemma 5.2 any point $x \in C_q$ satisfies $\|x - q\| \leq 1.3\varepsilon f(q)$. In particular, there is such a point $x \in V_p \cap V_q$ since $p \in N_q$. With $\|x - q\| \leq 1.3\varepsilon f(q)$ and $x \in V_p \cap V_q$ we have $\|p - q\| \leq 2.6\varepsilon f(q)$. For $\varepsilon \leq 0.01$ we can apply the Normal Variation Lemma 3.3 to deduce $\angle(\mathbf{n}_p, \mathbf{n}_q) \leq 0.03$. Thus, we have

$$\angle_a(\mathbf{v}_q, \mathbf{v}_p) \leq \angle_a(\mathbf{v}_q, \mathbf{n}_q) + \angle(\mathbf{n}_q, \mathbf{n}_p) + \angle_a(\mathbf{n}_p, \mathbf{v}_p)$$
$$\leq 0.14$$

which satisfies the normal condition for $\alpha = 0.14$. ∎

Next, we aim to prove the converse of the above theorem, that is, a (ρ, α)-flat sample point is an interior sample when ρ and α are sufficiently small. In other

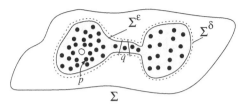

Figure 5.2. Σ^ε shown with the solid curves whereas Σ^δ is shown with the dotted curve. The point p is a boundary sample point in Σ^ε because of the small hole. This point may turn into an interior sample point for Σ^δ in which the hole may disappear. This is prohibited by the Boundary Assumption 5.1(i). The point q is a boundary sample point whose restricted Voronoi cell does not intersect that of any interior sample point violating the Boundary Assumption 5.1(ii).

words, these sample points cannot be boundary samples. This is the statement of the Boundary Sample Theorem 5.2.

For further development we will need to relate h_p with the local feature size $f(p)$. Since the Voronoi cell V_p contains the centers of the two medial balls at p, h_p is an upper bound on $f(p)$. Actually, for surfaces without boundary, it can be shown that h_p approximates the radius of the smaller of the two medial balls at p within a small factor of $\tilde{O}(\varepsilon^{\frac{2}{3}})$ (Exercise 3 in Chapter 6). We need a similar property for surfaces with boundary. However, for such surfaces h_p may not approximate $f(p)$ within a small factor dependent on ε. Nevertheless, we can bound the error with a surface-dependent constant which we use in the proof. Let $\Delta_p = \frac{h_p}{f(p)}$. We have an upper bound on $h_p = ||p^- - p||$ assuming that not all data points lie on a plane. By our assumption that Σ is compact and has a positive local feature size everywhere, $f(p)$ is greater than a surface-dependent constant. Thus, we have a surface-dependent constant, say Δ, so that $\Delta_p \leq \Delta$ for all $p \in \Sigma$.

The proof that the boundary sample points cannot be flat needs some assumptions. The first assumption (i) says that boundary sample points remain as boundary even if Σ^ε is expanded with a small collar around its boundary (see Figure 5.2). Assumption (ii) stipulates that the boundaries are "well separated" disallowing situations as shown in Figure 5.2.

Assumption 5.1 (Boundary Assumption).

(i) We assume that both surfaces Σ^ε and Σ^δ define the same set of boundary sample points when $\delta = 1.3\Delta\varepsilon$ and $\Delta = \max \Delta_p$.

(ii) The restricted Voronoi cell of each boundary sample point in $\mathrm{Vor}\ P|_{\Sigma^\varepsilon}$ intersects the restricted Voronoi cell of at least one interior sample point.

The Boundary Assumption 5.1(i) is used to show the next lemma which leads to the Boundary Sample Theorem 5.2. This lemma says that a sample point satisfying the ratio condition that has a pole vector approximating the normal is an interior sample. Suppose p is such a sample point. The surface Σ has to lie within the cocone in V_p because of the ratio condition and the pole vector approximating the normal. This means that the subset of Σ^ε in V_p is small and, in particular, when expanded with a collar intersects V_p completely. This violates the Boundary Assumption 5.1(i) if p is a boundary sample. We formalize this argument now.

Lemma 5.3 (Interior). *Let p be a sample point which satisfies the ratio condition for $\rho = 1.3\varepsilon$. If $\angle_a(\mathbf{v}_p, \mathbf{n}_p) \leq 0.2$, p is an interior sample point when $\varepsilon \leq \frac{0.01}{1.3\Delta}$.*

Proof. Suppose, on the contrary, p is a boundary sample point. Since the ratio condition holds, we have $||x - p|| \leq \rho h_p = \rho \Delta_p f(p)$ for any point $x \in C_p$. With $\rho = 1.3\varepsilon$, we have $||x - p|| \leq \delta f(p)$ where $\delta = \Delta\rho = 1.3\Delta\varepsilon$. Therefore, for any $x \in C_p$ we have

$$||x - p|| \leq \delta f(p). \tag{5.2}$$

Let y be any point on Σ with $||y - p|| \leq \delta f(p)$. The condition $\varepsilon \leq \frac{0.01}{1.3\Delta}$ gives $\delta < 2$. We can apply the proof of the Edge Normal Lemma 3.4 to claim $\angle_a(\overrightarrow{py}, \mathbf{n}_p) \geq \frac{\pi}{2} - \arcsin\frac{\delta}{2}$. Since $\angle_a(\mathbf{v}_p, \mathbf{n}_p) \leq 0.2$ by condition of the lemma, we have

$$\angle_a(\mathbf{v}_p, \overrightarrow{py}) \geq \frac{\pi}{2} - \arcsin\frac{\delta}{2} - 0.2$$
$$> \frac{3\pi}{8}.$$

It implies that any point $y \in \Sigma$ with $||y - p|| \leq \delta f(p)$ cannot lie on the boundary of the double cone defining C_p. In other words, $\Sigma \cap V_p \in C_p$. Therefore, by Inequality 5.2 any point $y \in \Sigma \cap V_p$ satisfies $||y - p|| \leq \delta f(p)$. According to the Boundary Assumption 5.1 the surface $\Sigma^\delta \supseteq \Sigma^\varepsilon$ must define p as a boundary sample point. But, that would require a boundary point of Σ^δ to be in the interior of V_p. This would in turn require a point $y \in \Sigma$ with $||y - p|| > \delta f(p)$ to be in V_p. We reach a contradiction as each point $y \in \Sigma \cap V_p$ is at most $\delta f(p)$ distance away from p. ∎

Theorem 5.2 (Boundary Sample). *Boundary sample points cannot be (ρ, α)-flat for $\rho = 1.3\varepsilon$, $\alpha = 0.14$, and $\varepsilon \leq \frac{0.01}{1.3\Delta}$.*

Proof. Let p be a boundary sample point. Suppose that, on the contrary, p is $(1.3\varepsilon, 0.14)$-flat. Consider an interior sample point q so that $V_q|_\Sigma \cap V_p|_\Sigma \neq \emptyset$ (Boundary Assumption 5.1(ii)). The sample point p is a cocone neighbor of q since $C_q \cap \Sigma = V_q \cap \Sigma$. The normal condition requires that $\angle_a(\mathbf{v}_p, \mathbf{v}_q) \leq 0.14$. Also, $\|q - p\| \leq 2.6\varepsilon f(q)$ due to the ratio condition. It implies that $\angle(\mathbf{n}_p, \mathbf{n}_q) \leq 0.03$ (Normal Variation Lemma 3.3). Thus,

$$\angle_a(\mathbf{v}_p, \mathbf{n}_p) \leq \angle_a(\mathbf{v}_p, \mathbf{v}_q) + \angle_a(\mathbf{v}_q, \mathbf{n}_q) + \angle(\mathbf{n}_q, \mathbf{n}_p)$$
$$\leq 0.14 + 0.021 + 0.03 = 0.191.$$

Thus, p satisfies the conditions of the Interior Lemma 5.3 and hence is an interior sample point reaching a contradiction. ∎

5.3 Boundary Detection

The algorithm for boundary detection first computes the set of interior sample points, R, that are (ρ, α)-flat where ρ and α are two user-supplied parameters to check the ratio and normal conditions. If ρ and α are small enough, the Interior Sample Theorem 5.1 guarantees that R is not empty. In a subsequent phase R is expanded to include all interior sample points in an iterative procedure. A generic iteration proceeds as follows. Let p be any cocone neighbor of a sample point $q \in R$ so that $p \notin R$ and p satisfies the ratio condition. If $\mathbf{v}_p$ and $\mathbf{v}_q$ make small angle up to orientation, that is, if $\angle_a(\mathbf{v}_p, \mathbf{v}_q) \leq \alpha$, we include p in R. If no such sample point can be found, the iteration stops.

There is a subtle difference between the initial phase and the expansion phase of the boundary detection. The initial phase checks the normal condition for all cocone neighbors (step 3 in ISFLAT) whereas the expansion phase checks this condition only for cocone neighbors that have already been detected as interior (step 6 in BOUNDARY). We argue that R includes all and only interior sample points at the end. The rest of the sample points are detected as boundary ones.

The following routine ISFLAT checks the ratio and normal conditions to detect flat sample points. The input is a sample point $p \in P$ with two parameters ρ and α. The return value is TRUE if p is (ρ, α)-flat and FALSE otherwise. The routine BOUNDARY uses ISFLAT to detect the boundary sample points.

ISFLAT($p \in P, \alpha, \rho$)
```
1   compute the radius r_p and the height h_p;
2   if r_p ≤ ρh_p
3       if ∠_a(v_p, v_q) ≤ α ∀q with p ∈ N_q
4           return TRUE;
5   return FALSE.
```

BOUNDARY(P, α, ρ)

```
1   R := ∅;
2   for all p ∈ P do
3       if ISFLAT(p, α, ρ)
4           R := R ∪ p;
5   endfor
6   while (∃p ∉ R) and (∃q ∈ R with p ∈ N_q) do
        and (r_p ≤ ρh_p) and (∠_a(v_p, v_q) ≤ α)
7       R := R ∪ p;
8   endwhile
9   return P \ R.
```

5.3.1 Justification

Now we argue that BOUNDARY outputs all and only boundary sample points. We need an interior assumption that says that all interior sample points have well-sampled neighborhoods.

Assumption 5.2 (Interior Assumption). *Each interior sample point is path connected to a deep interior sample point where the path lies only inside the restricted Voronoi cells of the interior sample points.*

Theorem 5.3. BOUNDARY *outputs all and only boundary sample points when* $\rho = 1.3\varepsilon$, $\alpha = 0.14$, *and* $\varepsilon \leq \frac{0.01}{1.3\Delta}$.

Proof. Inductively assume that the set R computed by BOUNDARY contains only interior sample points. Initially, the assumption is valid since steps 2 and 3 compute the set of flat sample points, R, which must be interior due to the Boundary Sample Theorem 5.2. The Boundary Assumption 5.1(ii) and the Interior Assumption 5.2 imply that each component of Σ^ε must have a deep interior sample point. Thus, R cannot be empty initially. In the *while* loop if a sample point p is included in the set R, it must satisfy the ratio condition. Also, there exists $q \in R$ so that $\angle_a(v_p, v_q) \leq 0.14$ since $\alpha = 0.14$ radians. Since q is an interior sample point by inductive assumption $\angle_a(v_q, n_q) \leq 2 \arcsin \frac{\varepsilon}{1-\varepsilon}$ (Interior Normal Lemma 5.1). It follows that $\angle_a(v_q, n_q) \leq 0.161$. Since p is a cocone neighbor of q, we have $\|q - p\| \leq 2.6\varepsilon f(q)$. Applying the Normal Variation Lemma 3.3 we get $\angle(n_q, n_p) \leq 0.03$ for $\varepsilon \leq 0.01$. Therefore,

$$\angle_a(v_p, n_p) \leq \angle_a(v_p, n_q) + \angle(n_q, n_p) \leq 0.2.$$

It follows from the Interior Lemma 5.3 that q is an interior sample point proving the inductive hypothesis.

Now we argue that each interior sample point p is included in R at the end of the *while* loop. The Interior Assumption 5.2 implies that one can reach p walking through adjacent cocones from a deep interior sample point. The proof of the Interior Sample Theorem 5.1 can be applied to show that any interior sample point that is a cocone neighbor of a sample point in R satisfies the condition of the *while* loop. It follows that p is encountered in the *while* loop during some iteration and is included in R.   ■

5.3.2 Reconstruction

The COCONE algorithm described in Chapter 4 can be used to complete the surface reconstruction after the boundary sample points are detected. In the COCONE algorithm a sample point p chooses all triangles incident to it whose dual Voronoi edges are intersected by the cocone C_p. But, this causes the boundary sample points to choose undesirable triangles since the estimated normals at these sample points are not correct. So, in the modified algorithm BOUNDCOCONE, the boundary sample points are not allowed to choose any triangles. The desired triangles incident to boundary sample points are chosen by some interior sample points. As a result "garbage" triangles are eliminated and clean holes appear at the undersampled regions. Also, the manifold extraction step needs to be slightly modified so that it does not prune any boundary triangle incident to a boundary sample point.

BOUNDCOCONE(P, α, ρ)

1   compute Vor P;
2   B :=BOUNDARY(P, α, ρ);
3   for each $p \in P \setminus B$ do
4   mark the triangle dual e where $e \cap C_p \neq \emptyset$;
5   endfor
6   $T := \emptyset$;
7   for each $\sigma \in \mathrm{Del}P$ do
8   if σ is marked by all its vertices not in B
9         $T:=T \cup \sigma$;
10   endif
11 endfor
12 extract a manifold from T using pruning and walking.

Figure 5.3 shows some examples of the boundary detection using BOUNDCOCONE. Obviously, in practice, sometimes the assumptions made for BOUNDCOCONE do not hold and the output may produce some artifacts.

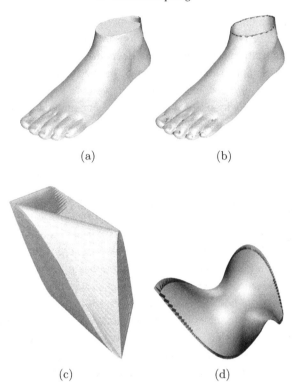

(a)   (b)

(c)   (d)

Figure 5.3. Reconstruction of the dataset FOOT: (a) without boundary detection; the big hole above the ankle is covered with triangles and (b) with boundary detection using the algorithm BOUNDCOCONE; the hole above the ankle is well detected. MONKEY saddle: (c) without boundary detection and (d) with boundary detection.

5.4 Notes and Exercises

The material for this chapter is taken from Dey and Giesen [30]. Undersampling is one of the major problems for surface reconstruction in practice. Systematic treatment of undersampling is scarce in the literature. Dey and Giesen gave the first provable algorithm for undersampling detection under some reasonable assumptions. The questions of relaxing these conditions and proving homeomorphisms between the reconstructed and original surfaces remain open. In practice, when BOUNDCOCONE is applied to reconstruct surfaces with boundaries sometimes it detects small holes in undersampled regions along with the intended boundaries. Theoretically, these small holes are correctly detected. However, often applications require that only the intended boundaries and not these small holes be detected. It would be interesting to find a solution which can recognize only distinct boundaries.

Recall that the presented theory is based on the assumption that the sampled surface Σ is C^2-smooth. However, it is observed that the boundary detection algorithm also detects undersampling in nonsmooth surfaces. The ability to handle nonsmooth surfaces stems from the fact that nonsmooth surfaces may be approximated with a smooth one that interpolates the sample points. Such a surface exists by a well-known result in mathematics that the class of C^2-smooth surfaces is dense in the class of C^0-smooth surfaces. For example, one can resort to the implicit surface that is C^2-smooth and interpolates the sample points using natural coordinates as explained in Boissonnat and Cazals [16] (see Section 9.7). These smooth surfaces have high curvatures near the sharp features of the original nonsmooth surface. The theory can be applied to the approximating smooth surface to ascertain that the sample points in the vicinity of sharp features act as boundary sample points in the vicinity of high curvatures for the smooth surface. Reconstructing nonsmooth surfaces with topological guarantees under the ε-sampling theory becomes difficult since the local feature size becomes zero at nonsmooth regions. Recently, Chazal, Cohen-Steiner, and Lieutier [19] proposed a sampling theory that alleviates this problem.

We assumed that the input point set samples a subset of a surface without boundary. It is not true that all surfaces with boundaries can be viewed as a subset of a surface without boundary. For example, nonorientable surfaces in $\mathbb{R}^3$ such as Möbius strip cannot be a subset of any surface without boundary. It remains open to develop a general reconstruction algorithm for any C^2-smooth, compact surface with boundaries (Exercise 6). Also, we did not prove any topological equivalence between the output and input surfaces. It remains open to develop an algorithm with such guarantees (Exercise 2).

Exercises

1. Let P oversample a C^2-smooth surface Σ, that is, P is unnecessarily dense. Devise an algorithm to eliminate points from P so that Σ can still be reconstructed from the decimated P.

2°. Let Σ be a C^2-smooth surface with a boundary C. Suppose P is an ε-sample of Σ where the local feature size function is defined with respect to the medial axis of Σ taking C into account. Also, assume that the points $P' \subset P$ that sample C are known. Design an algorithm to reconstruct Σ from P with a proof of homeomorphism.

3°. Devise an algorithm to detect the boundary sample points whose proof does not depend upon a global constant like Δ.

4°. Prove or disprove that only the ratio condition as presented in this chapter is sufficient for detection of the boundary sample points.

5. Prove the Voronoi Cell Lemma 3.10 for Σ^ε when ε is sufficiently small.

6°. BOUNDCOCONE and its proof depends on the fact that the surface Σ^ε is orientable. Devise an algorithm for reconstructing nonorientable surfaces.

6

Watertight Reconstructions

Most of the surface reconstruction algorithms face a difficulty when dealing with undersampled surfaces and noise. While the algorithm described in Chapter 5 can detect undersampling, it leaves holes in the surface near the undersampled regions. Although this may be desirable for reconstructing surfaces with boundaries, many applications such as CAD designs require that the output surface be *watertight*, that is, a surface that bounds a solid. Ideally, this means that the watertight surface should be a compact 2-manifold without any boundary. The two algorithms that are described in this chapter produce these types of surfaces when the input sample is sufficiently dense. However, the algorithms are designed keeping in mind that the sample may not be sufficiently dense everywhere. So, in practice, the algorithms may not produce a perfect manifold surface but their output is watertight in the following sense:

> *Watertight surface*: A 2-complex embedded in $\mathbb{R}^3$ whose underlying space is a boundary of the closure of a 3-manifold in $\mathbb{R}^3$.

Notice that the above definition allows the watertight surface to be nonmanifold. The closure of a 3-manifold can indeed introduce nonmanifold property; for example, a surface pinched at a point can be in the closure of a 3-manifold.

6.1 Power Crust

In Chapter 4, we have seen that the poles for a dense point sample lie quite far away from all samples (proof of the Pole Lemma 4.1) and hence from the surface. Indeed, they lie close to the medial axis. The Delaunay balls circumscribing the tetrahedra that are dual to the poles are called *polar balls*. These balls have their centers at the poles and they approximate the medial balls. The

POWERCRUST algorithm is based on the observation that a solid is equal to the union of all the inner (outer) medial balls of its bounding surface. Since the polar balls approximate the medial balls, the boundary of the union of inner (outer) polar balls approximates the bounding surface.

For simplicity and also for a technical reason we assume that the sampled surface Σ has a single component in this section. Also, assume that Σ does not have any boundary. Such a surface partitions $\mathbb{R}^3$ into two components. The unbounded component of $\mathbb{R}^3 \backslash \Sigma$ is denoted Ω_O. The rest, that is, $\mathbb{R}^3 \backslash \Omega_O$ is denoted Ω_I. Notice that Ω_O is open where Ω_I is closed with Σ on its boundary. For the analysis we need the normals of Σ oriented. As before we orient the normal $\mathbf{n}_x$ at any point $x \in \Sigma$ outward, that is, toward Ω_O.

When Σ is connected, there are two sets of medial balls. The inner medial balls have their centers in Ω_I while the outer medial balls have their centers in Ω_O. The surface Σ bounds the union of both sets of medial balls. In other words, Σ consists of points where the inner medial balls meet with the outer ones. Likewise we can separate the polar balls into inner and outer ones. The inner ones have their centers in Ω_I whereas the outer ones have their centers in Ω_O. The union of inner polar balls does not necessarily meet the union of outer polar balls in a surface. Nevertheless, the points lying in both unions and the points lying in neither of the unions are close to Σ. A surface is extracted out of these points by using *power diagrams* of the polar balls.

6.1.1 Definition

Power Diagrams

A power diagram is a generalization of the Voronoi diagram where the input points and distances are weighted. A *weighted point* $\hat{p}$ is a point $p \in \mathbb{R}^3$ with a weight w_p, that is, $\hat{p} = (p, w_p)$. The weighted point $\hat{p}$ can be thought of as a ball B_{p,w_p}. Conversely, a ball $B_{p,r}$ can be thought of as a weighted point $\hat{p} = (p, r)$. The *power distance* between two points $\hat{p}$ and $\hat{q}$ is given by

$$\pi(\hat{p}, \hat{q}) = \| p - q \|^2 - w_p^2 - w_q^2.$$

See Figure 6.1 for a geometric interpretation of the power distance of an unweighted point $\hat{x} = (x, 0)$ from a weighted one in $\mathbb{R}^2$. Let $\hat{P}$ denote a set of weighted points where P is the set of corresponding unweighted points. A *power cell* $V_{\hat{p}}$ for a weighted point $\hat{p} \in \hat{P}$ is defined as

$$V_{\hat{p}} = \{ x \in \mathbb{R}^3 \mid \pi(x, \hat{p}) \leq \pi(x, \hat{q}) \; \forall \hat{q} \in \hat{P} \}.$$

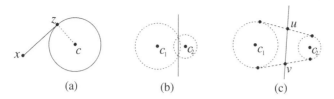

(a)   (b)   (c)

Figure 6.1. (a) $\pi(x, \hat{c})$ is the squared length of the tangent xz. (b) The cells of $\hat{c}_1$ and $\hat{c}_2$ are the half planes on the left and right respectively of the solid line. The line passes through the intersection of the two circles. (c) Similar to (b), the dividing line passes through the midpoints u and v of the bitangents.

The facets and hence all faces of a power cell are linear. A point x in such a facet satisfies the equation

$$\|p - x\|^2 - w_p^2 = \|q - x\|^2 - w_q^2$$
$$\text{or, } \|p\|^2 - 2p^T x - w_p^2 = \|q\|^2 - 2q^T x - w_q^2$$

which is an equation of a plane.

Definition 6.1. *For a set of weighted points $\hat{P} \subset \mathbb{R}^3$, the* power diagram Pow $\hat{P}$ *is the 3-complex made by the faces of the power cells $\{V_{\hat{p}} \mid \hat{p} \in \hat{P}\}$.*

If the two balls corresponding to the two weighted points determining a facet meet, the facet lies on the plane passing through the circle where the boundaries of the two balls meet. As the ordinary unweighted Voronoi diagram, the power diagram defines a dual triangulation called the weighted Delaunay triangulation. Precisely, for a weighted point set $\hat{P}$, the weighted Delaunay triangulation is a simplicial complex where a simplex σ is in the triangulation if the power cells in Pow $\hat{P}$ for the vertices of σ have a nonempty intersection.

See Figure 6.2 for a power diagram of a set of points in the plane. Notice that the power cell of a weighted point may be empty or may not contain the point. However, such anomalies occur only when a weighted point lies completely inside another one. In our case these situations will not arise.

Let P be a sufficiently dense sample of Σ. Recall that each sample point $p \in P$ defines two poles in the Voronoi diagram Vor P. These two poles lie in different components of $\mathbb{R}^3$ separated by Σ. The pole in the unbounded component Ω_O is called the *outer pole* and the pole in the bounded component Ω_I is called the *inner pole*. The set of inner poles, C_I, defines a weighted point set $\hat{C}_I$ where the weight of each pole is equal to the radius of the corresponding polar ball. Similarly, the set of outer poles, C_O, defines a weighted point set $\hat{C}_O$. The entire set of poles $C = C_I \cup C_O$ defines the weighted point set $\hat{C} = \hat{C}_I \cup \hat{C}_O$.

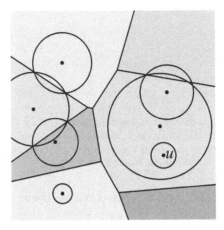

Figure 6.2. Power diagram of a set of points in the plane. A power cell of a weighted point may be empty or may not contain the point; $\hat{u}$ is such a weighted point.

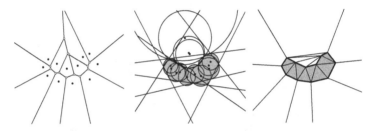

Figure 6.3. Power crust of a set of points in the plane: (left) the Voronoi diagram of the points, (middle) the polar balls including the infinite ones; the inner polar balls are shaded, (right) the inner power cells are shaded; the power crust edges drawn with thick segments separate the inner cells from the outer ones.

Definition 6.2. *The power crust* $\operatorname{Pwc} P$ *of* P *is defined as the subcomplex in* $\operatorname{Pow} \hat{C}$ *where a face* $F \in \operatorname{Pow} \hat{C}$ *is in* $\operatorname{Pwc} P$ *if a cell corresponding to an inner pole and a cell corresponding to an outer pole meet in* F.

Figure 6.3 illustrates the concept of the power crust for a set of points in the plane.

According to the definition, $\operatorname{Pwc} P$ is a collection of vertices, edges, and facets where a cell for an inner pole meets a cell for an outer pole. Consider such an edge. The sequence of cells around it should at least change from an inner pole to an outer one and again from an outer pole to an inner one. This implies the following lemma.

Lemma 6.1. *Each edge in* $\operatorname{Pwc} P$ *has an even number (greater than zero) of facets incident to it.*

The above lemma implies that $\mathrm{Pwc}\,P$ cannot have an edge with a single or no facets incident to it. This contributes to the watertightness of $\mathrm{Pwc}\,P$. Also, since each point of P has an inner pole and an outer pole, it is incident to cells in $\mathrm{Pow}\,\hat{C}$ where at least one corresponds to an inner pole and another corresponds to an outer pole. Therefore, we have:

Lemma 6.2. *Each point of a ε-sample P belongs to* $\mathrm{Pwc}\,P$ *if ε is sufficiently small.*

6.1.2 Proximity

The power crust $\mathrm{Pwc}\,P$ is geometrically close to Σ. Also, the normals to the facets of $\mathrm{Pwc}\,P$ match closely with the normals of Σ at nearby points. We will see that these properties together ensure that the underlying space of $\mathrm{Pwc}\,P$ is homeomorphic to Σ.

The union of the inner and outer polar balls plays a vital role in establishing the geometric and normal proximity of $\mathrm{Pwc}\,P$ to Σ. Let U_I and U_O denote the union of the inner and outer polar balls respectively.

Geometric Proximity

First, observe that any point on $\mathrm{Pwc}\,P$ is either in both of U_I and U_O or in neither of them. Specifically, let x be any point on a facet F in $\mathrm{Pwc}\,P$. The facet F belongs to two cells for two poles, say $c_1 \in C_I$ and $c_2 \in C_O$. By the property of the power diagram, the facet F is either in both polar balls if they intersect, or in neither of them if they do not. In the first case, clearly $x \in U_I \cap U_O$. In the other case x cannot belong to any polar ball since the power distance $\pi(x, \hat{c}_1)$ of x for the polar ball $\hat{c}_1$ is minimum among all poles and it is positive.

The next lemma states that points which belong to both of U_I and U_O or to neither of their interiors are very close to Σ. We will skip the proof (see Exercise 8).

Lemma 6.3. *Let x be a point so that either $x \in U_I \cap U_O$ or $x \notin \mathrm{Int} U_I \cup \mathrm{Int} U_O$. For a sufficiently small ε, $\|x - p\| = \tilde{O}(\varepsilon)f(p)$ where $p \in P$ is the nearest sample point to x.*

We already know that any point in the underlying space $|\mathrm{Pwc}\,P|$ of $\mathrm{Pwc}\,P$ is in either $U_I \cap U_O$ or in $\mathbb{R}^3 \setminus (U_I \cup U_O)$. Therefore, the above lemma along with the ε-sampling condition leads to the following theorem.

Theorem 6.1 (PC-Hausdorff). *For a sufficiently small ε, let P be a ε-sample of Σ. Each point $x \in |\mathrm{Pwc}\,P|$ is within $\tilde{O}(\varepsilon)f(\tilde{x})$ distance of Σ where $\tilde{x}$ is* the closest point to x on Σ. Conversely, each point $x \in \Sigma$ is within $\tilde{O}(\varepsilon) f(x)$ distance of $|\mathrm{Pwc}\,P|$.

Normal Proximity

The boundaries of U_I and U_O remain almost parallel to the surface Σ. To describe this phenomenon precisely, we need to define a normal for each point on the union boundaries. For a polar ball, orient the normal to its boundary to point outward, that is, away from the center. The normals on the boundaries of U_I and U_O are well defined for points that belong to a single polar ball. The points that belong to more than one polar ball do not have well defined normals. Therefore, when we talk about a normal at a point x on the boundary of U_I (or U_O), we mean the normal to the boundary of any polar ball incident to x. The following lemma is the key to establishing the normal proximity. We will not prove this lemma here though a general version of this lemma is proved in Section 7.3 in the context of noisy samples. The corollary of the General Normal Theorem 7.1 has the same condition as that of the following lemma with $\delta = \tilde{O}(\varepsilon)$.

Lemma 6.4. *Let x be any point in an inner polar ball $B_{c,r}$ where $\|x - \tilde{x}\| = \tilde{O}(\varepsilon) f(\tilde{x})$ for a sufficiently small ε. One has $\angle(\mathbf{n}_{\tilde{x}}, \overrightarrow{cx}) = \tilde{O}(\sqrt{\varepsilon})$.*

In the above lemma, $B_{c,r}$ is an inner polar ball containing x. It is possible that x does not belong to the cell of $c \in C_I$. The next lemma considers the polar ball whose power distance to x is the least, that is, x belongs to the cell of the center of that polar ball.

Lemma 6.5. *For a sufficiently small ε, let x be a point within $\tilde{O}(\varepsilon) f(\tilde{x})$ distance from its closest point $\tilde{x}$ in Σ. If c is the inner pole where x belongs to the cell of c, $\angle(\mathbf{n}_{\tilde{x}}, \overrightarrow{cx}) = \tilde{O}(\sqrt{\varepsilon})$.*

Proof. Let $B_{c,r}$ be the inner polar ball centering c. If $x \in B_{c,r}$, Lemma 6.4 establishes the claim.

Consider the other case when x does not belong to $B_{c,r}$. In that case it can be shown that the distance of x to $B_{c,r}$ is $\tilde{O}(\varepsilon) f(\tilde{x})$. The closest point of x to $B_{c,r}$ lies on the segment xc. Let this point be z. The point z is $\tilde{O}(\varepsilon) f(\tilde{x})$ away from its closest point $\tilde{z}$ on Σ since this distance is no more than the sum of the distances of x from Σ and of z from x. By Lipschitz property of f this distance is also no more than $\tilde{O}(\varepsilon) f(\tilde{z})$. Now Lemma 6.4 applied to z gives that the angle between $\mathbf{n}_{\tilde{z}}$ and $\overrightarrow{cz}$ is $\tilde{O}(\sqrt{\varepsilon})$. Since the normals at $\tilde{z}$ and $\tilde{x}$ make at most $\tilde{O}(\varepsilon)$ angle (Normal Variation Lemma 3.3), the claimed bound follows. ∎

Notice that the above Lemma also holds for outer poles.

The above lemma and some more observations together lead to the following result about the normals of the facets in Pwc P.

Theorem 6.2 (PC-Normal). *Let P be an ε-sample of Σ where ε is sufficiently small. Let $\mathbf{n}_F$ be the normal to any facet F in Pwc P and x be the point in Σ closest to F. Then, $\angle_a(\mathbf{n}_F, \mathbf{n}_x) = \tilde{O}(\sqrt{\varepsilon})$.*

Proof. Let y be the point in F closest to x. We know from PC-Hausdorff Theorem 6.1 that $\|x - y\| = \tilde{O}(\varepsilon) f(x)$. Let c and c' be the inner and outer poles respectively whose cells share F. Lemma 6.5 implies $\angle(\mathbf{n}_x, \overrightarrow{cy}) = \tilde{O}(\sqrt{\varepsilon})$ and $\angle(\mathbf{n}_x, \overrightarrow{yc'}) = \tilde{O}(\sqrt{\varepsilon})$. This implies that $\angle(\overrightarrow{cy}, \overrightarrow{c'y}) = \pi - \tilde{O}(\sqrt{\varepsilon})$ which also means $\angle(\overrightarrow{cc'}, \overrightarrow{cy}) = \tilde{O}(\sqrt{\varepsilon})$. We are done since the line containing cc' is perpendicular to the plane of F and hence

$$\angle_a(\mathbf{n}_F, \mathbf{n}_x) = \angle_a(\overrightarrow{cc'}, \mathbf{n}_x) \leq \angle_a(\overrightarrow{cc'}, \overrightarrow{cy}) + \angle_a(\overrightarrow{cy}, \mathbf{n}_x)$$
$$= \tilde{O}(\sqrt{\varepsilon}).$$

∎

6.1.3 Homeomorphism and Isotopy

Lemma 6.5 is the key to establishing the homeomorphism between Σ and $|\text{Pwc } P|$, the underlying space of Pwc P. Consider the function $\nu : \mathbb{R}^3 \setminus M \to \Sigma$ where $\nu(x) = \tilde{x}$ and M is the medial axis of Σ. We show that the restriction of ν to $|\text{Pwc } P|$ realizes this homeomorphism.

Theorem 6.3. *$|\text{Pwc } P|$ is homeomorphic to Σ where P is a sufficiently dense sample of Σ.*

Proof. Consider the restriction $\nu' : |\text{Pwc } P| \to \Sigma$ of ν. Since $|\text{Pwc } P|$ avoids the medial axis (PC-Hausdorff Theorem 6.1) for a sufficiently small ε, the map ν' is well defined. It is also continuous since ν is. We show that ν' is one-to-one. If not, at least two points x, x' exist on $|\text{Pwc } P|$ where $\nu'(x) = \nu'(x') = \tilde{x}$. The point x, x', and $\tilde{x}$ lie on the line ℓ normal to Σ at $\tilde{x}$. By PC-Hausdorff Theorem 6.1, both x and x' are within $\tilde{O}(\varepsilon) f(\tilde{x})$ distance from $\tilde{x}$. We claim that ℓ intersects $|\text{Pwc } P|$ only at a single point within $\tilde{O}(\varepsilon) f(\tilde{x})$ distance, thereby contradicting the existence of x and x' as assumed. To prove the claim assume without loss of generality that x is further from $\tilde{x}$ than x' is. Consider two functions Π_I and Π_O that assign to each point $z \in \mathbb{R}^3$ the minimum power distance to any pole in C_I

and C_O respectively. Consider moving a point z from $\tilde{x}$ toward x. Lemma 6.5 implies that the vectors from the nearest (in terms of power distance) pole in C_I and C_O to z make an angle $\tilde{O}(\sqrt{\varepsilon})$ with the line ℓ. This means that either the function Π_I monotonically increases while Π_O monotonically decreases or Π_I monotonically increases while Π_O monotonically decreases as z moves from $\tilde{x}$ to x. It follows that the two functions become equal only at a single point. Since each point on $|\text{Pwc } P|$ has equal minimum power distances to the poles in C_I and to the poles in C_O, we must have $x = x'$.

Consider the set $\Sigma' = \nu'(|\text{Pwc } P|)$. Obviously, ν' maps $|\text{Pwc } P|$ surjectively onto Σ'. Since $|\text{Pwc } P|$ is compact, so is Σ'. The inverse map of ν' from Σ' to $|\text{Pwc } P|$ is continuous since the inverse of a continuous map between two compact spaces is also continuous. Therefore, ν' is a homeomorphism between $|\text{Pwc } P|$ and Σ'. The only thing that remains to be shown is that $\Sigma' = \Sigma$.

Notice that Σ' is a manifold without boundary since Pwc P does not have any edge with a single facet incident on it (Lemma 6.1). Then Σ' being a submanifold of Σ can differ from it by a component. But, that is impossible since we assume that Σ has a single component. ■

We already indicated in Section 1.1 that two homeomorphic surfaces can be embedded in $\mathbb{R}^3$ in ways that are fundamentally different. So, it is desirable that we prove a stronger topological relation between Σ and $|\text{Pwc } P|$. We show that, not only are they homeomorphic but are isotopic as well. This means one can deform $\mathbb{R}^3$ continuously so that $|\text{Pwc } P|$ is taken to Σ.

Theorem 6.4 (PC-Isotopy). *Let P be an ε-sample of Σ. $|\text{Pwc } P|$ is isotopic to Σ if ε is sufficiently small.*

Proof. For isotopy we define a map $\xi : \mathbb{R}^3 \times [0, 1] \to \mathbb{R}^3$ so that $\xi(|\text{Pwc } P|, 0) = |\text{Pwc } P|$ and $\xi(|\text{Pwc } P|, 1) = \Sigma$ and $\xi(\cdot, t)$ is a continuous, one-to-one, and onto map for all $t \in [0, 1]$. Consider a tubular neighborhood N_Σ of Σ as

$$N_\Sigma = \{x \mid d(x, \Sigma) \leq c\varepsilon f(\tilde{x})\}$$

where each point y of $|\text{Pwc } P|$ is within $c\varepsilon f(\tilde{y})$ distance and $c\varepsilon < 1$ is sufficiently small. For a sufficiently small ε, such a c exists by the PC-Hausdorff Theorem 6.1. In $\mathbb{R}^3 \setminus N_\Sigma$ we define ξ to be identity for all $t \in [0, 1]$. For any point $x \in N_\Sigma$ we define ξ as follows. Consider the line segment g passing through x and normal to Σ with endpoints g_i and g_o on the two boundaries of N_Σ. Since $c\varepsilon < 1$, the tubular neighborhood N_Σ avoids the medial axis and hence g intersects Σ in exactly one point, say at u. Also, by arguments in the

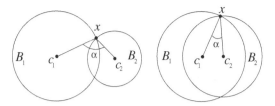

Figure 6.4. Shallow intersection (left) and deep intersection (right) between two balls.

proof of Theorem 6.3, g intersects $|\text{Pwc } P|$ only at a single point, say at w. In N_Σ we define $w_t = \xi(w, t) = tu + (1 - t)w$ and let $\xi(\cdot, t)$ linearly map the segments $g_i w$ to $g_i w_t$, and $w g_o$ to $w_t g_o$. That is,

$$\xi(x, t) = w_t + (x - w)\frac{g_i - w_t}{g_i - w}, \quad x \text{ is in } g_i w$$

$$= w_t + (x - w)\frac{g_o - w_t}{g_o - w}, \quad x \text{ is in } g_o w.$$

Clearly, ξ is continuous, one-to-one, and onto for each $t \in [0, 1]$ with

$$\xi(|\text{Pwc } P|, 0) = |\text{Pwc } P| \quad \text{and} \quad \xi(|\text{Pwc } P|, 1) = \Sigma.$$

∎

6.1.4 Algorithm

We compute the power crust by identifying the cells corresponding to the inner and outer poles and then computing the facets separating a cell of an inner pole from a cell of an outer pole. The poles are labeled inner or outer by computing how deeply the corresponding polar balls intersect. It is important for this labeling algorithm that the surface Σ has a single connected component.

The labeling algorithm is a simple traversal of the Delaunay graph structure. It utilizes the following properties of the polar balls. If two polar balls intersect, their depth of intersection depends on their types. If one of them is inner and the other is outer, the intersection is shallow. On the other hand, if both of them are inner or outer, the intersection is deep . We formalize this idea.

Let two balls B_1 and B_2 intersect and x be any point on the circle in which their boundaries intersect. We say that B_1 and B_2 intersect at an angle α if the vectors $\overrightarrow{c_1 x}$ and $\overrightarrow{c_2 x}$ make an angle α where c_1 and c_2 are the centers of B_1 and B_2 respectively (see Figure 6.4).

Lemma 6.6. *Let B_1 and B_2 be two polar balls that intersect. For a sufficiently small ε the following hold.*

(i) If B_1 is an inner and B_2 is an outer polar ball, they intersect at an angle of
$\pi - \tilde{O}(\sqrt{\varepsilon})$.

(ii) If both of B_1 and B_2 are inner or outer polar balls, and there is a facet
F in $\mathrm{Pow}\,\hat{C}$ between the cells of c_1 and c_2 with a point $x \in F$ where
$\|x - \tilde{x}\| = \tilde{O}(\varepsilon)f(\tilde{x})$, then B_1 and B_2 intersect at an angle of $\tilde{O}(\sqrt{\varepsilon})$.

Proof. Consider (i). Let y be a point on the circle where the boundaries of
B_1 and B_2 intersect. Since y belongs to $U_I \cap U_O$, Lemma 6.3 asserts that
$\|y - \tilde{y}\| = \tilde{O}(\varepsilon)f(\tilde{y})$.

Let $\mathbf{n}_{\tilde{y}}$ be the oriented outer normal. By Lemma 6.4 we get that the angle
between $\mathbf{n}_{\tilde{y}}$ and the vector $\overrightarrow{c_i x}$ is $\tilde{O}(\sqrt{\varepsilon})$ if c_i is an inner pole, and the angle is
$\pi - \tilde{O}(\sqrt{\varepsilon})$ if c_i is an outer pole. Since c_1 and c_2 are poles with opposite labels
in case (i), the claimed angle bound follows.

Consider (ii). The poles have same labels, say inner in case (ii). Both polar
balls have a point, namely x with $\|x - \tilde{x}\| = \tilde{O}(\varepsilon)f(\tilde{x})$. Therefore, the vectors
$\overrightarrow{c_1 x}$ and $\overrightarrow{c_2 x}$ make an angle of $\tilde{O}(\sqrt{\varepsilon})$ with $\mathbf{n}_{\tilde{x}}$ according to Lemma 6.4. The
claimed angle bound is immediate.   ∎

Now we describe the labeling algorithm for the poles. The angle at which
two polar balls centering c and c' intersect is denoted $\angle c, c'$.

LABELPOLE(Vor P,C,Pow $\hat{C}$)

1   label all poles in C outer;
2   choose any sample p on Conv P;
3   mark the finite pole c of p inner;
4   push c into a stack S;
5   while $S \neq \emptyset$ do
6       $c := \mathrm{pop}\,S$;
7   mark c processed;
8   for each pole c' adjacent to c in Pow $\hat{C}$ do
9   if $(\angle c, c' > \frac{2\pi}{3})$ and $(c'$ is not processed)
10   label c' inner;
11   push c' into S;
12   endif
13   endfor
14 endwhile
15 return C with labels.

Notice that we chose an angle threshold of $\frac{2\pi}{3}$ somewhat arbitrarily to decide
if two balls are intersecting deeply or not. The point is that any angle $\tilde{O}(\sqrt{\varepsilon})$

will work as long as ε is sufficiently small. Assuming $\varepsilon < 0.1$, the angle of $\frac{2\pi}{3}$ is a safe choice. The correctness of LABELPOLES follows from the next lemma.

Lemma 6.7 (Label). *Each pole is labeled correctly by* LABELPOLE.

Proof. Consider the graph of the power crust edges. Since Σ has a single component, this graph is connected. We call two inner polar balls adjacent if they contribute a facet in Pow $\hat{C}$ and the facet has an edge in the power crust.

The first inner polar ball marked by LABELPOLE is correctly labeled as the finite pole of a sample point on the convex hull is necessarily inner. This sample point, as all others, lie on the power crust. Since the graph of the power crust edges is connected, all inner polar balls contributing an edge on the power crust are labeled by LABELPOLE. Also, since each polar ball has a sample point on its boundary which appears as an endpoint of a power crust edge, Lemma 6.6 can be applied assuring that all of them are labeled correctly. ∎

Now we enumerate the steps of the power crust.

POWERCRUST(P)

1 compute Vor P;
2 compute all poles C in Vor P;
3 compute Pow $\hat{C}$;
4 $C := $LABELPOLE(Vor P, C, Pow $\hat{C}$);
5 mark each facet of Pow $\hat{C}$ separating a cell of an
   inner pole from that of an outer pole;
6 output the 2-complex made by the marked facets.

The PC-Hausdorff Theorem 6.1, the PC-Normal Theorem 6.2, the PC-Isotopy Theorem 6.4, and the Label Lemma 6.7 make the following theorem.

Theorem 6.5. *Given an ε-sample of a smooth, compact surface Σ without boundary, the* POWERCRUST *computes a 2-complex* Pwc P *with the following properties if ε is sufficiently small.*

(i) Each point $x \in |$Pwc $P|$ has $\|x - \tilde{x}\| = \tilde{O}(\varepsilon)f(\tilde{x})$.
(ii) Each facet $F \in$ Pwc P has a normal $\mathbf{n}_F$ with $\angle_a(\mathbf{n}_F, \mathbf{n}_x) = \tilde{O}(\sqrt{\varepsilon})$ where x is the point in Σ closest to F.
(iii) $|$Pwc $P|$ is isotopic to Σ.

The POWERCRUST algorithm computes two Voronoi diagrams. The first one in step 1 takes $O(n^2)$ time and space in the worst case for a set of n points.

The power diagram computation in step 3 takes $O(m^2)$ time and space if m is the number of poles. Since we have at most two poles for each input point, we have $m \leq 2n$. Therefore, step 3 takes $O(n^2)$ time and space in the worst case. The complexity of all other steps are dominated by the Voronoi diagram computations. Therefore, POWERCRUST runs in $O(n^2)$ time and space in the worst case.

6.2 Tight Cocone

The output of POWERCRUST has each input sample point as a vertex. However, each of the vertices of Pwc P is not necessarily a point in P. The vertices of the power crust facets are the points whose nearest power distance to the poles is determined by three or more poles. Each sample point satisfies this property and so do other points. As a result, the number of vertices in the output surface is usually greater than the number of input points. In some cases, this increase in size can be a prohibitive bottleneck, especially when dealing with large data sets. Further, the power crust is a subcomplex of a Voronoi diagram and is not necessarily triangular. Of course, its polygonal facets can be triangulated but at the expense of increased size and many coplanar triangles. These limitations of POWERCRUST are remedied by the TIGHTCOCONE algorithm.

The overall idea of TIGHTCOCONE is to label the Delaunay tetrahedra computed from the input sample as *in* or *out* according to an initial approximation of the surface and then peeling off all *out* tetrahedra. This leaves the *in* tetrahedra, the boundary of whose union is output as the watertight surface. The output of BOUNDCOCONE described in Chapter 5 is taken as the initial approximated surface possibly with holes and other artifacts.

Since the output of TIGHTCOCONE is the boundary of the union of a set of tetrahedra, it is watertight by definition. However, apart from being watertight, the output also should approximate the geometry of the original sampled surface. For any such theoretical guarantee, we need the sample to be dense enough. Since the main motivation for designing TIGHTCOCONE is to consider undersampled point sets, we do not prove any guarantee about TIGHTCOCONE except that all guarantees for COCONE also hold for TIGHTCOCONE when the sample is sufficiently dense.

Although we do not attempt to design TIGHTCOCONE with theoretical guarantees, we make some decisions in the algorithm based on the assumption that the undersampling is not arbitrary. This means that BOUNDCOCONE computes most of the intended surface except with holes that are locally repairable. Of course, if this assumption is not obeyed, the output surface, though watertight may not be close to the original one and may even be empty.

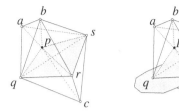

Figure 6.5. The umbrella of p has three triangles pqr, prs, and pqs. This umbrella separates the tetrahedra incident to p into two clusters: the upper cluster $\{absp, asqp, abpq, bqrp, brsp\}$ and the lower cluster $\{cqrp, csrp, cqsp\}$. Suppose the walk entered p with the pair $(p, bprs)$. The right picture shows that the unexplored point q has an umbrella. Therefore, the pair $(q, bprq)$ is entered into the stack since q is a good and unexplored point.

6.2.1 Marking

The BOUNDCOCONE algorithm as described in Chapter 5 computes a preliminary surface possibly with holes and other artifacts at the undersampled regions. The sample points in the well-sampled regions have their neighborhoods well approximated. Specifically, the set of surface triangles incident to these points form a *topological disk*. We call the points *good* whose incident surface triangles form a topological disk. The rest of the points are called *poor*.

Definition 6.3. *The union of surface triangles incident to a good point p is called its* umbrella *denoted as* U_p.

The algorithm to mark tetrahedra walks through the Delaunay triangulation in a depth first manner using the vertex and triangle adjacencies. It maintains a stack of pairs (p, σ) where p is a good point and σ is a tetrahedron incident to p which has been marked *out*. Suppose the pair (p, σ) is currently popped out from the stack. The umbrella U_p locally separates the tetrahedra incident to p into two clusters, one on each side (see Figure 6.5). The cluster that contains σ is marked *out* since σ is already marked *out*. The other cluster gets the marking *in*. This is done by initiating a local walk from σ that traverses all tetrahedra through triangle adjacency without ever crossing a triangle in U_p and marking each tetrahedron as *out*. The rest of the tetrahedra that are not encountered in this walk get the *in* marking. During this local walk in the *out* cluster, when a vertex q of U_p is reached through a tetrahedron σ', the pair (q, σ') is pushed into the stack if q is good and is not explored yet (see Figure 6.5).

Now we face the question of initiating the stack. For this we assume that Del P is augmented with "infinite" tetrahedra that are incident to a triangle on the convex hull of P and a point at infinity. The stack is initiated with a good point on the convex hull paired with an incident infinite tetrahedron.

MARK(Del P)

1   push an infinite tetrahedron incident to a good point
    on the convex hull to stack S;
2   let T_p be the set of tetrahedra incident to p in Del P;
3   while $S \neq \emptyset$ do
4       $(p, \sigma) := \text{pop } S$;
5   mark p processed;
6       $G := \{\sigma\}$;
7   while $(\exists \sigma \in G)$ and $(\sigma' \in T_p \setminus G)$ and $(\sigma \cap \sigma' \notin U_p)$ do
8           $G := G \cup \{\sigma'\}$;
9   for all good vertex q of σ' do
10   if $(q \in U_p)$ and $(q$ not processed$)$
11   push (q, σ') to S;
12   endfor
13   endwhile
14   mark each $\sigma \in G$ *out*;
15   mark each $\sigma \in T_p \setminus G$ *in*;
16 endwhile.

For most of the data in practice, the surface computed by BOUNDCOCONE is well connected, that is, all triangles incident to good points can be reached from any other good point via a series of triangle adjacencies. Assuming this connectivity of the preliminary surface computed by BOUNDCOCONE, the above procedure marks all tetrahedra that are incident to at least one good sample point. However, the tetrahedra whose vertices are all poor are not marked by this step. We call them *poor tetrahedra*. The intended output surface is the boundary of the union of a set of tetrahedra. Accordingly, the poor tetrahedra should be marked *in* or *out*. We follow a heuristic here based on the assumption that the undersampling is local.

In the justification of poor tetrahedra marking we assume an intended ideal surface that is the boundary of a set of tetrahedra. These tetrahedra are referred as the ones lying inside the intended surface and the rest lying in its outside. Of course, here we deviate from the mathematical precision, but it makes the description more intuitive.

The poor tetrahedra whose vertices lie in a single undersampled region tend to be small when undersampling is local. We choose to mark them *in* and the

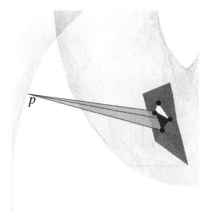

Figure 6.6. The four vertices marked with dark circles border a hole. The poor tetrahedron with these four vertices is marked *in*. The sharp tip *p* of the long tetrahedron is a good point which marks it *out*. When this tetrahedron is peeled, the triangle opposite to *p* fills the hole partially. The other triangle of the hole also gets into the output by a similar peeling.

peeling process later is not allowed to peel them away. This allows the surface to get repaired in the undersampled region. See Figure 6.6 for an illustration.

Other poor tetrahedra that connect vertices from different undersampled regions tend to be big. If such a big poor tetrahedron lies outside the intended surface, we need to take it out. So, it should be marked *out*. On the other hand, if this big poor tetrahedron lies inside the intended surface, we need to mark it as *in*. Otherwise, a large void/tunnel in the surface is created by taking out this tetrahedron. We eliminate this dilemma using the assumption that undersampling is local. Call a triangle in a tetrahedron *small* if its circumradius is the least among all triangles in the tetrahedron. If a poor tetrahedron has a triangle with vertices from the same undersampled region, then that triangle is small. The poor tetrahedra lying inside the intended surface have to be reached by the peeling process that peels away all *out* marked tetrahedra. This means that the inner poor tetrahedra have to be reached through the small triangle. We take this observation into account during peeling while dealing with the poor tetrahedra and defer designating them during the marking step.

6.2.2 *Peeling*

After the marking step, a walk is initiated to peel off the tetrahedra that are marked *out* and some others. The boundary of the union of the remaining

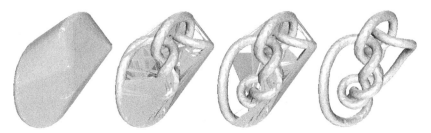

Figure 6.7. The boundary of the union of peeled tetrahedra as peeling process progresses.

tetrahedra form the watertight surface. This is also the surface of the union of the peeled tetrahedra (see Figure 6.7).

The walk maintains a stack of surface triangles that form the boundary of the union of the tetrahedra peeled so far. It is initiated with all convex hull triangles. At any generic step, a triangle, say t, is popped out from the stack. One of the tetrahedra incident to t is already peeled. If the other incident tetrahedron, say σ, is also already peeled the triangle t separates two *out* tetrahedra and is not put in the output. Otherwise, there are two possibilities. If σ is not poor and marked *in*, we put t in the output list. In the other case either σ is marked *out* or σ is poor. When σ is marked *out* the walk should move into σ through t, which is done by replacing t with the other three triangles of σ into the stack. If σ is a poor tetrahedron, the walk is also allowed to move into σ through t only if t is not the small triangle in σ. This is done to protect peeling of the inner poor tetrahedra as we discussed before. Notice that if σ is a poor tetrahedron outside the intended surface, it will be eventually reached by the peeling process at triangles other than the small one. But, if σ is a poor tetrahedron inside, it can only be reached from outside through its small triangle due to the assumption that undersampling is local. The walk terminates with the surface triangles in the output list when there are no more triangles to process from the stack.

PEEL(Del P)

1　　push all convex hull triangles in Del P to stack S;
2　　mark all infinite tetrahedra *peeled*;
3　　$T := \emptyset$;
4　　while $S \neq \emptyset$ do
5　　　$t := $ pop S;
6　　　if $\exists \sigma \in$ Del P incident to t *and* not marked *peeled*
7　　　　if (σ is not poor) *and* (marked *in*)
8　　　　　$T := T \cup t$;

```
9      else
10         if (σ is marked out) or (σ is poor and t is
             not the small triangle in σ)
11             mark σ peeled;
12             push all triangles of σ other than t to S;
13         endif
14      endif
15   endif
16 endwhile
17 return T.
```

TIGHTCOCONE(P)
```
1   compute Del P;
2   MARK(Del P);
3   T := PEEL(Del P);
4   output T.
```

The complexity of TIGHTCOCONE is dominated by the Delaunay triangulation computation in step 1. The marking and peeling steps are mere traversal of the Delaunay triangulation data structure. Therefore, in the worst case TIGHTCOCONE takes $O(n^2)$ time and space for a set of n input points. However, unlike POWERCRUST, it computes the Delaunay/Voronoi data structure only once.

6.3 Experimental Results

In Figure 6.8, we show the results of POWERCRUST and TIGHTCOCONE on two data sets. In MANNEQUIN there are undersamplings in eyes, lips, and ears which produce holes. TIGHTCOCONE closes all these holes. In particular, in the ear there is a relatively large hole since points cannot be sampled for occlusion. This hole is nicely filled. The PIG data has severe undersampling in the hoofs, ears, and nose. They are mostly due to the fact that these thin and highly curved regions should have more sample points to capture the features properly. POWERCRUST fills all holes and produces a watertight surface for this difficult data set.

The time and space complexities of both TIGHTCOCONE and POWERCRUST are $O(n^2)$ where n is the number of input points. However, in practice this quadratic behavior is not observed. Table 6.1 shows the timings of POWERCRUST and TIGHTCOCONE for four data sets on a PC with 733 MHz Pentium III CPU and 512 MB memory.

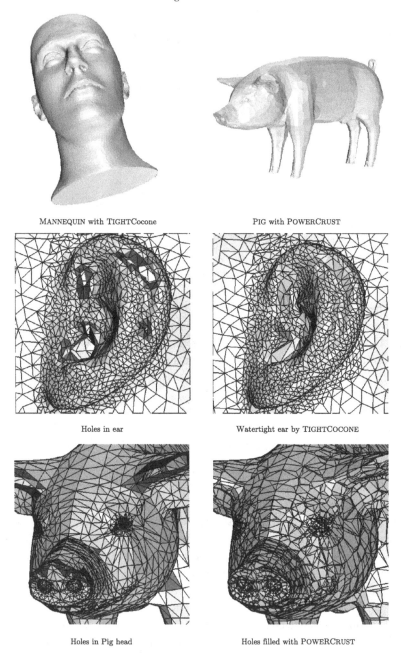

Figure 6.8. Results of POWERCRUST and TIGHTCOCONE. Holes in the surface computed by BOUNDCOCONE are filled. Triangles bordering the holes are shaded darker.

Table 6.1. *Time data*

Object	# points	POWERCRUST (s)	TIGHTCOCONE (s)
PIG	3,511	11	5
MANNEQ	12,772	54	23
CLUB	16,864	55	43
HORSE	48,485	163	152

6.4 Notes and Exercises

Amenta, Choi, and Kolluri [7] designed the POWERCRUST algorithm. The material on the power crust in this chapter is taken from this paper. The labeling algorithm in the original paper is intended for surfaces with multiple components. However, the proof given in the paper does not work for surfaces with multiple components. This is why we choose to describe the algorithm for surfaces with a single component.

In the paper [7], Amenta, Choi, and Kolluri also prove that the poles approximate a subset of the medial axis. Specifically, the Hausdorff distance between the poles and the medial axis approaches zero as ε does so. In a simultaneous work Boissonnat and Cazals [16] also establish this result. The Exercises 3 and 4 are set keeping this result in mind. In Chapter 7, we will establish a similar result for noisy samples.

The material on the TIGHTCOCONE algorithm is taken from the paper by Dey and Goswami [33]. The main advantage of this algorithm is that it does not introduce any extra points as vertices in the output surface. The POWERCRUST, on the other hand, introduces extra points. For example, for the PIG data set, POWERCRUST generates 28,801 points from an input set of 3,511 points.

Both POWERCRUST and TIGHTCOCONE can handle a small amount of noise. However, it may happen that these algorithms fail completely when the noise is beyond a certain limit.

Exercises

1. Prove that the plane of a facet shared by two cells of $\hat{c}$ and $\hat{c}'$ in a power diagram is perpendicular to the line containing c and c'.
2. Let bd U_I denote the boundary of the union of inner polar balls. Show that bd U_I is homeomorphic to Σ when the input sample P is sufficiently dense.
3^h. Let $B_{m,r}$ be a finite medial ball which touches Σ at x_1 and x_2. Let $\angle x_1 m x_2 \geq \varepsilon^{\frac{1}{3}}$. Let p be the nearest sample point to m. Prove that the distance of m to

the nearest pole of p is $\tilde{O}(\varepsilon^{\frac{2}{3}})r$ where the sampling density ε is sufficiently small.

4. Prove the converse of the statement in 3, that is, if c is the center of a polar ball, then there is a medial ball $B_{m,r}$ so that the distance of m to c is $\tilde{O}(\varepsilon^{\frac{2}{3}})r$ when ε is sufficiently small.

5. Prove or disprove that any 2-complex is watertight if and only if each edge has even number of facets incident to it.

6. Prove that the output of TIGHTCOCONE is homeomorphic to Σ if the input point set P is sufficiently dense.

7. Redesign TIGHTCOCONE so that the marking and peeling phases are combined, that is, both are done simultaneously.

8. Prove Lemma 6.3 and Lemma 6.4 [7].

9°. Design a labeling algorithm for poles where the sampled surface may have multiple components. Prove that the algorithm labels all poles correctly.

7
Noisy Samples

In the previous chapters we have assumed that the input points lie exactly on the sampled surface. Unfortunately, in practice, the input sample often does not satisfy this constraint. Noise introduced by measurement errors scatters the sample points away from the surface. Consequently, all analysis as presented in the previous chapters becomes invalid for such input points. In this chapter we develop a noise model that accounts for the scatter of the inputs and then analyze noisy samples based on this model. We will see that, as in the noise-free case, some key properties of the sampled surface can be computed from the Delaunay triangulation of a noisy sample. Specifically, we show that normals of the sampled surface can still be estimated from the Delaunay/Voronoi diagrams. Furthermore, the medial axis and hence the local feature sizes of the sampled surface can also be estimated from these diagrams. These results will be used in Chapters 8 and 9 where we present algorithms to reconstruct surfaces from noisy samples.

7.1 Noise Model

In the noise-free case ε-sampling requires each point on the surface have a sample point within a distance of ε times the local feature size. When noise is allowed, the sample points need not lie exactly on the surface and may scatter around it. Therefore, the sampling model needs to specify both a *tangential scatter*, that is, the sparseness of the points along the tangential directions of the surface and also a *normal scatter*, that is, the sparseness of the points along the normal directions. We use two independent parameters ε and δ for these two scatters to reveal the dependence of the approximation errors on these two parameters separately.

We also need a third parameter to specify a local uniformity condition in the sampling. In the noise-free case we do not need any such condition. However, in the noisy case, the points can collaborate to form a dense sample of a spurious surface. For example, a set of points near the actual sampled surface can form a dense sample of a spurious toroidal handle. In that case, an ambiguity creeps in as the input becomes a dense sample of two topologically different surfaces. We prevent this ambiguity by a local uniformity condition.

As before we assume that the sampled surface $\Sigma \subset \mathbb{R}^3$ is a compact C^2-smooth surface without boundary. Recall that for any point $x \in \mathbb{R}^3 \setminus M$, $\tilde{x}$ denotes its closest point on Σ.

Definition 7.1. *A point set $P \subset \mathbb{R}^3$ is a $(\varepsilon, \delta, \kappa)$-sample of Σ if the following conditions hold.*

(i) $\tilde{P} = \{\tilde{p}\}_{p \in P}$ is a ε-sample of Σ,
(ii) $\|p - \tilde{p}\| \leq \delta f(\tilde{p})$,
(iii) $\|p - q\| \geq \varepsilon f(\tilde{p})$ for any point $p \in P$ and its κth nearest sample point q.

The first condition says that the projection of the input point set P on the surface makes a dense sample and the second one says that P is close to the surface. The third condition enforces the sample to be locally uniform. We will see that the third condition is not needed for the analyses of the normal and medial axis approximation results in Sections 7.3 and 7.4 respectively. However, it is needed for the algorithms that estimate the normals and features based on these analyses. When the third condition is ignored, we say P is a $(\varepsilon, \delta, -)$-sample.

The analysis that we are going to present holds for surfaces that may not be connected. However, for simplicity in presentation, we assume that Σ is connected. We have already observed that such a surface partitions $\mathbb{R}^3$ into two components, Ω_I and Ω_O where Ω_O is the unbounded component of $\mathbb{R}^3 \setminus \Sigma$ and $\Omega_I = \mathbb{R}^3 \setminus \Omega_O$. As before assume the normal $\mathbf{n}_x$ at any point $x \in \Sigma$ to be directed locally outward, that is, toward Ω_O.

In the analysis we concentrate only on the bounded component Ω_I together with the inner medial axis. The results also hold for the unbounded component and outer medial axis except for the points at infinity. To avoid these points, one can take a large enough bounded open set containing Σ and then extend the results to the outer medial axis defined with maximal empty balls within the bounded set. This does not make any change to the inner medial axis though. For a point $x \in \Sigma$, let m_x denote the center of the inner medial ball meeting Σ at x and ρ_x its radius. In what follows assume that P is a $(\varepsilon, \delta, \kappa)$-sample of Σ for $0 < \varepsilon < 1, 0 < \delta < 1$, and $\kappa \geq 1$.

It follows almost immediately from the sampling conditions that all points of Σ and all points not far away from Σ have sample points nearby. The Close Sample Lemma 7.1 and Corollary 7.1 formalize this idea.

Lemma 7.1 (Close Sample). *Any point* $x \in \Sigma$ *has a sample point within* $\varepsilon_1 f(x)$ *distance where* $\varepsilon_1 = (\delta + \varepsilon + \delta\varepsilon)$.

Proof. From the sampling condition (i), we must have a sample point p so that $\|x - \tilde{p}\| \leq \varepsilon f(x)$. Also, $\|p - \tilde{p}\| \leq \delta f(\tilde{p}) \leq \delta(1 + \varepsilon)f(x)$. Thus,

$$\|x - p\| \leq \|x - \tilde{p}\| + \|\tilde{p} - p\|$$
$$\leq \varepsilon f(x) + \delta(1 + \varepsilon)f(x)$$
$$= (\delta + \varepsilon + \delta\varepsilon)f(x).$$

∎

Since $f(x) \leq \rho_x$ for any point $x \in \Sigma$, the following corollary is immediate.

Corollary 7.1. *Any point* $y \in \mathbb{R}^3$ *with* $\|y - \tilde{y}\| \leq \delta\rho_{\tilde{y}}$ *has a sample point within* $\varepsilon_2\rho_{\tilde{y}}$ *distance where* $\varepsilon_2 = (2\delta + \varepsilon + \delta\varepsilon)$.

7.2 Empty Balls

A main ingredient in our analysis will be the existence of large balls that remain empty of the points from P. They in turn lead to the existence of large Delaunay balls that circumscribe Delaunay tetrahedra in Del P. The centers of such Delaunay balls which are also Voronoi vertices in Vor P play crucial roles in the algorithms for normal and feature approximations. In this section, we present two lemmas that assure the existence of large empty balls with certain conditions.

The Empty Ball Lemma 7.2 below assures that for each point $x \in \Sigma$ there is a large empty ball of radius almost as large as (i) $f(x)$ and (ii) ρ_x. Notice the differences between the distances of these balls from x. Also, see Figure 7.1.

Lemma 7.2 (Empty Ball). *Let* $B_{m,r}$ *be a ball and* $x \in \Sigma$ *be a point so that either*

(i) $\tilde{m} = x$, $\|m - x\| = f(x)$, *and* $r = (1 - 3\delta)f(x)$, *or*
(ii) $m = m_x$ *and* $r = (1 - \delta)\rho_x$.

Then, $B_{m,r}$ *is empty of points in* P.

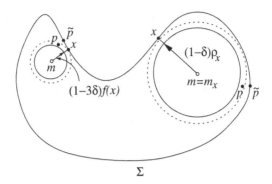

Figure 7.1. Illustration for the Empty Ball Lemma 7.2. The dotted big balls are not empty of sample points but their slightly shrunk copies (shown with solid boundaries) are.

Proof. Let p be any point in P (Figure 7.1). For (i) we have

$$f(\tilde{p}) \leq f(x) + \|x - \tilde{p}\|$$
$$\leq f(x) + \|x - m\| + \|m - \tilde{p}\|$$
$$= 2f(x) + \|m - \tilde{p}\|.$$

Therefore,

$$\|m - p\| \geq \|m - \tilde{p}\| - \|p - \tilde{p}\|$$
$$\geq \|m - \tilde{p}\| - \delta f(\tilde{p})$$
$$\geq \|m - \tilde{p}\| - \delta(2f(x) + \|m - \tilde{p}\|)$$
$$= (1 - \delta)\|m - \tilde{p}\| - 2\delta f(x)$$
$$\geq (1 - 3\delta)f(x)$$

as $\|m - \tilde{p}\| \geq \|m - x\| = f(x)$. Hence, p cannot be in the interior of $B_{m,r}$. Now consider (ii). We get

$$\|m_x - p\| \geq \|m_x - \tilde{p}\| - \|p - \tilde{p}\|$$
$$\geq \|m_x - \tilde{p}\| - \delta f(\tilde{p})$$
$$\geq \|m_x - \tilde{p}\| - \delta\|m_x - \tilde{p}\|$$
$$= (1 - \delta)\|m_x - \tilde{p}\|$$
$$\geq (1 - \delta)\rho_x$$

as $\|m_x - \tilde{p}\| \geq \|m_x - x\| = \rho_x$. Again, p cannot lie in the interior of $B_{m,r}$. ∎

Next, we show that, for each point x of Σ, there is a nearby large ball which is not only empty but also has a boundary that passes through a sample point

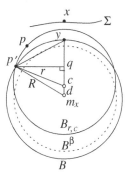

Figure 7.2. Illustration for the Deformed Ball Lemma 7.3.

close to x. Eventually this ball will be deformed to a Delaunay ball for medial axis point approximations.

Lemma 7.3 (Deformed Ball). *For each point $x \in \Sigma$ there is an empty ball $B_{c,r}$ with $c \in \Omega_I$ that enjoys the following properties when ε and δ are sufficiently small.*

(i) m_x is in $B_{c,r}$, $(1 - 2\sqrt{\varepsilon_2})\rho_x \leq r \leq \rho_x$, and $\|c - m_x\| \leq 2\sqrt{\varepsilon_2}\rho_x$ where $\varepsilon_2 = \tilde{O}(\varepsilon + \delta)$ is defined in Corollary 7.1,

(ii) The boundary of $B_{c,r}$ contains a sample point p within a distance $\varepsilon_3 \rho_x$ from x where $\varepsilon_3 = 2\varepsilon_2^{\frac{1}{4}} + \delta$.

Proof. We describe a construction of $B_{c,r}$ which is also used later. Consider the empty ball $B = B_{m_x,R}$ whose boundary passes through a point y where $\tilde{y} = x$, $\|y - x\| = \delta\rho_x$, and $R = (1 - \delta)\rho_x$. Such a ball exists by the Empty Ball Lemma 7.2.

Shrinking: Let $B^\beta = B_{m_x,\beta R}$ for $\beta < 1$. The ball B^β is obtained by shrinking B by a factor of β. The ball B and hence B^β are empty.

Rigid motion: Translate B^β rigidly by moving the center along the direction $\overrightarrow{m_x x}$ until its boundary hits a sample point $p \in P$. Let this new ball be denoted $B_{c,r}$, refer to Figure 7.2.

Obviously, $r = \beta R$. Let $d = \|c - m_x\|$. First, we claim

$$(1 - \beta)R \leq d \leq (1 - \beta)R + \varepsilon_2\rho_x. \tag{7.1}$$

The first half of the inequality holds since B is empty of sample points and hence B^β has to move out of it to hit a sample point. The second half of the inequality holds since from Corollary 7.1, a ball centered at y with radius $\varepsilon_2 \rho_x$ cannot be empty of sample points.

Next, we obtain an upper bound on $\|y - p\|$. Since

$$\|p' - q\|^2 = \|c - p'\|^2 - \|c - q\|^2 = \|m_x - p'\|^2 - \|m_x - q\|^2,$$

we have

$$r^2 - \|c - q\|^2 = R^2 - \|m_x - q\|^2$$
$$\text{or, } r^2 - \|c - q\|^2 = R^2 - (d + \|c - q\|)^2$$
$$\text{or, } r^2 = R^2 - d^2 - 2d\|c - q\|$$
$$\text{or, } \|c - q\| = \frac{R^2 - r^2 - d^2}{2d}.$$

Hence,

$$\|y - p\|^2 \le \|y - p'\|^2 = \|p' - q\|^2 + \|q - y\|^2$$
$$= R^2 - (d + \|c - q\|)^2 + (R - (d + \|c - q\|))^2$$
$$= 2R^2 - Rd - \frac{R}{d}(R^2 - r^2)$$

which, by Inequality 7.1, gives

$$\|y - p\|^2 \le \frac{\varepsilon_2(1 + \beta)}{(1 - \delta)(1 - \beta) + \varepsilon_2} R^2. \qquad (7.2)$$

Since we want both $\|c - m_x\|$ and $\|x - p\|$ to be small, we take $\beta = 1 - \sqrt{\varepsilon_2}$. Hence, with $R = (1 - \delta)\rho_x$,

$$r = \beta R = (1 - \delta)(1 - \sqrt{\varepsilon_2})\rho_x$$

which gives, for sufficiently small δ and ε,

$$(1 - 2\sqrt{\varepsilon_2})\rho_x \le r \le \rho_x.$$

Also,

$$\|c - m_x\| = d$$
$$\le (1 - \beta)R + \varepsilon_2\rho_x$$
$$\le ((1 - \delta)\sqrt{\varepsilon_2} + \varepsilon_2)\rho_x$$
$$\le 2\sqrt{\varepsilon_2}\rho_x$$

for $\varepsilon_2 < 1, \delta < 1$. Given that ε and δ are sufficiently small, $\sqrt{\varepsilon_2}\rho_x$ is small implying that m_x stays inside $B_{c,r}$. In addition, from Inequality 7.2 we have

$$\|y - p\| \le \sqrt{\left(\frac{2 - \sqrt{\varepsilon_2}}{1 - \delta + \sqrt{\varepsilon_2}}\right)}\varepsilon_2^{\frac{1}{4}} R \le 2\varepsilon_2^{\frac{1}{4}}\rho_x.$$

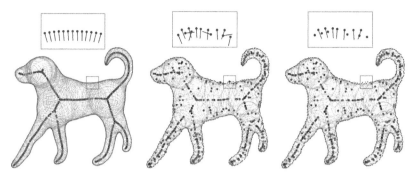

Figure 7.3. Black dots are the centers of Delaunay balls. Left: the normals are esti-mated correctly by pole vectors in the noise-free case. Left-middle: pole vectors do not estimate the normals correctly when noise is present. Right: vectors from the sample points to the center of the big Delaunay balls estimate the normals even when noise is present.

The bound on $\|p - x\|$ follows as $\|x - y\| = \delta \rho_x$ and $\|p - x\| \leq \|y - p\| + \|x - y\|$. ■

In the above proof, if we make the ball $B_{c,r}$ smaller, we will get a sample point closer to x. For example, if we choose β to be a constant, say $\frac{3}{4}$, the above proof gives $\varepsilon_3 = \tilde{O}(\sqrt{\varepsilon_2}) = \tilde{O}(\sqrt{\varepsilon + \delta})$. Also, the entire proof remains valid when we replace ρ_x with $f(x)$. We will use this version of the lemma in the next chapter.

7.3 Normal Approximation

In noise-free case we saw that poles help approximate the normals (Pole Lemma 4.1). When noise is present poles may come arbitrarily close to the surface and the pole vector may not approximate the normals. Figure 7.3 il-lustrates this point. Nevertheless, some Voronoi vertices that are the centers of some large Delaunay balls still help in estimating the normal directions. This idea is formalized in the analysis below.

7.3.1 Analysis

The normal approximation theorem says that if there is a large empty ball incident to a sample point p, then the vector from p to the center of the ball approximates the normal direction $\mathbf{n}_{\tilde{p}}$. The idea is that one cannot tilt a large ball too much and keep it empty if it is anchored at p and has its center in the direction of $\mathbf{n}_{\tilde{p}}$.

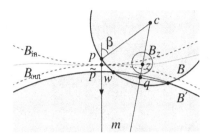

Figure 7.4. Illustration for the General Normal Theorem 7.1.

Theorem 7.1 (General Normal). *Let $p \in P$ be incident to a ball $B_{c,r}$ empty of sample points where $r = \lambda f(\tilde{p})$ and $c \in \Omega_I$. One has*

$$\sin \angle(\overrightarrow{cp}, \mathbf{n}_{\tilde{p}}) \leq \left(4 + \frac{3}{\sqrt{\lambda}}\right)\sqrt{\delta} + \left(2 + \frac{3}{\lambda}\right)\varepsilon_1$$

for a sufficiently small $\varepsilon > 0$ and $\delta > 0$.

Proof. Let $B = B_{c,r}$ and $\beta = \angle(\overrightarrow{cp}, \mathbf{n}_{\tilde{p}})$. Let B_{in} and B_{out} be two balls with radius $f(\tilde{p})$ that tangentially meet the surface at point $\tilde{p}$ as in Figure 7.4. Let m be the center of B_{out}. We know the surface Σ is outside these two balls. By the Empty Ball Lemma 7.2, the ball $B' = B_{m,(1-3\delta)f(\tilde{p})}$, a shrunk copy of B_{out}, is empty of sample points. Therefore, no sample point is inside the shaded area of Figure 7.4.

OBSERVATION A. Let D be the disk bounded by the circle in which the boundaries of B and B' intersect. Let cm intersect D at q. As β increases, the radius of D increases, that is, $\|w - q\|$ increases and vice versa.

OBSERVATION B. Suppose that $\sin \beta$ has the claimed bound when $\|w - q\| = \sqrt{2}\varepsilon_1 f(\tilde{p})$. Then, if we show $\|w - q\| < \sqrt{2}\varepsilon_1 f(\tilde{p})$, we are done following Observation A.

Assume $\|w - q\| = \sqrt{2}\varepsilon_1 f(\tilde{p})$. Let z be the intersection point between Σ and the segment mc.

Consider the triangle formed by p, m, and c. We have

$$(1 - \delta)f(\tilde{p}) \leq \|m - p\| \leq (1 + \delta)f(\tilde{p})$$

and

$$\|c - p\| = \|c - w\| = \lambda f(\tilde{p})$$

and also

$$\|c - m\| = \sqrt{\|c - w\|^2 - \|w - q\|^2} + \sqrt{\|m - w\|^2 - \|w - q\|^2}.$$

We obtain

$$\cos \beta = \frac{\|c - m\|^2 - \|c - p\|^2 - \|m - p\|^2}{2\|c - p\|\|m - p\|}$$

$$\geq \frac{\left(\sqrt{\lambda^2 - 2\varepsilon_1^2} + \sqrt{(1 - 3\delta)^2 - 2\varepsilon_1^2}\right)^2 - \lambda^2 - (1 + \delta)^2}{2\lambda(1 + \delta)}$$

which after some calculations gives

$$1 - \cos \beta \leq \left(7 + \frac{4}{\lambda}\right)\delta + 2\left(1 + \frac{2}{\lambda^2}\right)\varepsilon_1^2.$$

Hence,

$$\sin \beta \leq 2 \sin \frac{\beta}{2} = \sqrt{2(1 - \cos \beta)}$$

$$\leq \sqrt{\left(14 + \frac{8}{\lambda}\right)\delta + 4\left(1 + \frac{2}{\lambda^2}\right)\varepsilon_1^2}$$

$$\leq \left(4 + \frac{3}{\sqrt{\lambda}}\right)\sqrt{\delta} + \left(2 + \frac{3}{\lambda}\right)\varepsilon_1. \tag{7.3}$$

Now we show that $\|w - q\| < \sqrt{2}\varepsilon_1 f(\tilde{p})$ as required by Observation B. Again, first assume that $\|w - q\| = \sqrt{2}\varepsilon_1 f(\tilde{p})$. One can show $\|\tilde{p} - z\| \leq 3\|\tilde{p} - m\| \tan \beta$. Therefore, from equation 7.3 $\|\tilde{p} - z\| = \tilde{O}(\varepsilon_1 + 2\sqrt{\delta})f(\tilde{p})$ which by Lipschitz property gives $f(z) < \sqrt{2}f(\tilde{p})$ given a sufficiently small δ and ε. We know $B_z = B_{z,\varepsilon_1 f(z)}$ with radius $\varepsilon_1 f(z) < \sqrt{2}\varepsilon_1 f(\tilde{p})$ has to contain at least one sample point by the Close Sample Lemma 7.1. This is impossible since B_z has a radius at most $\sqrt{2}\varepsilon_1 f(\tilde{p}) = \|w - q\|$ which means it lies completely in the shaded area. Therefore, $\|w - q\| \neq \sqrt{2}\varepsilon_1 f(\tilde{p})$. Now consider increasing $\|w - q\|$ beyond this distance while keeping z fixed. Notice that now z is not the intersection point between Σ and the segment mc. It is obvious that B_z remains inside the shaded area. Therefore, again we reach a contradiction to the Close Sample Lemma 7.1. Hence, $\|w - q\|$ cannot be larger than $\sqrt{2}\varepsilon_1 f(\tilde{p})$. ∎

The General Normal Theorem 7.1 gives a general form of the normal approximation under a fairly general sampling assumption. One can derive different normal approximation bounds under different sampling assumptions from this general result. For example, if P is a $(\varepsilon, \varepsilon^2, -)$-sample we get an $\tilde{O}(\varepsilon)$ bound on the normal approximation error for a large Delaunay ball with $\lambda = \Omega(1)$.

In the case where P is a $(\varepsilon, \varepsilon, -)$-sample, this error bound becomes $\tilde{O}(\sqrt{\varepsilon})$. When there is no noise, that is, P is a $(\varepsilon, 0, -)$-sample, we obtain $\tilde{O}(\varepsilon)$ error bound that agrees with the Normal Lemma 3.2. Another important implication of the General Normal Theorem is that the Delaunay balls need not be too big to give good normal estimates. One can observe that if λ is only $\sqrt{\max\{\varepsilon, \delta\}}$, we get $\tilde{O}(\varepsilon^{\frac{1}{2}} + \delta^{\frac{1}{4}})$ error. The algorithmic implication of this fact is that a lot of Delaunay balls can qualify for normal approximation.

We also observe that the proof of the General Normal Theorem 7.1 remains valid even if the sample point p is replaced with any point $x \in \mathbb{R}^3$ meeting the conditions as stated in the corollary below. We use this fact later in feature approximation.

Corollary 7.2. *Let $x \in \mathbb{R}^3$ be any point with $\|x - \tilde{x}\| \leq \delta\rho_{\tilde{x}}$ and $B_{c,r}$ be any empty ball incident to x so that $r = \Omega(\rho_{\tilde{x}})$ and $c \in \Omega_l$. Then, $\angle(\overrightarrow{cx}, \mathbf{n}_{\tilde{x}}) = \tilde{O}(\varepsilon + \sqrt{\delta})$ for sufficiently small ε and δ.*

7.3.2 Algorithm

We know from the General Normal Theorem 7.1 that if there is a big Delaunay ball incident to a sample point p, the vector from the center of the ball to p estimates the normal direction at the point $\tilde{p}$. On the other hand, the Deformed Ball Lemma 7.3 assures that, for each point $x \in \Sigma$, there is a sample point p within $\tilde{O}(\varepsilon^{\frac{1}{4}} + \delta^{\frac{1}{4}})f(x)$ distance with an empty ball of radius $\Omega(f(x))$. This means there is a big Delaunay ball incident to p where the vector $\overrightarrow{cp}$ approximates $\mathbf{n}_{\tilde{p}}$ and hence $\mathbf{n}_x$. Algorithmically we can exploit this fact by picking up sample points that are incident to big Delaunay balls only if we have a scale to measure "big" Delaunay balls. For this we assume the third condition in the sampling which says that the sample is locally uniform.

Let d_p be the distance of p to its κth nearest neighbor. The locally uniform condition in the noise model gives $d_p \geq \varepsilon f(\tilde{p})$. Therefore, any Delaunay ball incident to p with radius more than τd_p will give a normal approximation with an error

$$\tilde{O}\left(\left(1 + \frac{1}{\sqrt{\tau\varepsilon}}\right)\sqrt{\delta} + \left(1 + \frac{1}{\tau\varepsilon}\right)\varepsilon\right)$$

according to the General Normal Theorem 7.1. If we assume that P is a $(\varepsilon, \varepsilon^2, \kappa)$-sample, the error bound is $\tilde{O}(\varepsilon + \frac{1}{\tau} + \sqrt{\frac{\varepsilon}{\tau}})$. Notice that the error decreases as τ increases. However, we cannot increase τ arbitrarily since then no Delaunay ball may meet the condition that its radius is at least as large as τd_p.

In fact, we also need an upper bound on d_p to assert that it is not arbitrarily large.

Lemma 7.4 (κ-Neighbor). $d_p \leq \varepsilon' f(\tilde{p})$ where $\varepsilon' = \left(\varepsilon + \frac{4\kappa + \varepsilon}{1 - 4\kappa\varepsilon}\right)\varepsilon$.

Proof. Consider the sample $\tilde{P}$ which is locally uniform. It is an easy consequence of the sampling condition (i) and the Lipschitz property of f that, for each $x \in \Sigma$ there exists a sample point p so that $\|\tilde{p} - x\| \leq \frac{\varepsilon}{1-\varepsilon} f(\tilde{p})$. This means that, for sufficiently small ε, balls of radius $2\varepsilon f(\tilde{p}) > \frac{\varepsilon}{1-\varepsilon} f(\tilde{p})$ around each point $\tilde{p} \in \tilde{P}$ cover Σ. Consider the graph where a point $\tilde{p} \in \tilde{P}$ is joined with $\tilde{q} \in \tilde{P}$ with an edge if the balls $B_{\tilde{p}, r_1}$ and $B_{\tilde{q}, r_2}$ intersect where $r_1 = 2\varepsilon f(\tilde{p})$ and $r_2 = 2\varepsilon f(\tilde{q})$. Take a simple path Π of κ edges in this graph with one endpoint at $\tilde{p}$. An edge between any two points $\tilde{q}_i$ and $\tilde{q}_j$ in the graph has a length at most $2\varepsilon(f(\tilde{q}_i) + f(\tilde{q}_j))$. The path Π thus has length at most

$$\ell = 2\varepsilon(f(\tilde{p}) + 2f(\tilde{q}_1) + \cdots + 2f(\tilde{q}_{\kappa-1}) + f(\tilde{q}_\kappa))$$

where $\tilde{q}_i, i = 1, \ldots, \kappa$ are the vertices ordered along the path. Denoting $f_{\max}$ as the maximum of the feature sizes of all vertices on the considered path we get

$$\ell \leq 4\kappa\varepsilon f_{\max}$$
$$\leq \frac{4\kappa\varepsilon}{1 - 4\kappa\varepsilon} f(\tilde{p}).$$

The distance from p to the farthest point, say q, among the κ closest points to p cannot be more than the distance

$$\|p - \tilde{p}\| + \|\tilde{p} - \tilde{q}\| + \|\tilde{q} - q\|$$

which is no more than

$$\varepsilon^2 f(\tilde{p}) + \frac{4\kappa\varepsilon}{1 - 4\kappa\varepsilon} f(\tilde{p}) + \frac{\varepsilon^2}{1 - 4\kappa\varepsilon} f(\tilde{p}) \leq \varepsilon' f(\tilde{p}).$$

∎

The previous lemma and the locally uniform sampling condition together confirm that a Delaunay ball with radius τd_p has at least $\tau\varepsilon f(\tilde{p})$ radius and at most $\tau \tilde{O}(\varepsilon) f(\tilde{p})$ radius. The quantity τd_p can be made as small as $\sqrt{\varepsilon} f(\tilde{p})$ to give an $\tilde{O}(\sqrt{\varepsilon})$ error. This means the Delaunay ball with radius as small as $\sqrt{\varepsilon} f(\tilde{p})$ provides a good approximation of the true normal. This explains why a large number of Delaunay balls give good normal approximations in

practice. See Figure 7.3 for an illustration in two dimensions. Thus, we have
the following algorithm:

APPROXIMATENORMAL(P,τ)

1   compute Del P;
2   for each $p \in P$ do
3   compute d_p;
4   if there is a Delaunay ball incident to p with radius larger than τd_p
5   compute the largest Delaunay ball $B_{c,r}$ incident to p;
6   store the normal direction at p as pc;
7   endif
8   endfor.

Notice that, alternatively we could have eliminated the parameter τ in the
algorithm by looking for the largest Delaunay ball incident to a set of k-
nearest neighbors of p for some suitable k. Again, thanks to the Deformed
Ball Lemma 7.3, we are assured that for a suitable k, one or more neighbors
have Delaunay balls with radius almost equal to the medial balls. However, this
approach limits the number of sample points where the normals are estimated.
Because of our earlier observation, the normals can be estimated at more points
where the Delaunay ball is big but not necessarily as big as the medial balls.
However, as we see next, for feature approximation we need the Delaunay balls
almost as big as the medial ones.

7.4 Feature Approximation

We approximate the local feature size at a sample point p by first approximating
the medial axis with a set of discrete points and then measuring the distance of
p from this set. In the noise-free case it is known that poles approximate the
medial axis. Therefore, feature sizes can be estimated by computing distance to
the poles. Unfortunately, as we have seen already, the poles do not necessarily
lie near the medial axis when noise is present. We circumvented this difficulty by
considering big Delaunay balls for normal approximations. The big Delaunay
balls were chosen by an input threshold. The case for feature approximations
is more difficult. This is because unlike normal approximations, not all centers
of the big Delaunay balls approximate the medial axis. Only the centers of the
Delaunay balls that approximate the medial balls lie near the medial axis. These
Delaunay balls are difficult to choose with a size threshold. If the threshold
is relatively small, a number of centers remain which do not approximate the
medial axis. See the right picture in Figure 7.3. On the other hand, if the threshold
is large, the medial axis for some parts of the models may not be approximated

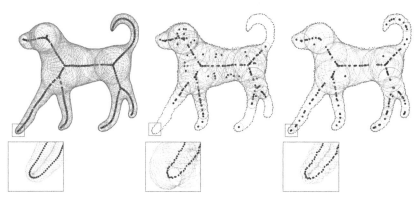

Figure 7.5. Left: poles approximate the medial axis when no noise is present. Middle: Delaunay balls of big size are selected to eliminate unwanted centers, some significant parts of the medial axis are not approximated. Right: centers of polar balls chosen with the nearest neighbors approach approximate the medial axis everywhere. Approximated feature sizes are indicated in the highlighted boxes.

at all; see the middle picture in Figure 7.5. As a result no threshold may exist for which large Delaunay balls' centers approximate the medial axis. The HORSE data in Figure 7.9 is another such example in three dimensions.

We design a different algorithm to choose the Delaunay balls for approximating the medial axis. We consider k-nearest neighbors for some k and take the largest polar ball's center among these neighbors to approximate the medial axis. Our analysis leads to this algorithm. It frees the user from the burden of choosing a size threshold. Experiments suggest that k can be chosen fairly easily, generally in the range of 5–10. The most important thing is that a k can be found for which the medial axis is well approximated where no such size threshold may exist.

We are guaranteed by the Deformed Ball Lemma 7.3 that there are lots of sample points which are incident to big Delaunay balls. The furthest Voronoi vertices from these sample points in Ω_I and Ω_O approximate the inner and outer medial axis respectively. For a point $p \in P$, we call the furthest Voronoi vertex from p in $V_p \cap \Omega_I$ as the inner pole p^+ of p. Similarly, one may define the outer pole p^- of p which resides in Ω_O.

It turns out that the entire medial axis cannot be approximated by poles. Certain parts of the medial axis needs to be excluded. This exclusion is also present in the medial axis approximations with poles in the noise-free case (Exercises 3 and 4 in Chapter 6). Of course, the excluded part is small. In fact, it vanishes to zero in the limit that ε and δ go to zero. Let x and x' be two points where the medial ball B centered at m meets Σ. Call $\angle xmx'$ the *medial angle*

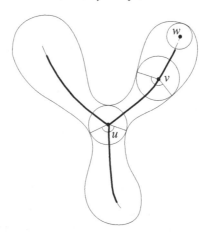

Figure 7.6. The medial angles at u, v are indicated. The medial angle at w is zero. M_α for a small α is shown with thicker curves.

at m if it is the largest angle less than π made by any two such points of $B \cap \Sigma$. Let $M_\alpha \subseteq M$ be the subset where each point $m \in M_\alpha$ has a medial angle at least α (see Figure 7.6).

7.4.1 Analysis

We show that each medial axis point m_x with a large enough medial angle is approximated by a pole. The idea is as follows. Consider the large ball incident to a sample point p guaranteed by the Deformed Ball Lemma 7.3. We deform it to a large Delaunay ball centering the pole p^+. First, during this deformation the ball cannot be tilted too much since the vector from the center to p has to approximate the normal $\mathbf{n}_{\tilde{p}}$ by the General Normal Theorem 7.1. Second, the center in the tilted direction cannot move too much due to Lemma 7.5 as stated below. The result of these constraints is that the center p^+ of the Delaunay ball remains close to the center of the original ball which in turn is close to m_x.

Lemma 7.5. *Let $B = B_{c,r}$ be an empty ball whose boundary passes through a sample point p. Let z be a point on Σ and the distance from z to the boundary of B be less than $\varepsilon' \rho_z$. Suppose B is expanded to an empty ball $B' = B_{c',r'}$ where c' is on the ray $\overrightarrow{pc}$ and $\mathrm{bd}\, B'$ passes through p (Figure 7.7). If $\beta \rho_z \leq r \leq \rho_z$, one has*

$$\|c - c'\| \leq \frac{(\varepsilon_1 + \varepsilon')(2 + \varepsilon')}{2\beta(1 - \cos \angle pcz) - 2\varepsilon_1 - 2\varepsilon' \cos \angle pcz} \rho_z.$$

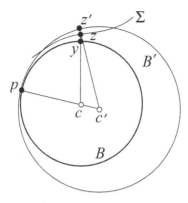

Figure 7.7. Illustration for Lemma 7.5.

Proof. Let y be the closest point to z on the boundary of B. Obviously, y, c, and z are collinear. Let z' be the point where the line of $c'z$ intersects the boundary of B' (see Figure 7.7). We have $\|y - z\| \leq \varepsilon' \rho_z$. Since a ball centered at z with radius $\varepsilon_1 f(z)$ cannot be empty of sample points by the Close Sample Lemma 7.1, we have $\|z' - z\| \leq \varepsilon_1 f(z) \leq \varepsilon_1 \rho_z$.

Consider the triangle made by c, c', and z. For convenience write $\angle pcz = \alpha$, $\|c - c'\| = \Delta c$, $\|z - z'\| = \Delta z$, and $\|y - z\| = \Delta y$.

$$\|c' - z\|^2 = (\Delta c)^2 + \|c - z\|^2 + 2\Delta c \|c - z\| \cos\alpha$$

or, $(r + \Delta c - \Delta z)^2 = (\Delta c)^2 + (r + \Delta y)^2 + 2\Delta c(r + \Delta y)\cos\alpha$

from which we get

$$\Delta c = \frac{(r + \Delta y)^2 - (r - \Delta z)^2}{2(r - \Delta z) - 2(r + \Delta y)\cos\alpha}$$

$$= \frac{(\Delta y + \Delta z)(2r + \Delta y - \Delta z)}{2r(1 - \cos\alpha) - 2\Delta z - 2\Delta y \cos\alpha}$$

$$\leq \frac{(\varepsilon_1 + \varepsilon')(2 + \varepsilon')}{2\beta(1 - \cos\alpha) - 2\varepsilon_1 - 2\varepsilon' \cos\alpha} \rho_z.$$

by plugging in $\Delta z \leq \varepsilon_1 \rho_z$, $\Delta y \leq \varepsilon' \rho_z$, and $\beta\rho_z \leq r \leq \rho_z$. ∎

Theorem 7.2 (Medial Axis Approximation). *For each point $m_x \in M_\alpha$ in Ω_I where $\alpha = \varepsilon^{\frac{1}{4}} + \delta^{\frac{1}{4}}$ with ε and δ being sufficiently small, there is a sample point p within $\tilde{O}(\varepsilon^{\frac{1}{4}} + \delta^{\frac{1}{4}})\rho_x$ distance of x so that the pole p^+ lies within $\tilde{O}(\varepsilon^{\frac{1}{4}} + \delta^{\frac{1}{4}})\rho_x$ distance from m_x.*

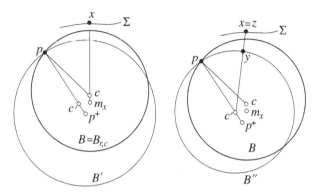

Figure 7.8. Illustration for the Medial Axis Approximation Theorem 7.2. The ball $B_{c,r}$ is deformed to the Delaunay ball $B' = B_{p^+,r'}$. The ball $B'' = B_{c',\|p-c'\|}$ on the right is a shrunk version of B'.

Proof. Consider the ball $B = B_{c,r}$ guaranteed by the Deformed Ball Lemma 7.3 whose boundary passes through a sample point p. We have

$$r \geq (1 - 2\sqrt{\varepsilon_2})\rho_x,$$

$$\|p - x\| \leq \varepsilon_3 \rho_x, \text{ and}$$

$$\|c - m_x\| \leq 2\sqrt{\varepsilon_2}\rho_x.$$

Let $B' = B_{p^+,r'}$ where p^+ is the inner pole of p and $r' = \|p - p^+\|$. The ball B' is Delaunay and has radius $r' \geq r \geq (1 - 2\sqrt{\varepsilon_2})\rho_x$.

Focus on the two balls B and B' passing through p (see Figure 7.8). The ball B has m_x inside it which means that its radius is at least $(1 - \delta)f(\tilde{p})/2$. So, the radius of B' being bigger than that of B is also at least $(1 - \delta)f(\tilde{p})/2$. Therefore, by plugging $\lambda = \Omega(1)$ in the General Normal Theorem 7.1, the vectors $\overrightarrow{pc}$ and $\overrightarrow{pp^+}$ make $\tilde{O}(\varepsilon + \sqrt{\delta})$ angle with $\mathbf{n}_{\tilde{p}}$ and at most double of this angle among them. Let c' be the point on the segment pp^+ so that pc' has the same length as pc. Clearly,

$$\|c - c'\| \leq \|p - c\|\angle cpc' \leq (1 - 2\sqrt{\varepsilon_2})\tilde{O}(\varepsilon + \sqrt{\delta})\rho_x. \tag{7.4}$$

Now we can bound the distance $\|c - p^+\|$ if we have a bound on $\|c' - p^+\|$. We will apply Lemma 7.5 to the ball $B'' = B_{c',\|p-c'\|}$ to bound $\|c' - p^+\|$. Since $m_x \in M_\alpha$ there are two points x and x' in Σ so that $\angle xm_xx' \geq \alpha$. Take z in Lemma 7.5 as the point x or x' which makes the angle $\angle zm_xp$ at least $\alpha/2$.

With this set up we show that β and ε' in Lemma 7.5 are $1 - \tilde{O}(\sqrt{\varepsilon} + \sqrt{\delta})$ and $\tilde{O}(\sqrt{\varepsilon} + \sqrt{\delta})$ respectively. Since the radius of B'' is $r \geq (1 - 2\sqrt{\varepsilon_2})\rho_x = (1 - 2\sqrt{\varepsilon_2})\rho_z$, the claim for β follows.

For ε', consider the point y where the ray $\overrightarrow{c'z}$ meets the boundary of B'', refer to Figure 7.8. We have $\|m_x - c'\| \le \|c - m_x\| + \|c - c'\| = \tilde{O}(\sqrt{\varepsilon} + \sqrt{\delta})\rho_x$ and hence

$$\|y - z\| = \|c' - z\| - \|c' - y\| \le \|m_x - z\| + \|c' - m_x\| - \|c' - y\|$$

$$\le \rho_z + \tilde{O}(\sqrt{\varepsilon} + \sqrt{\delta})\rho_z - (1 - 2\sqrt{\varepsilon_2})\rho_z$$

$$= \tilde{O}(\sqrt{\varepsilon} + \sqrt{\delta})\rho_z.$$

So, we can apply Lemma 7.5 with $\varepsilon' = \tilde{O}(\sqrt{\varepsilon} + \sqrt{\delta})$ and $\beta = 1 - \tilde{O}(\sqrt{\varepsilon} + \sqrt{\delta})$. Observe that, since the points c' and m_x are nearby, the angle $\angle pc'y$ is almost equal to $\angle zm_x p$. So, we can take $\angle pc'y \ge \frac{\alpha}{4}$. With $\alpha = \varepsilon^{\frac{1}{4}} + \delta^{\frac{1}{4}}$, Lemma 7.5 gives

$$\|p^+ - c'\| = (\tilde{O}(\sqrt{\varepsilon} + \sqrt{\delta})/\Omega(\varepsilon^{\frac{1}{4}} + \delta^{\frac{1}{4}}))\rho_z = \tilde{O}(\varepsilon^{\frac{1}{4}} + \delta^{\frac{1}{4}})\rho_z.$$

The claim of the theorem follows as

$$\|p^+ - m_x\| \le \|p^+ - c'\| + \|c' - m_x\|$$

$$= \tilde{O}(\varepsilon^{\frac{1}{4}} + \delta^{\frac{1}{4}})\rho_x + \tilde{O}(\varepsilon^{\frac{1}{2}} + \delta^{\frac{1}{2}})\rho_x$$

$$= \tilde{O}(\varepsilon^{\frac{1}{4}} + \delta^{\frac{1}{4}})\rho_x.$$

■

For each point $x \in \Sigma$ where $m_x \in M_\alpha$, the previous theorem guarantees the existence of a sample point p whose pole approximates m_x. Actually, the proof technique can be used to show that any Delaunay ball with radius almost as big as ρ_x and incident to a sample point close to x has its center close to m_x.

Theorem 7.3 (Feature). *Let $x \in \Sigma$ be a point so that $m_x \in M_\alpha$ for $\alpha = \varepsilon^{\frac{1}{4}} + \delta^{\frac{1}{4}}$ where ε and δ are sufficiently small. For any point $p \in P$ within $\varepsilon_3\rho_x$ distance of x and with an incident Delaunay ball of radius at least $(1 - \tilde{O}(\sqrt{\varepsilon} + \sqrt{\delta}))\rho_x$, the pole p^+ lies within $\tilde{O}(\varepsilon^{\frac{1}{8}} + \delta^{\frac{1}{8}})\rho_x$ distance from m_x.*

Proof. [sketch]. Notice that if $\mathbf{n}_{\tilde{p}}$ and $\mathbf{n}_x$ make small angle, we will be done. Then, we have two segments pp^+ and xm_x almost parallel where p and x are close. Also, these segments can be shown to be of almost same lengths by the given condition and a proof similar to that of the Medial Axis Approximation Theorem 7.2. This would imply m_x and p^+ are close.

Observe that we cannot assert that $\angle(\mathbf{n}_{\tilde{p}}, \mathbf{n}_x)$ is small directly from the Normal Variation Lemma 3.3. We could have applied this lemma had the distance between $\tilde{p}$ and x been $\tilde{O}(\varepsilon)f(x)$. The Deformed Ball Lemma 7.3 only gives that this distance is at most $\tilde{O}(\varepsilon)\rho_x$ and not $\tilde{O}(\varepsilon)f(x)$. Since p and x are at most $\varepsilon_3\rho_x$ apart and the distance of p^+ to p and hence to x is $\Omega(\rho_x)$, $\angle pp^+x = \tilde{O}(\varepsilon_3)$. By Corollary 7.2, it can be shown that p^+x makes $\tilde{O}(\sqrt{\varepsilon_3})$ angle with $\mathbf{n}_x$. Therefore, pp^+ makes $\tilde{O}(\sqrt{\varepsilon_3})$ angle with $\mathbf{n}_x$. It is easy to show that ρ_x is at least $\Omega(f(\tilde{p}))$. So, the angle between pp^+ and $\mathbf{n}_{\tilde{p}}$ is $\tilde{O}(\sqrt{\varepsilon_3})$ completing the claim that $\angle(\mathbf{n}_{\tilde{p}}, \mathbf{n}_x) = \tilde{O}(\sqrt{\varepsilon_3}) = \tilde{O}(\varepsilon^{\frac{1}{8}} + \delta^{\frac{1}{8}})$.   ■

7.4.2 Algorithm

The Medial Axis Approximation Theorem 7.2 and the Feature Theorem 7.3 suggest the following algorithm for feature approximation at points $x \in \Sigma$ where $m_x \in M_{\varepsilon^{\frac{1}{4}}}$. The Medial Axis Approximation Theorem 7.2 says that x has a sample point p within a neighborhood of $\varepsilon_3\rho_x$ whose pole p^+ approximates m_x. Also, the Feature Theorem 7.3 says that *all* sample points within $\varepsilon_3\rho_x$ neighborhood of x with a large enough Delaunay ball have their poles approximate m_x. Therefore, if we take the pole of a sample point q whose distance to q is largest among all sample points within a small neighborhood of x, we will get an approximation of m_x.

We search the neighborhood of x by taking k nearest neighbors of a sample point s close to x. If we assume that P is a $(\varepsilon, \varepsilon, \kappa)$-sample for some $\kappa \geq 1$, k nearest neighbors cannot be arbitrarily close to x. Notice that if we do not prevent oversampling by the third condition of noisy sampling, we cannot make this assertion. In the algorithm, we simply allow a user supplied parameter k to search the k nearest neighbors. Since we want to cover all points of Σ, we simply take all points of P and carry out the following computations.

For each point $p \in P$ we select k-nearest neighbors for a suitable k. Let N_p be this set of neighbors. First, for each $q \in N_p$, we determine the Voronoi vertex v_q in V_q which is furthest from q. This is one of the poles of q. Let $\ell_1(q) = \|v_q - q\|$. Select the point $p_1 \in N_p$ so that $\ell_1(p_1)$ is maximum among all points in N_p. By Medial Axis Approximation Theorem 7.2 and the Feature Theorem 7.3, v_{p_1} approximates a medial axis point m_x if $x \in M_{\varepsilon^{\frac{1}{4}}}$. However, we do not know if m_x is an inner medial axis point or an outer one. Without loss of generality assume that m_x is an inner medial axis point. To approximate the outer medial axis point for x, we determine the Voronoi vertex u_q in V_q for each $q \in N_p$ so that $\overrightarrow{qu_q}$ makes more than $\frac{\pi}{2}$ angle with $\overrightarrow{p_1 v_{p_1}}$. Let $\ell_2(q) = \|u_q - q\|$. Then, we select the point $p_2 \in N_p$ so that $\ell_2(p_2)$ is maximum among all points in N_p. Again, appealing to the Medial Axis Approximation Theorem 7.2 and the Feature Theorem 7.3 for outer medial axis, we can assert that u_{p_2} approximates a medial axis point for x.

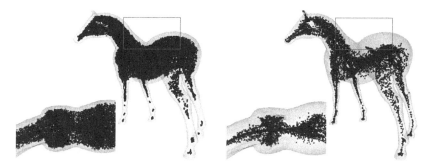

Figure 7.9. Left: medial axis approximated by centers of big Delaunay balls for a noisy HORSE. For a chosen threshold, some parts of the legs do not have medial axis approximated though still many centers lie near the surface. Right: medial axis well approximated by the poles as computed by APPROXIMATEFEATURE.

APPROXIMATEFEATURE(P,k)

1   compute Del P;
2    $L := \emptyset$;
3   for each $p \in P$ compute k nearest neighbors N_p;
4   compute $p_1 \in N_p$ whose distance to one of its pole v_{p_1}
         is maximum among all points in N_p;
5   compute $p_2 \in N_p$ with a pole v_{p_2} so that $\angle(\overrightarrow{p_2 v_{p_2}}, \overrightarrow{p_1 v_{p_1}}) \geq \frac{\pi}{2}$
         and $\|p_2 - v_{p_2}\|$ is maximum among all such points $p_2 \in N_p$;
6        $L := L \cup \{v_{p_1}, v_{p_2}\}$;
7   endfor
8   for each $p \in P$ store the distance of p to L.

As we have observed already, a subset of the medial axis is not approximated by the poles. These are exactly the points on the medial axis which have a small medial angle. The implication of this exclusion is that features cannot be properly estimated for points whose closest point on the medial axis resides in the excluded part. However, if the sampling is sufficiently dense, the excluded part is indeed small in most cases. Figure 7.9 shows the result of feature approximations for a three-dimensional model.

7.5 Notes and Exercises

The material in this chapter is taken from Dey and Sun [39]. The noise model with a condition for each of tangential scatter, normal scatter, and local uniformity was first proposed by Dey and Goswami [34]. They used the same parameter ε for both the scatters. Later, Kolluri [63] proposed a slightly different model in the context of smoothing noisy point samples.

In the noise-free case normals can be approximated by poles as we have seen already. Amenta, Choi, and Kolluri [7] as well as Boissonnat and Cazals [16] showed independently that poles also approximate the medial axis. Later, Dey and Zhao [42] and Chazal and Lieutier [20] showed how to approximate the medial axis with a subset of Voronoi facets and not necessarily with a set of discrete points.

In case of noise, an analysis of normals with big Delaunay balls appeared in Dey and Sun [40] and also in Mederos et al. [67]. Normal approximation under the general noise model as adopted in this chapter was put forward by Dey and Sun [39]. They also provided the analysis and the algorithm for feature approximation under this noise model.

For noisy point samples, optimization-based techniques also work well for normal approximations in practice. See, for example, Mitra, Nguyen, and Guibas [69] and Pauly, Keiser, Kobbelt, and Gross [75]. A comparison between the optimization and the Delaunay-based approaches can be found in Dey, Li, and Sun [37].

Exercises

1. Show an example where a point set P is a $(\varepsilon, \delta, -)$-sample of two topologically different surfaces.

2. Call a point set P a (ε, κ)-sample of Σ if (i) each point $x \in \Sigma$ has a point in P within $\varepsilon f(x)$ distance and (ii) each point $p \in P$ has its κth nearest neighbor at least $\varepsilon f(\tilde{p})$ distance away. Show that P is also a $(\varepsilon', \varepsilon'', \kappa)$-sample of Σ for some ε' and ε'' dependent upon ε.

3. Formulate and prove a version of the Empty Ball Lemma 7.2 when P is a (ε, κ)-sample.

4. In the proof of the Deformed Ball Lemma 7.3 if we choose β to be a fraction, say $\frac{3}{4}$, what bound do we get for ε_3?

5. Derive from the General Normal Theorem 7.1 that the pole vectors in noise-free samples approximate the normals within an angle of $\arcsin 5\varepsilon$ when ε is sufficiently small.

6. Prove Feature Theorem 7.3 rigorously.

8

Noise and Reconstruction

The algorithms for surface reconstruction in previous chapters assume that the input is noise-free. Although in practice all of them can handle some amount of displacements of the points away from the surface, they are not designed in principle to handle such data sets. As a result when the points are scattered around the sampled surface, these algorithms are likely to fail. In this chapter we describe an algorithm that is designed to tolerate noise in data.

The algorithm works with the Delaunay/Voronoi diagrams of the input points and draws upon some of the principles of the power crust algorithm. The power crust algorithm exploits the fact that the union of the polar balls approximates the solid bounded by the sampled surface. Obviously, this property does not hold in the presence of noise. Nevertheless, we have observed in Chapter 7 that, under some reasonable noise model, some of the Delaunay balls remain relatively big and can play the role of the polar balls. These balls are identified and partitioned into inner and outer balls. We show that the boundary of the union of the outer (or inner) big Delaunay balls is homeomorphic to the sampled surface. This immediately gives a homeomorphic surface reconstruction though the reconstructed surface may not interpolate the sample points. The algorithm can be extended to compute a homeomorphic surface interpolating a subset of the input sample points. These points reside on the outer (or inner) big Delaunay balls. The rest of the points are deleted. The Delaunay triangulation of the chosen sample points restricted to the boundary of the chosen big Delaunay balls is output as an approximation to the sampled surface. Figure 8.1 illustrates this algorithm in two dimensions.

8.1 Preliminaries

As before we will assume that the sampled surface Σ is smooth, compact, and has no boundary. Also, we will assume that Σ is connected. The requirement

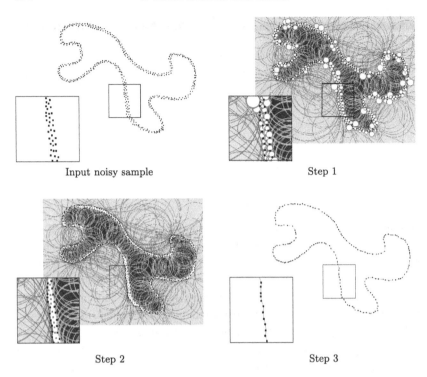

Input noisy sample   Step 1

Step 2   Step 3

Figure 8.1. Step 1: big Delaunay balls (shaded) are separated from small ones (un-shaded), Step 2: outer and inner big Delaunay balls are separated, Step 3: only the points on the outer balls are retained and the curve (surface) is reconstructed from them.

of connectedness is no more for mere simplicity but is indeed needed for the algorithm. Inner and outer big Delaunay balls are separated by a labeling step similar to that of POWERCRUST, which we already know requires Σ to be connected. As in Chapter 7, we use the notations Ω_O to denote the unbounded component of $\mathbb{R}^3 \setminus \Sigma$ and $\Omega_I = \mathbb{R}^3 \setminus \Omega_O$. The normals of Σ are oriented to point outside, that is, toward Ω_O.

We will follow the noise model presented in Chapter 7. This noise model allows two separate parameters for the horizontal and the normal scatters. For simplicity we will make this general noise model a little more specific by assuming P to be a $(\varepsilon, \varepsilon^2, \kappa)$-sample of Σ. First, this removes one parameter from the general model. Second, the quadratic dependence of the normal scatter on ε makes the presentation simpler. Notice that the analysis we are going to present can be extended to the general model by carrying around an extra parameter δ in all calculations.

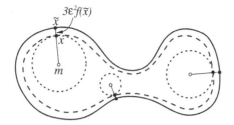

Figure 8.2. Feature balls for three different positions for x are shown with the dotted boundary. The points x, $\tilde{x}$, and the center m are collinear.

Recall that, for a point $x \in \mathbb{R}^3$ that is not on the medial axis, $\tilde{x}$ denotes its closest point in Σ. Under the assumed noise model, the following claims follow from the Close Sample Lemma 7.1 and the κ-Neighbor Lemma 7.4.

Lemma 8.1 (Sampling).

(i) Any point $x \in \Sigma$ has a sample point within $\varepsilon_1 f(x)$ distance where $\varepsilon_1 = \varepsilon(1 + \varepsilon + \varepsilon^2)$.

(ii) Any sample point $p \in P$ has its κth closest sample point within $\varepsilon_2 f(\tilde{p})$ distance where $\varepsilon_2 = \left(\varepsilon + \frac{4\kappa + \varepsilon}{1 - 4\kappa\varepsilon}\right)\varepsilon = \tilde{O}(\varepsilon)$.

From this point onward we consider Ω_I to state all definitions and results unless specified otherwise. It should be clear that they also hold for Ω_O. We have already seen in the previous chapter (Empty Ball Lemma 7.2) that there are empty balls with radius almost as large as local feature sizes and with a boundary point close to Σ. These balls, which we call *feature balls* (Figure 8.2) will play an important role in the proofs. Because of their importance in the proofs, we give a formal definition of them.

Definition 8.1. *Let $B_{m,r}$ be the ball with the following conditions:*

(i) $m \in \Omega_I$; the boundary of $B_{m,r}$ has a point x where $\|x - \tilde{x}\| \leq 3\varepsilon^2 f(\tilde{x})$,
(ii) $r = (1 - 3\varepsilon^2)f(\tilde{x})$, and
(iii) the center m lies on the line of $\mathbf{n}_{\tilde{x}}$. In other words, $\tilde{m} = \tilde{x}$.

Call $B_{m,r}$ a feature ball.

The particular choice of the term $3\varepsilon^2$ in the definition of the feature balls is motivated by the Empty Ball Lemma 7.2. One can substitute δ with ε^2 in this lemma to claim that the feature balls are empty.

Also, the following observation will be helpful for our proofs. It says that if a ball with two points x and y on its boundary is big relative to the feature size of $\tilde{x}$, it remains big relative to the feature size of $\tilde{y}$ if x and y are close to Σ. The parameters λ and ε' will be close to 1 and ε respectively when we use this lemma later.

Lemma 8.2. *Let* $B = B_{c,r}$ *be a ball with two points* x *and* y *on its boundary where* $\|x - \tilde{x}\| \leq \varepsilon' f(\tilde{x}), \|y - \tilde{y}\| \leq \varepsilon' f(\tilde{y}).$ *Then,* $r \geq \frac{\lambda(1-\varepsilon')}{1+2\lambda+\varepsilon'} f(\tilde{y})$ *given that* $r \geq \lambda f(\tilde{x})$ *for* $\lambda > 0.$

Proof. We get

$$r \geq \lambda f(\tilde{x})$$
$$\geq \lambda(f(\tilde{y}) - \|\tilde{x} - \tilde{y}\|)$$
$$\geq \lambda(f(\tilde{y}) - \|x - \tilde{x}\| - \|x - y\| - \|y - \tilde{y}\|)$$
$$\geq \lambda(f(\tilde{y}) - \varepsilon' f(\tilde{x}) - 2r - \varepsilon' f(\tilde{y}))$$

from which it follows that

$$(1 + 2\lambda + \varepsilon')r \geq \lambda(1 - \varepsilon')f(\tilde{y})$$
$$\text{or,}\ r \geq \frac{\lambda(1 - \varepsilon')}{1 + 2\lambda + \varepsilon'} f(\tilde{y}).$$

∎

8.2 Union of Balls

As we indicated before, our goal is to filter out a subset of points from P that lie on big Delaunay balls. We do this by choosing Delaunay balls that are big compared to the distances between sample points and their κth nearest neighbors. Let d_p denote the distance to the κth nearest neighbor of a sample point $p \in P$. For an appropriate constant $K > 0$, we define

$\mathcal{B}(K) =$ set of Delaunay balls $B_{c,r}$ where $r > Kd_p$ for all points $p \in P$ incident on the boundary of $B_{c,r}$.

Since we know that $d_p \geq \varepsilon f(\tilde{p})$ by the sampling condition, we have

Observation 8.1. *Let* $B_{c,r} \in \mathcal{B}(K)$ *be a Delaunay ball with* $p \in P$ *on its boundary. Then,* $r > K\varepsilon f(\tilde{p}).$

By definition $\mathbb{R}^3 = \Omega_I \cup \Omega_O.$ So, we can write $\mathcal{B}(K) = \mathcal{B}_I \cup \mathcal{B}_O$ where $\mathcal{B}_I$ is the set of balls having their centers in Ω_I and $\mathcal{B}_O$ is the set of balls with their centers in $\Omega_O.$ We call the balls in $\mathcal{B}_I$ the *inner* big Delaunay balls and the ones in $\mathcal{B}_O$ the *outer* big Delaunay balls.

We will filter out those points from P that lie on the balls in $\mathcal{B}(K)$. A decomposition of $\mathcal{B}(K)$ induces a decomposition on these points, namely

$$P_I = \{p \in P \cap B \mid B \in \mathcal{B}_I\} \quad \text{and} \quad P_O = \{p \in P \cap B \mid B \in \mathcal{B}_O\}.$$

Notice that P_I and P_O may not be disjoint and they decompose only the set of points incident to the balls in $\mathcal{B}(K)$ and not necessarily the set P.

In the analysis to follow we will assume that ε is a sufficiently small positive value no more than 0.01. With this assumption we have

$$\varepsilon_1 = \varepsilon(1 + \varepsilon + \varepsilon^2) \leq 1.1\varepsilon.$$

We will use the General Normal Theorem 7.1 in the analysis. Substituting $\delta = 3\varepsilon^2$ and $\varepsilon_1 \leq 1.1\varepsilon$ we get the following corollary.

Corollary 8.1. *Let $B_{c,r}$ be a Delaunay ball whose boundary contains a sample point $p \in P$. Let c lie in Ω_I. If $r = \lambda f(\tilde{p})$ then the sin of the angle the vector $\vec{cp}$ makes with n_p is at most*

$$\left(2.2 + 4\sqrt{3} + \frac{3\sqrt{3}}{\sqrt{\lambda}} + \frac{3.3}{\lambda}\right)\varepsilon$$

when $\varepsilon \leq 0.01$ is sufficiently small.

In the rest of the chapter we use

$$\varepsilon_3 = \varepsilon_1 + 3\varepsilon^2 \quad \text{and} \quad \varepsilon_4 = \left(\frac{7\varepsilon_3}{(1 - 3\varepsilon^2) + 4\varepsilon_3}\right)^{\frac{1}{2}}(1 - 3\varepsilon^2).$$

Notice that $\varepsilon_3 = \tilde{O}(\varepsilon)$ and $\varepsilon_4 = \tilde{O}(\sqrt{\varepsilon})$.

The next lemma shows that not only do we have large Delaunay balls in Del P but also many of them covering almost the entire Ω_I.

Lemma 8.3 (Delaunay Ball). *For each point $x \in \Omega_I$ with $\|x - \tilde{x}\| = 3\varepsilon^2 f(\tilde{x})$, there is a Delaunay ball that enjoys the following properties when ε is sufficiently small.*

(i) The radius of the Delaunay ball is at least $\frac{3}{4}(1 - 3\varepsilon^2)f(\tilde{x})$.

(ii) The boundary of the Delaunay ball contains a sample point $p \in P_I$ within a distance $\varepsilon_4 f(\tilde{x}) = \tilde{O}(\sqrt{\varepsilon})f(\tilde{x})$ from x.

Proof. Consider the feature ball $B = B_{m,r}$ whose boundary meets x. By definition,

$$r = (1 - 3\varepsilon^2)f(\tilde{x}).$$

We construct the Delaunay ball as claimed by deforming B as follows.

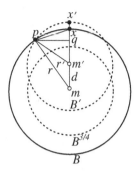

Figure 8.3. Deformation of B to B'.

Shrinking: Let $B^{3/4} = B_{m,3r/4}$ be a shrunk copy of B. The ball B and hence $B^{3/4}$ are empty.

Translation: Translate $B^{3/4}$ rigidly by moving the center m along the direction $\overrightarrow{mx}$ until its boundary hits a sample point $p \in P$. Let this new ball be $B' = B'_{m',r'}$, refer to Figure 8.3.

Delaunay deformation: Deform B' further to a larger Delaunay ball $B'' = B_{m'',r''}$ which we show has the claimed properties. The center m' of B' belongs to the Voronoi cell V_p since B' is empty of points from P. Move the center m' of B' continuously in V_p always increasing the distance $\|m' - p\|$ till m' meets a Voronoi vertex, say m'', in V_p. This motion is possible as the distance function from p reaches its maxima only at the Voronoi vertices.

Let x' be the closest point to x on the boundary of B'. The Sampling Lemma 8.1(i) implies that the point x has a sample point within $(\varepsilon_1 + 3\varepsilon^2)f(\tilde{x})$ distance. We have

$$\|x' - x\| \le (\varepsilon_1 + 3\varepsilon^2)f(\tilde{x}) = \varepsilon_3 f(\tilde{x}) \tag{8.1}$$

since otherwise there is an empty ball centering x with radius $\varepsilon_3 f(\tilde{x})$.

Claim 8.1. $\|x - p\| \le \varepsilon_4 f(\tilde{x})$.

First, we observe that both B and B' contain their centers in their intersection. Since B' has a radius smaller than B, it is sufficient to show that B' contains m inside. During the rigid translation when the ball $B^{3/4}$ touches B at x, its center moves by $\frac{1}{4}r$ distance. After that, we move $B^{3/4}$ by the distance $\|x' - x\| \le$

$\varepsilon_3 f(\tilde{x})$ (Inequality 8.1). Thus,

$$\|m - m'\| \leq \frac{1}{4}r + \varepsilon_3 f(\tilde{x}). \tag{8.2}$$

Therefore, the distance between m and m' is less than $\frac{3}{4}r$ for sufficiently small ε implying that m is in B'.

Now we prove the claimed bound for $\|x - p\|$. The point p can only be on that part of the boundary of B' which is outside the empty ball B. This with the fact that the centers of B and B' are in their intersection imply that the largest distance from x to p is realized when p is on the circle where the boundaries of B and B' intersect. Consider this situation as in Figure 8.3.

Let $d = \|m' - m\|$. First, observe that

$$\frac{1}{4}r \leq d \leq \frac{1}{4}r + \varepsilon_3 f(\tilde{x}). \tag{8.3}$$

The first half of the inequality holds since B is empty of samples and hence $B^{\frac{3}{4}}$ has to move out of it to hit a sample point. The second half of the inequality follows from Inequality 8.2. Since

$$\|p - q\|^2 = \|m - p\|^2 - \|m - q\|^2,$$
$$= r^2 - (\|m' - q\| + d)^2$$

and also

$$\|p - q\|^2 = \|m' - p\|^2 - \|m' - q\|^2,$$
$$= (r')^2 - \|m' - q\|^2$$

we have

$$\|m' - q\| = \frac{r^2 - (r')^2 - d^2}{2d}.$$

Hence,

$$\begin{aligned}
\|x - p\|^2 &= \|p - q\|^2 + \|q - x\|^2 \\
&= r^2 - (d + \|m' - q\|)^2 \\
&\quad + (r - (d + \|m' - q\|))^2 \\
&= 2r^2 - rd - \frac{r}{d}(r^2 - r'^2) \\
&\overset{\text{Ineq. 8.3}}{\leq} \frac{\varepsilon_3(1 + \frac{3}{4})}{\frac{1}{4}(1 - 3\varepsilon^2) + \varepsilon_3}r^2 \\
&\leq \varepsilon_4 f(\tilde{x}).
\end{aligned}$$

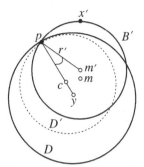

Figure 8.4. The balls B' and D incident to p. The reduced ball D' shown with dotted circle contains m.

Claim 8.2. $m'' \in \Omega_I$.

To prove this claim we first show that the radius r' of B', which is $\frac{3}{4}r = \frac{3}{4}(1 - 3\varepsilon^2)f(\tilde{x})$, is also large compared to $f(\tilde{p})$. Observe that $\|x' - \tilde{x}\|$ is at most $\varepsilon_3 f(\tilde{x})$ if $\tilde{x}$ lies between x and x' (Inequality 8.1). If $\tilde{x}$ does not lie between x and x', the distance $\|x' - \tilde{x}\|$ is no more than $\|x - \tilde{x}\|$ which and is at most $3\varepsilon^2 f(\tilde{x})$ since B is a feature ball (refer to Figure 8.2). Hence, $\|x' - \tilde{x}\| \leq \max\{\varepsilon_3, 3\varepsilon^2\}f(\tilde{x})$. We have $\varepsilon_3 > 3\varepsilon^2$. Therefore, we can say $\|x' - \tilde{x}\| \leq \varepsilon_3 f(\tilde{x})$. We know $\|p - \tilde{p}\| \leq \varepsilon^2 f(\tilde{p})$. So, we can apply Lemma 8.2 with $\varepsilon' = \varepsilon_3$ and $\lambda = \frac{3}{4}(1 - 3\varepsilon^2)$ to deduce that $r' = \|p - m'\| \geq \beta f(\tilde{p})$ where

$$\beta = \frac{3}{10} \frac{(1 - 3\varepsilon^2)(1 - \varepsilon_3)}{1 + \tilde{O}(\varepsilon)}.$$

This means

$$r' \geq \left(\frac{3}{10} - \tilde{O}(\varepsilon)\right) f(\tilde{p}). \tag{8.4}$$

Now we show that the center of B' cannot reach a point in Σ during its deformation to B'' establishing $m'' \in \Omega_I$. Suppose not, that is, the center of B' reaches a point $y \in \Sigma$ during the deformation. Then, we reach a contradiction.

First, observe that m' is in Ω_I as it is only within $\frac{1}{4}r + \varepsilon_3 f(\tilde{x})$ distance away from m. Next, consider the two balls B' and $D = B_{y, \|y-p\|}$ meeting at p (Figure 8.4). Both have radii larger than $(\frac{3}{10} - \tilde{O}(\varepsilon))f(\tilde{p})$ (Inequality 8.4) which is at least $\frac{f(\tilde{p})}{4}$ for sufficiently small ε. Both vectors $\overrightarrow{yp}$ and $\overrightarrow{m'p}$ make at most 35ε angle with $\mathbf{n}_{\tilde{p}}$ (Corollary 8.1) and hence make an angle of at most 70ε among themselves. Consider a smaller version of D by moving its center towards p till its radius becomes same as that of B'. Let this new ball be

$D' = B_{c,\|p-c\|}$ (Figure 8.4). We show that this D' and hence D contain m. We have

$$\|m - c\| \le \|m - m'\| + \|m' - c\|$$

$$\le \frac{1}{4}(1 - 3\varepsilon^2)f(\tilde{x}) + \varepsilon_3 f(\tilde{x}) + 70\varepsilon r'$$

$$= \left(\frac{1}{4} + \tilde{O}(\varepsilon)\right)(1 - 3\varepsilon^2)f(\tilde{x}).$$

On the other hand, the radius $\|p - c\|$ of D' is $r' = \frac{3}{4}(1 - 3\varepsilon^2)f(\tilde{x})$. Therefore, $\|m - c\|$ is smaller than this radius for a sufficiently small ε. Hence, m is in D' and therefore in D. Now we claim that y and m are far away and thus y cannot have any sample point nearby contradicting the Sampling Lemma 8.1. Let z be the point on the medial axis so that $\|\tilde{x} - m\| = f(\tilde{x}) = \|\tilde{x} - z\|$. Then, $\|y - m\| + 2\|\tilde{x} - m\| \ge \|y - z\| \ge f(y)$ giving $3\|y - m\| \ge f(y)$ or $\|y - m\| \ge f(y)/3$. Since D contains m, the ball centered at y with radius $\|y - m\|$ lies completely inside D and thus cannot contain any sample point. This means y cannot have a sample point within $f(y)/3$ distance, a contradiction to the Sampling Lemma 8.1 when ε is sufficiently small. This completes the claim that the center of B' always remains in Ω_I while deforming B' to B''.

Claim 8.3. $B'' \in \mathcal{B}_I$.

The ball B'' contains four sample points including p on its boundary. For any of these sample points u, we have $\|u - \tilde{u}\| \le \varepsilon^2 f(\tilde{u})$ by the sampling condition. Therefore, applying Lemma 8.2 to B'' with points p, $u \ne p$, and $\lambda = (\frac{3}{10} - \tilde{O}(\varepsilon))$ we get

$$r'' \ge \frac{\lambda(1 - \varepsilon^2)}{1 + 2\lambda + \varepsilon^2}f(\tilde{u}) \ge \left(\frac{3}{16} - \tilde{O}(\varepsilon)\right)f(\tilde{u}).$$

Also, we have $d_u \le \varepsilon_2 f(\tilde{u})$ from the Sampling Lemma 8.1. Thus, B'' is in $\mathcal{B}(K)$ if

$$\frac{(\frac{3}{16} - \tilde{O}(\varepsilon))}{2} > K\varepsilon_2, \quad \text{or} \quad 1 > \tilde{O}(\varepsilon) + 11K\varepsilon_2,$$

a condition which is satisfied for a sufficiently small ε. Since $m'' \in \Omega_I$ by Claim 8.2, we have $B'' \in \mathcal{B}_I$.

Lemma claims: Clearly,

$$r'' \ge r' \ge \frac{3}{4}(1 - 3\varepsilon^2)f(\tilde{x}).$$

This proves (i). Claim 8.3 proves $p \in P_I$ which together with the Claim 8.1 gives (ii).   ■

8.3 Proximity

We aim to prove that the boundary of $\bigcup \mathcal{B}_I$ is homeomorphic and close to Σ. The proof can be adapted in a straightforward manner for a similar result between the boundary of $\bigcup \mathcal{B}_O$ and Σ. We define

$$S_I = \mathrm{bd}\left(\bigcup \mathcal{B}_I\right),$$

$$S_O = \mathrm{bd}\left(\bigcup \mathcal{B}_O\right).$$

In the next two lemmas we establish that each point in S_I has a nearby point on Σ.

Lemma 8.4. *Let x be a point lying in Ω_O where $x \in S_I$. Then, $\|x - \tilde{x}\| \leq \frac{\varepsilon_1}{1-2\varepsilon_1} f(\tilde{x})$.*

Proof. Let $x \in B_{c,r}$ where $B_{c,r} \in \mathcal{B}_I$. The line segment joining x and c must intersect Σ since c lies in Ω_I while x lies in Ω_O. Let this intersection point be z. We claim that $\|x - z\| \leq \varepsilon_1 f(z)$. Otherwise, there is a ball inside $B_{c,r}$ centering z and radius at least $\varepsilon_1 f(z)$. This ball is empty since $B_{c,r}$ is empty. This violates the Sampling Lemma 8.1 for z. This means that the closest point $\tilde{x} \in \Sigma$ to x has a distance $\|x - \tilde{x}\| \leq \|x - z\| \leq \varepsilon_1 f(z)$. We also have $\|z - \tilde{x}\| \leq 2\|x - z\|$. Applying the Lipschitz property of f, we get the desired bound for $\|x - \tilde{x}\|$.   ■

Lemma 8.5. *Let x be a point lying in Ω_I where $x \in S_I$. Then, for a sufficiently small ε, $\|x - \tilde{x}\| \leq 36\varepsilon f(\tilde{x})$.*

Proof. Let $y \in \Omega_I$ be a point where $\tilde{y} = \tilde{x}$ and $\|y - \tilde{x}\| = 3\varepsilon^2 f(\tilde{x})$. Observe that x, y, and $\tilde{x}$ are collinear. If x lies between $\tilde{x}$ and y, then $\|x - \tilde{x}\| \leq 3\varepsilon^2 f(\tilde{x})$ which is no more than $36\varepsilon f(\tilde{x})$.

So, assume that x is further away from $\tilde{x}$ than y is. Consider a Delaunay ball $B = B_{c,r} \in \mathcal{B}_I$ for y guaranteed by the Delaunay Ball Lemma 8.3. This ball has a sample point $p \in P$ on the boundary so that $\|y - p\| \leq \varepsilon_4 f(\tilde{x})$. Moreover, $r \geq \frac{3}{4}(1 - 3\varepsilon^2) f(\tilde{x})$. This ball was obtained by deforming a ball $B' = B_{m',r'}$ whose boundary passes through p and a point x' where $\|y - x'\| \leq \varepsilon_3 f(\tilde{x})$. Also, $r' = \frac{3}{4}(1 - 3\varepsilon^2) f(\tilde{x})$. Focus on the two balls B and B' incident to p. Since y and p and hence $\tilde{x}$ and p are close, both B and B' have radii larger

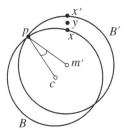

Figure 8.5. The balls B and B' incident to p. The point x' is furthest from x when B is the smallest possible.

than $\frac{3}{5}f(\tilde{p})$ when ε is sufficiently small. By Corollary 8.1, we obtain that the vectors $\overrightarrow{pc}$ and $\overrightarrow{pm'}$ make 23ε angle with $-\mathbf{n}_{\tilde{p}}$ and hence make an angle of 46ε among them.

We know that B has a radius at least as large as B' (proof of the Delaunay Ball Lemma 8.3). The points $x, x', \tilde{x}$, and y are collinear and y separates x and x'. Further, x cannot lie inside a Delaunay ball. With these constraints, the distance between x and x' is the most when x lies on the boundary of B and B is the smallest possible (see Figure 8.5). This means we can assume that both B and B' have the same radius to estimate the worst upper bound on $\|x - x'\|$. In that configuration, $\|x - x'\| \le \|c - m'\| \le 46r'\varepsilon$ which is at most $34\varepsilon(1 - 3\varepsilon^2)f(\tilde{x})$. Therefore,

$$\|x - \tilde{x}\| \le \|x - y\| + \|y - \tilde{x}\|$$
$$\le \|x - x'\| + \|x' - \tilde{x}\|$$
$$\le (34\varepsilon(1 - 3\varepsilon^2) + \varepsilon_3)f(\tilde{x})$$
$$\le 36\varepsilon f(\tilde{x}).$$

■

From Lemma 8.4 and Lemma 8.5 we get the following theorem.

Theorem 8.1 (Small Hausdorff). *For a sufficiently small ε, each point x on S_I has a point in Σ within $36\varepsilon f(\tilde{x})$ distance.*

Lemma 8.6. *Let x be any point on the boundary of a ball $B_{c,r} \in \mathcal{B}_I$, we have $r \ge (K/2)\varepsilon f(\tilde{x})$ for a sufficiently small ε.*

Proof. Suppose the claim is not true. Then, consider a vertex $p \in P_I$ on the Delaunay ball $B_{c,r}$. Since this ball is in $\mathcal{B}_I$, we have $r \ge K\varepsilon f(\tilde{p})$. Since

$\|x - p\| \le 2r$, we have $\|x - p\| \le K \varepsilon f(\tilde{x})$ by our assumption. This means $\|x - \tilde{p}\| \le K \varepsilon f(\tilde{x}) + \varepsilon^2 f(\tilde{p})$. Since $\tilde{x}$ is closer to x than $\tilde{p}$, we have

$$\|\tilde{x} - \tilde{p}\| \le \|\tilde{x} - x\| + \|x - \tilde{p}\|$$
$$\le 2 \left(K \varepsilon f(\tilde{x}) + \varepsilon^2 f(\tilde{p}) \right).$$

Using the Lipschitz property of f we get

$$f(\tilde{x}) \le \left(\frac{1 + 2\varepsilon^2}{1 - 2K\varepsilon} \right) f(\tilde{p}).$$

Therefore by our assumption,

$$r < \left(\frac{K}{2} \right) \left(\frac{1 + 2\varepsilon^2}{1 - 2K\varepsilon} \right) \varepsilon f(\tilde{p}).$$

We reach a contradiction if $\frac{K(1+2\varepsilon^2)}{2(1-2K\varepsilon)} \le K$, a condition which is satisfied for a sufficiently small ε. ∎

Theorem 8.2 (Normal Approximation). *Let x be a point in S_l where $B_{c,r} \in \mathcal{B}_l$ contains x. For a sufficiently small ε, $\angle(\mathbf{n}_{\tilde{x}}, \overrightarrow{cx}) = 25\sqrt{\varepsilon} + \frac{26}{\sqrt{K}} + \frac{8}{K}$.*

Proof. We apply the General Normal Theorem 7.1 to x. Lemma 8.6 gives $\lambda = \frac{K\varepsilon}{2}$ and the Small Hausdorff Theorem 8.1 gives $\delta = 36\varepsilon$. With these substitutions we get the required angle bound. ∎

8.4 Topological Equivalence

We have all ingredients to establish a homeomorphism between Σ and S_l using the map ν. Recall that ν maps all points of $\mathbb{R}^3$ except the medial axis points of Σ to their closest point in Σ.

Although the next theorem is stated for a large K, it is not as large in practice. The large value of K is due to the slacks introduced at various places of the analysis.

Theorem 8.3. *For any $K > 400$ there exists a $\varepsilon > 0$ and $\kappa \ge 1$ so that if P is a $(\varepsilon, \varepsilon^2, \kappa)$-sample of a surface Σ, the restriction ν' of ν to S_l defines a homeomorphism between S_l and Σ.*

Proof. For any fixed $K > 0$, Lemmas 8.3 to 8.6 hold for a sufficiently small ε. In particular, the Small Hausdorff Theorem 8.1 asserts that each point x in S_l is within $\tilde{O}(\varepsilon) f(\tilde{x})$ distance from $\tilde{x}$. Therefore, all points of S_l are far away from the medial axis when ε is sufficiently small. Thus ν' is well defined. Since S_l

and Σ are both compact we only need to show that v' is continuous, one-to-one, and onto. The continuity of v' follows from the continuity of v.

To prove that v' is one-to-one, assume on the contrary that there are points x and x' in S_I so that $\tilde{x} = v'(x) = v'(x')$. Without loss of generality assume x' is further away from $\tilde{x}$ than x is. Let $x \in B_{c,r}$ where $B_{c,r} \in \mathcal{B}_I$. The line ℓ_x passing through x and x' is normal to Σ at $\tilde{x}$ and according to the Normal Approximation Theorem 8.2, ℓ_x makes an angle of at most $\alpha = 25\sqrt{\varepsilon} + \frac{26}{\sqrt{K}} + \frac{8}{K}$ with the vector $\overrightarrow{cx}$. This angle is less than $\frac{\pi}{2}$ for $K > 400$. Thus, while walking on the line ℓ_x toward the inner medial axis starting from $\tilde{x}$, we encounter a segment of length at least $2r\cos\alpha$ inside $B_{c,r}$. By the Small Hausdorff Theorem 8.1 both x and x' are within $36\varepsilon f(\tilde{x})$ distance from $\tilde{x}$. We reach a contradiction if $2r\cos\alpha$ is more than $72\varepsilon f(\tilde{x})$. Since $r > (K/2)\varepsilon f(\tilde{x})$ this contradiction can be reached for a sufficiently small ε. Then, x and x' are the same.

The map v' is also onto. Since S_I is a closed, compact surface without boundary and v' maps S_I continuously to Σ, $v'(S_I)$ must consist of closed connected components of Σ. By our assumption Σ is connected. This means $v'(S_I) = \Sigma$ and hence v' is onto. ∎

We can also show an isotopy between S_I and Σ using the proof technique of the PC-Isotopy Theorem 6.4 in Section 6.1. To carry out the proof we need (i) S_I lives in a small tubular neighborhood of Σ which is ensured by the Small Hausdorff Theorem 8.1 and (ii) the normals to Σ intersects S_I in exactly one point within this neighborhood which is shown in the proof of the above theorem.

8.4.1 Labeling

To apply the previous results, we need to label the balls in $\mathcal{B}_I$ and the ones in $\mathcal{B}_O$. As in POWERCRUST we achieve this by looking at how deeply the balls intersect. A ball in $\mathcal{B}_I$ can have only a shallow intersection with a ball in $\mathcal{B}_O$. However, adjacent balls in $\mathcal{B}_I$ or in $\mathcal{B}_O$ intersect deeply. In the case of POWERCRUST we took two balls adjacent if they contribute a facet in the power diagram. Here we will define the adjacency slightly differently without referring to the power diagram. We call two balls in $\mathcal{B}_I$ $(\mathcal{B}_O)$ *adjacent* if their boundaries intersect at a point lying in S_I $(S_O$ respectively). The adjacent balls in $\mathcal{B}_I$ or in $\mathcal{B}_O$ intersect deeply. We measure the depth of intersection as before, that is, by the angle at which two balls intersect. We say a ball B_1 intersects another ball B_2 at an angle α if there is a point x in the intersection of their boundaries and $\angle(\overrightarrow{c_1 x}, \overrightarrow{c_2 x}) = \alpha$ where c_1 and c_2 are the centers of B_1 and B_2 respectively.

Lemma 8.7. *Any two adjacent balls B_1 and B_2 in $\mathcal{B}_I$ intersect at an angle of at most $50\sqrt{\varepsilon} + \frac{52}{\sqrt{K}} + \frac{16}{K}$ when ε is sufficiently small.*

Proof. Let $x \in B_1 \cap B_2$ be a point in S_I. The angle at which B_1 and B_2 intersect at x is equal to the angle between the vectors $\overrightarrow{c_1 x}$ and $\overrightarrow{c_2 x}$ where c_1 and c_2 are the centers of B_1 and B_2 respectively. By the Normal Approximation Theorem 8.2 both $\angle(\mathbf{n}_{\tilde{x}}, \overrightarrow{c_1 x})$ and $\angle(\mathbf{n}_{\tilde{x}}, \overrightarrow{c_2 x})$ are at most $25\sqrt{\varepsilon} + \frac{26}{\sqrt{K}} + \frac{8}{K}$. This implies $\angle(\overrightarrow{c_1 x}, \overrightarrow{c_2 x})$ is no more than the claimed bound. ∎

Lemma 8.8. *For a sufficiently small ε, any ball $B_1 \in \mathcal{B}_I$ intersects any other ball $B_2 \in \mathcal{B}_O$ at an angle more than $\pi/2 - \arcsin((2/K)(1 + \tilde{O}(\varepsilon)))$.*

Proof. The line segment joining the center c_1 of B_1 and the center c_2 of B_2 intersects Σ as c_1 lies in Ω_I where c_2 lies in Ω_O. Let this intersection point be x. Without loss of generality, assume that x lies inside B_1. Let C be the circle of intersection of the boundaries of B_1 and B_2 and d be its radius. Clearly, d is smaller than the distance of x to the closest sample point as B_1 is empty. This fact and the Sampling Lemma 8.1 imply

$$d \leq \varepsilon_1 f(x). \tag{8.5}$$

Next, we obtain a lower bound on the radius of B_1 in terms of $f(x)$. Let the segment $c_1 c_2$ intersect the boundary of B_1 at y. The Sampling Lemma 8.1 implies $\|x - y\| \leq \varepsilon_1 f(x)$. This also means $\|x - \tilde{y}\| \leq 2\varepsilon_1 f(x)$. By Lipschitz property of f, we have

$$f(\tilde{y}) \geq (1 - 2\varepsilon_1) f(x).$$

The radius r of B_1 satisfies (Lemma 8.6)

$$\begin{aligned} r &\geq (K/2)\varepsilon f(\tilde{y}) \\ &\geq (K/2)\varepsilon(1 - 2\varepsilon_1) f(x). \end{aligned} \tag{8.6}$$

Combining Inequalities 8.5 and 8.6 we obtain that, for a point z on the circle C, $\overrightarrow{zc_1}$ makes an angle at least $\pi/2 - \arcsin((2/K)(1 + \tilde{O}(\varepsilon)))$ with the plane of C. The angle at which B_1 and B_2 intersect is greater than this angle. ∎

Lemmas 8.7 and 8.8 say that, for a sufficiently large K and a small ε, one can find an angle $\theta > 0$ so that the adjacent balls in $\mathcal{B}_I$ and $\mathcal{B}_O$ intersect at an angle less than θ whereas a ball from $\mathcal{B}_I$ intersects a ball from $\mathcal{B}_O$ at an angle larger than θ. This becomes the basis of separating the inner balls from the outer ones. The boundary of the union of the outer balls, or the inner big balls can be output as the approximated surface. Alternatively, one can apply a technique to smooth this boundary. In fact, it is known how to produce a surface from the union of a set of balls with C^2-smoothness. These surfaces are called *skin surfaces*. However, these surfaces may not interpolate the input points. We take the help of the restricted Delaunay triangulation to compute a surface interpolating through the points on the outer (or inner) big Delaunay balls. The restricted Delaunay surfaces Del $P_I|_{S_I}$ and Del $P_O|_{S_O}$ can be shown to be homeomorphic to S_I and S_O respectively by showing that (S_I, P_I) and (S_O, P_O) satisfy the topological ball property when ε is sufficiently small.

Theorem 8.4. *For sufficiently small $\varepsilon > 0$, Del $P_I|_{S_I}$ is homeomorphic to Σ. Further, each point x in Del $P_I|_{S_I}$ has a point in Σ within $\tilde{O}(\sqrt{\varepsilon})f(\tilde{x})$ distance and conversely, each point x in Σ has a point in Del $P_I|_{S_I}$ within $\tilde{O}(\sqrt{\varepsilon})f(x)$ distance.*

8.4.2 Algorithm

Now we have all ingredients to design an algorithm that computes a surface homeomorphic to Σ. We will describe the algorithm to compute Del $P_O|_{S_O}$. Clearly, it can be adapted to compute Del $P_I|_{S_I}$ as well. The algorithm uses three user-supplied parameters, κ, K, and θ. It first chooses each Delaunay ball whose radius is bigger than K times the distance between any sample point p on its boundary and the κth nearest sample point of p. Then, it starts walking from an infinite Delaunay ball circumscribing an infinite tetrahedron formed by a convex hull triangle and a point at infinity. This Delaunay ball is outer. The angle of intersection between an infinite Delaunay ball and other Delaunay balls intersecting it needs to be properly interpreted taking infinity into account. The algorithm continues to collect all big balls that intersect a ball already marked *outer* at an angle more than a threshold angle θ. Once all outer big Delaunay balls are identified, the set P_O is constructed.

To compute Del $P_I|_{S_I}$ we first compute Del P_I and then determine the Voronoi edges of Vor P_I that intersect S_I. The dual Delaunay triangles of these Voronoi edges along with their vertices and edges form Del $P_I|_{S_I}$.

RobustCocone(P,κ,K,θ)
1   compute Del P;
2   mark all infinite Dealuany balls;
3   for each tetrahedron $pqrs \in$ Del P do
4   let $B_{c,r}$ be the Delaunay ball of $pqrs$;
5   let the smallest κth neighbor distance for p, q, r, and s be d;

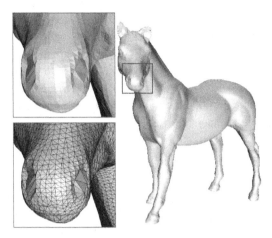

Figure 8.6. Surface reconstruction by ROBUSTCOCONE from a noise-free sample.

6   if $r \geq Kd$ then mark $B_{c,r}$;
7 endfor
8 initialize a stack S and a set U with all infinite Delaunay balls;
9 while $S \neq \emptyset$ do
10    $B := \text{pop } S$;
11   for each marked ball $B' \notin U$ do
12   if $B \neq B'$, and B and B' intersect at an angle less than θ
13          $U := U \cup B'$;
14   push B' into S;
15   endif
16   endfor
17 endwhile
18 let P_O be the vertex set of tetrahedra circumscribed by balls in U;
19 compute Vor P_O;
20 $E := \emptyset$;
21 for each Voronoi edge $e \in \text{Vor } P_O$ do
22   if one vertex of e is in a ball in U and
          the other is in none of them
23       $E := E \cup \text{dual } e$;
24   endif
25 endfor
26 output E.

In Figures 8.6 and 8.7, we show the results of a slightly modified ROBUST-
COCONE. It first filters the points as described using the parameters $K = 0.5$

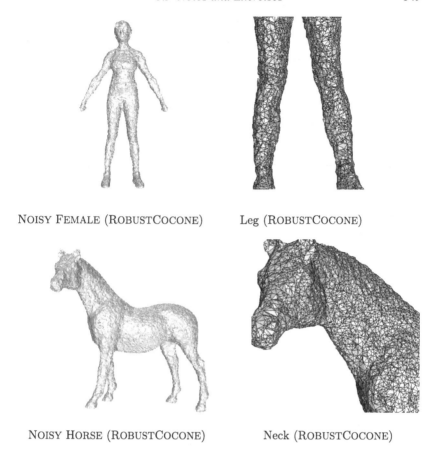

NOISY FEMALE (ROBUSTCOCONE)   Leg (ROBUSTCOCONE)

NOISY HORSE (ROBUSTCOCONE)   Neck (ROBUSTCOCONE)

Figure 8.7. Reconstruction by ROBUSTCOCONE on noisy samples.

and $\kappa = 3$. Then, instead of computing the restricted Delaunay triangulation Del $P_O|_{S_O}$, it applies TIGHTCOCONE on the filtered point set. ROBUSTCOCONE performs much better than TIGHTCOCONE alone on noisy data where noise is reasonably high. One aspect of the algorithm is that it tends to produce much less nonmanifold vertices and edges. It should be clear that the ROBUSTCOCONE is able to handle noise-free data sets as well. Figure 8.6 shows an example.

8.5 Notes and Exercises

The ROBUSTCOCONE algorithm presented in this chapter is taken from Dey and Goswami [34]. This paper showed that the idea of power crust can be applied to noisy point cloud data.

The noise model is reasonable though variations in the sampling conditions are certainly possible. The sampling condition (ii) requires a quadratic dependence (ε^2) on the sampling parameter. One can relax this condition to be linearly dependent on ε by trading off the normal approximation guarantee. Corollary 8.1 will give an $\tilde{O}(\sqrt{\varepsilon})$ approximation to normals at the sample points. This will in turn give an $\tilde{O}(\sqrt{\varepsilon})f(\tilde{x})$ bound on the distances between any point x in S_I and $\tilde{x}$ in Σ in Lemma 8.5. As a consequence the Normal Approximation Theorem 8.2 will provide an $\tilde{O}(\varepsilon^{\frac{1}{4}} + \frac{1}{\sqrt{K\sqrt{\varepsilon}}} + \frac{1}{K\sqrt{\varepsilon}})$ approximation for the normals which will mean that $K\sqrt{\varepsilon}$ has to be large, or K has to be large, say $\Omega(\frac{1}{\varepsilon})$, to have a good normal approximations. This observation suggests that larger the noise amplitude, the bigger the parameter K should be for choosing big Delaunay balls. It would be interesting to see what kind of other tradeoffs can be achieved between the guarantees and the noise models.

We have assumed Σ to be connected. All definitions and proofs can be easily extended to the case when Σ has multiple components. However, it is not clear how to extend the labeling algorithm to separate the balls on two sides of a component of Σ when it has multiple components. It is important that all the big Delaunay balls on one side remain connected through the adjacency relation as defined in Section 8.4.1. When Σ has multiple components, we cannot appeal to Theorem 8.3 to claim the connectedness among the big Delaunay balls since the surface S_I may not be connected as Σ is not. This is also a bottleneck for the POWERCRUST algorithm [7]. It would be interesting to devise a labeling algorithm which can handle multiple components with guarantee.

The ROBUSTCOCONE algorithm requires that the sampled surface have no boundary. It is not clear how the algorithm should be adapted for surfaces with boundary. A reconstruction of surfaces with boundaries from noiseless point samples can be done by the BOUNDCOCONE algorithm described in Chapter 5. However, noise together with boundaries pose a difficult challenge. The spectral crust of Kolluri, O'Brien, and Shewchuk [64] is shown to work well for such data sets though no proofs are given.

Exercises

1^h. Consider the set of inner and outer big Delaunay balls $\mathcal{B}_I$ and $\mathcal{B}_O$ respectively. Consider the following algorithm for reconstructing Σ. Compute the power diagram of the centers of the balls in $\mathcal{B}_I \cup \mathcal{B}_O$ with their radii as the weights. Then output the facets that separate a power cell of an inner ball center from that of an outer ball center. Show that the surface output by this algorithm is homeomorphic to Σ if the sample is sufficiently dense.

2. Let $\phi(x) = (x - \tilde{x})^T \mathbf{n}_{\tilde{x}}$ for a point $x \in \mathbb{R}^3$. Consider the offset surface $\Sigma_{-\varepsilon}$ defined as:

$$\Sigma_{-\varepsilon} = \{x \mid |\phi(x)| = \varepsilon f(x) \text{ and } \phi(x) \text{ is negative}\}.$$

   (i) Is $\phi(x)$ continuous if Σ is C^1-smooth? What if Σ is C^2-smooth?
   (ii) Give an example that shows $\Sigma_{-\varepsilon}$ is not necessarily C^1-smooth even if Σ is.
   (iii) Prove that $\Sigma_{-\varepsilon}$ is homeomorphic to Σ for a sufficiently small ε.

3. Suppose one adopts the following intersection depth check to collect all outer big Delaunay balls. Let B be any big Delaunay ball that has been already collected. Let t be the tetrahedron circumscribed by B. For depth intersection with B check all the balls circumscribing the tetrahedra sharing a triangle with t. Does this algorithm work?

4^h. Carry out the entire analysis of topological and geometric guarantees of S_I assuming that P is a $(\varepsilon, \varepsilon, \kappa)$-sample for suitable ε and κ.

5°. Prove that the Cocone algorithm applied to the points on the union of inner big Delaunay balls produces a surface homeomorphic to Σ for a sufficiently small ε in the noise model.

6. Instead of choosing big Delaunay balls with a threshold in RobustCocone one can choose the largest polar balls among k-nearest neighbors for some $k \geq 1$ as in the feature approximation algorithm in Chapter 7. Show that, for a $(\varepsilon, \varepsilon^2, \kappa)$-sample, the surface S_I defined with these balls is isotopic to the sampled surface if k is close to κ and ε is sufficiently small.

9

Implicit Surface-Based Reconstructions

In surface reconstruction, if the input point cloud is noisy, a surface fitting through the points can be too bumpy for practical use. A remedy to this problem is to define a target smooth implicit surface and project or generate points on this implicit surface for reconstruction. Of course, the main problem is to choose a suitable implicit surface that resembles the original surface which the input point cloud presumably sampled. This means we should prove that the chosen implicit surface is homeomorphic (isotopic) to the sampled surface and is also geometrically close to it. First, we outline a generic approach to achieve this and then specialize the approach to a specific type of implicit surface called MLS surface.

9.1 Generic Approach

Suppose $\mathcal{N} : \mathbb{R}^3 \to \mathbb{R}$ is an implicit function whose zero-level set $\mathcal{N}^{-1}(0)$ is of interest for approximating the sampled surface Σ. The gradient of $\mathcal{N}$ at x is

$$\nabla \mathcal{N}(x) = \left(\frac{\partial \mathcal{N}}{\partial x_1}(x) \quad \frac{\partial \mathcal{N}}{\partial x_2}(x) \quad \frac{\partial \mathcal{N}}{\partial x_3}(x) \right).$$

As before let $\Sigma \subset \mathbb{R}^3$ be a compact, smooth surface without boundary. For simplicity assume that Σ has a single connected component. As in previous chapters Ω_O denotes the unbounded component of $\mathbb{R}^3 \setminus \Sigma$ and Ω_I denotes $\mathbb{R}^3 \setminus \Omega_O$. For a point $z \in \Sigma$, $\mathbf{n}_z$ denotes the oriented normal of Σ at z where $\mathbf{n}_z$ points locally toward the unbounded component Ω_O. Let M be the medial axis of Σ.

The entire set $\mathcal{N}^{-1}(0)$ may not approximate Σ. Instead, only the subset of $\mathcal{N}^{-1}(0)$ close to Σ will be the implicit surface of our interest. For this we define a thickening of Σ.

Recall that, for a point $x \in \mathbb{R}^3 \setminus M$, $\tilde{x}$ denotes its closest point in Σ. Let $\phi(x)$ denote the signed distance of a point x to Σ, that is, $\phi(x) = (x - \tilde{x})^T \mathbf{n}_{\tilde{x}}$. For a

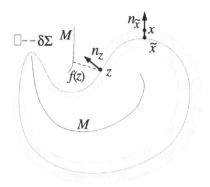

Figure 9.1. The set $\delta\Sigma$, medial axis, and normals.

real $\delta \geq 0$, define offset surfaces $\Sigma_{+\delta}$ and $\Sigma_{-\delta}$ where

$$\Sigma_{+\delta} = \{x \in \mathbb{R}^3 \mid \phi(x) = +\delta f(\tilde{x})\}$$

$$\Sigma_{-\delta} = \{x \in \mathbb{R}^3 \mid \phi(x) = -\delta f(\tilde{x})\}.$$

Let $\delta\Sigma$ be the region between $\Sigma_{-\delta}$ and $\Sigma_{+\delta}$, that is,

$$\delta\Sigma = \{x \in \mathbb{R}^3 \mid -\delta f(\tilde{x}) \leq \phi(x) \leq \delta f(\tilde{x})\}.$$

Figure 9.1 illustrates the above concepts.

We want to focus on the subset of the zero-level set $\mathcal{N}^{-1}(0)$ near Σ. So, we define $W = \mathcal{N}^{-1}(0) \cap \delta\Sigma$ for a small $\delta > 0$. The proofs of topological equivalence and geometric approximation between W and Σ use two key properties of $\mathcal{N}$.

9.1.1 Implicit Function Properties

HAUSDORFF PROPERTY. We say that $\mathcal{N}$ has the Hausdorff property for δ and δ' if $\delta' < \delta$ and

$$\mathcal{N}(x) > 0 \quad \text{when } x \in (\delta\Sigma \setminus \delta'\Sigma) \cap \Omega_O$$
$$< 0 \quad \text{when } x \in (\delta\Sigma \setminus \delta'\Sigma) \cap \Omega_I.$$

The above inequalities mean that $\mathcal{N}(x)$ crosses zero value in $\delta\Sigma$ only when x is in $\delta'\Sigma$. This implies that $\mathcal{N}^{-1}(0) \cap \delta\Sigma$ indeed resides in $\delta'\Sigma$.

GRADIENT PROPERTY. Let z be any point in Σ. Let $\ell_{\mathbf{n}_z}$ be the oriented line containing the normal $\mathbf{n}_z$ to Σ at z. Let $[\mathbf{u}]\mathcal{N}(x)$ be the directional derivative of $\mathcal{N}$ at x along the vector $\mathbf{u}$, that is, $[\mathbf{u}]\mathcal{N}(x)$ is $\mathbf{u}^T \nabla \mathcal{N}(x)$. We say $\mathcal{N}$ has the gradient property for δ if

$$[\mathbf{n}_z]\mathcal{N}(x) > 0 \quad \text{for any } x \in \ell_{\mathbf{n}_z} \cap \delta\Sigma.$$

The directional derivative $[\mathbf{n}_z]\mathcal{N}(x)$ is the projection of the gradient $\nabla\mathcal{N}(x)$ along $\ell_{\mathbf{n}_z}$. Therefore, the gradient property implies that $\nabla\mathcal{N}(x)$ is not zero in $\delta\Sigma$.

9.1.2 Homeomorphism Proof

We show that if $\mathcal{N}$ has the Hausdorff property for δ and δ', and the gradient property for δ' where $\delta' < \delta < 1$, the subset

$$W = \mathcal{N}^{-1}(0) \cap \delta\Sigma$$

is homeomorphic to Σ. First, observe that Hausdorff property implies W is indeed a subset of $\delta'\Sigma$. Second, the gradient property implies that $\nabla\mathcal{N}$ does not vanish in $\delta'\Sigma$. Therefore, by the implicit function theorem in differential topology, W is a compact, smooth 2-manifold.

Consider the map $\nu : \mathbb{R}^3 \setminus M \to \Sigma$ that takes a point $x \in \mathbb{R}^3$ to its closest point in Σ. We show that ν defines a homeomorphism when restricted to W. Let ν' denote this restriction.

Lemma 9.1. *If $\mathcal{N}$ has the Hausdorff property for δ and δ' where $\delta < 1$, ν' is well defined and surjective.*

Proof. Since $\delta < 1$, W avoids M as all points of W are in $\delta\Sigma$ by definition. Therefore, ν' avoids M and hence is well defined.

Let z be any point in Σ. The normal line $\ell_{\mathbf{n}_z}$, through z along the normal $\mathbf{n}_z$, intersects $\mathcal{N}^{-1}(0)$ within $\delta\Sigma$, thanks to the Hausdorff property. Thus, by definition of W, it intersects W at a point. Therefore, for each point $z \in \Sigma$, there is a point in W which is mapped by ν' to z. ∎

Lemma 9.2. *If $\mathcal{N}$ has the Hausdorff property for δ and δ' as well as the gradient property for δ' where $\delta' < \delta < 1$, ν' is injective.*

Proof. To prove the injectivity of ν', assume for the sake of contradiction that there are two points w and w' in W so that $\nu'(w) = \nu'(w') = z$. This means $\ell_{\mathbf{n}_z}$ intersects W at w and w' within $\delta'\Sigma$ (Hausdorff property). Without loss of generality assume that w and w' are two such consecutive intersection points. It follows that the oriented line $\ell_{\mathbf{n}_z}$ makes at least $\frac{\pi}{2}$ angle with one of the normals to W at w and w'. But, that is impossible since the gradient property implies that

$$\angle(\mathbf{n}_z, \nabla\mathcal{N}(x)) < \frac{\pi}{2}$$

for any point $x \in \ell_{\mathbf{n}_z} \cap \delta'\Sigma$. ∎

Theorem 9.1. *If $\mathcal{N}$ has the Hausdorff property for δ and δ' as well as the gradient property for δ' where $\delta' < \delta < 1$, ν' is a homeomorphism.*

Proof. The function ν' is continuous since ν is. Since W is compact, it is sufficient to establish that ν' is surjective and injective which are the statements of Lemma 9.1 and Lemma 9.2 respectively. ∎

Several implicit surfaces have been proposed with different algorithms for their computations in the literature. Among them we focus on the class of surfaces defined by a technique called *moving least squares*. These surfaces, generically, are called MLS surfaces.

9.2 MLS Surfaces

Our goal is to formulate an implicit surface that fits the input points well. In particular, we would like to prove the Hausdorff and the gradient property for the implicit function that defines the implicit surface. *Least squares* is a numerical technique developed to fit a function to a given input data. Let a function $\Phi : \mathbb{R}^3 \to \mathbb{R}$ be sampled at the points in $P \subset \mathbb{R}^3$. This means each point $p \in P$ has an associated function value $\phi_p = \Phi(p)$. Suppose we wish to design an implicit function $\mathcal{I} : \mathbb{R}^3 \to \mathbb{R}$ that fits the data points as close as possible with respect to some metric. If this metric is the sum of the squares of the errors at the data points, we get the well-known least squares solution. Specifically, we minimize the error

$$\Sigma_{p \in P}(\mathcal{I}(p) - \phi_p)^2 \tag{9.1}$$

to obtain a solution for $\mathcal{I}$. In our case we would like the implicit surface given by $\mathcal{I}^{-1}(0)$ to fit the given input points P. We modify the basic least squares technique as follows. First, each function value ϕ_p is replaced with a function $\phi_p : \mathbb{R}^3 \to \mathbb{R}$ where $\phi_p(p) = 0$. Then, taking

$$\mathcal{I}(x) = \Sigma_{i=1}^n c_i b_i(x) \tag{9.2}$$

where c_i is the coefficient for the ith basis function $b_i(x)$, one can minimize

$$\Sigma_{p \in P}(\mathcal{I}(x) - \phi_p(x))^2 \tag{9.3}$$

over the unknown coefficients. The intention here is that the resulting solution $\mathcal{I}$ fits each function $\phi_p(x)$ well and in particular when x is near p. Since $\phi_p(p) = 0$, this would mean that the implicit surface given by $\mathcal{I}^{-1}(0)$ fits the points in P. However, this does not happen in general as the least square fit given by the minimization of the expression in 9.3 does not give any preference to $\phi_p(x)$ when x is near p. We achieve this goal by weighting the contributions of the errors differently. We use a weight function $\theta_p : \mathbb{R}^3 \to \mathbb{R}$ for the point p so that it takes a larger value than all other weight functions when x is near p. So, we minimize

$$\Sigma_{p \in P}(\mathcal{I}(x) - \phi_p(x))^2 \theta_p(x).$$

The effects of the weights make the least square fit change or "move" which lead to the terminology *moving least squares* or MLS in short for the resulting implicit surface.

For simplicity we choose $\mathcal{I}(x) = c_0$ letting all other $c_i = 0$ in Equation 9.2. Notice that c_0 will be a function of x instead of a constant. The minimization leads to the equation

$$\Sigma_{p \in P} 2(c_0 - \phi_p(x))\theta_p(x) = 0$$

$$\text{or, } \mathcal{I}(x) = c_0 = \frac{\Sigma_{p \in P} \phi_p(x)\theta_p(x)}{\Sigma_{p \in P}\theta_p(x)}.$$

We would like the implicit surface $\mathcal{I}^{-1}(0)$ not only match the sampled surface in Hausdorff distance but also match its normals. So, we assume that each sample point is equipped with an estimated normal. Let $\mathbf{v}_p$ denote the assigned normal to the sample point p. Then, the gradient $\nabla \mathcal{I}(p)$ should approximate $\mathbf{v}_p$. Keeping this in mind we choose

$$\phi_p(x) = (x - p)^T \mathbf{v}_p.$$

With these choices the MLS surface is the zero-level set of

$$\mathcal{I}(x) = \frac{\Sigma_{p \in P}((x - p)^T \mathbf{v}_p)\theta_p(x)}{\Sigma_{p \in P}\theta_p(x)}. \tag{9.4}$$

9.2.1 Adaptive MLS Surfaces

Weighting Functions

The implicit function value $\mathcal{I}(x)$ at a point x should be primarily decided by the nearby sample points. That is exactly the reason why the MLS function weighs the sample points differently in a sum instead of giving them equal weights. We will adopt the noise model as in Chapter 8, that is, a $(\varepsilon, \varepsilon^2, -)$-

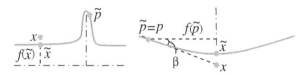

Figure 9.2. The solid curves and the dash–dot lines represent part of the surface and its medial axis respectively.

sample for a suitably small $\varepsilon > 0$. This model implies that the sample points within a sufficiently small neighborhood of a point x near Σ are predictably distributed within a small slab (Lemma 9.4). However, the surface Σ and its sample points outside this neighborhood could be arbitrarily distributed. Hence, we should design a weighting function such that the sample points outside the neighborhood have much less effect on the implicit function than those inside.

Our first step to meet the above requirements is to choose Gaussian functions as the weights since their widths can control the influence of the sample points. Therefore, the weighting function $\theta_p(x)$ is chosen as a Gaussian function with a support width h around p, that is,

$$\theta_p(x) = \exp^{\|x-p\|^2/h^2} . \tag{9.5}$$

Essentially, h determines the neighborhood from where the sample points have dominant effects on the implicit function. To make the implicit surface sensitive to features of Σ, one may take h to be a fraction of the local feature size. However, one needs to be more careful. If we simply take a fraction of $f(\tilde{x})$ as the width, that is, take $\exp^{-\frac{\|x-p\|^2}{[\rho f(\tilde{x})]^2}}$ as the weighting function for some $\rho < 1$, we cannot bound the effect of the far away sample points. Consider the left picture in Figure 9.2. The local feature size at the point $\tilde{p}$ can be arbitrarily small requiring the number of sample points around $\tilde{p}$ to be arbitrarily large to meet the sampling conditions. Consequently, the summation of the weights over those sample points which are outside $B_{x,f(\tilde{x})}$ becomes too large to be dominated by the contributions of the sample points in the neighborhood $B_{x,f(\tilde{x})}$ of x.

An alternative option is to take a fraction of $f(\tilde{p})$ as the width, that is, take $\exp^{-\frac{\|x-p\|^2}{[\rho f(\tilde{p})]^2}}$ as the weighting function. However, it also fails as illustrated in the right picture in Figure 9.2. The sample points such as p has a constant weight $\exp^{-\frac{1}{[\rho \cos \beta]^2}}$. As the summation extends outside the neighborhood of x, the contribution of the sample points remains constant instead of decreasing. As a result, one cannot hope to bound the outside contribution.

We overcome the difficulty by using a combination of the above two options, that is, by taking a fraction of $\sqrt{f(\tilde{x})f(\tilde{p})}$ as the width of the Gaussian

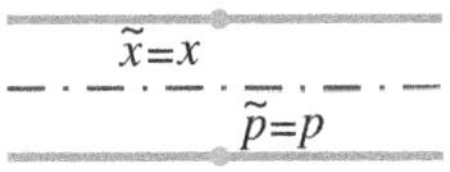

$$\overline{\tilde{x}=x}$$
$$— \cdot — \cdot — \cdot \overline{\tilde{p}=p} — \cdot — \cdot —$$

Figure 9.3. The solid and the dash–dot lines represent part of the surface and its medial axis respectively.

weighting functions. This takes into account the effects from both members, the contribution sender p and the contribution receiver x. Unlike $\exp^{-\frac{\|x-p\|^2}{[\rho f(\tilde{p})]^2}}$, such form of weighting function decreases as p goes away from x. In addition, such form of weighting function assigns a small value to the points that sample small features, which in turn cancels out the effect that small features require more sample points.

There is still one more difficulty. The function f, though continuous, is not smooth everywhere on Σ. The nonsmoothness appears where Σ intersects the medial axis of its own medial axis M. To make the implicit function smooth, we use a smooth function σ arbitrarily close to f where

$$|\sigma(x) - f(x)| \le \beta f(x) \tag{9.6}$$

for arbitrarily small $\beta > 0$. This is doable since the family of real-valued smooth functions over smooth manifolds is dense in the family of continuous functions and the minimal feature size is strictly positive for any manifold that is at least C^2-smooth. Finally, we choose a fraction (given by ρ) of $\sqrt{\sigma(\tilde{x})\sigma(\tilde{p})}$ as the width of the Gaussian weighting functions. Specifically, we take

$$\ln \theta_p(x) = -\frac{\sqrt{2}\|x - p\|^2}{\rho^2 \sigma(\tilde{p})\sigma(\tilde{x})}. \tag{9.7}$$

The factor $\sqrt{2}$ in the exponent is for the convenience in proofs as one may see later. In general, it is known that larger values of ρ make the MLS surface look smoother. To have a sense of appropriate values of ρ, consider the case where x is on the surface Σ. The sample points such as p in Figure 9.3 across the medial axis to point x should have little effect on the implicit function value at x. Taking $\rho \le 0.4$ makes the weight of p at x less than $\exp^{-25\sqrt{2}} \approx 5 \times 10^{-16}$ since $\|x - p\| \ge 2 \max\{f(\tilde{x}), f(\tilde{p})\}$.

AMLS Function

With the weighting function given by Equation 9.7 we define the implicit function. Since the weights adapt to the local feature size, we call this function *adaptive* MLS or AMLS in short. The implicit surface given by the AMLS function is referred as AMLS surface. Let

$$\mathcal{N}(x) = \sum_{p \in P} ((x - p)^T \mathbf{v}_p) \theta_p(x) \tag{9.8}$$

where θ_p is given by Equation 9.7. The AMLS function is given by

$$\mathcal{I}(x) = \frac{\mathcal{N}(x)}{\mathcal{W}(x)}$$

where

$$\mathcal{W}(x) = \sum_{p \in P} \theta_p(x).$$

Obviously, the implicit functions $\mathcal{N}$ and $\mathcal{I}$ have exactly the same zero-level set, that is, $\mathcal{I}^{-1}(0) = \mathcal{N}^{-1}(0)$. Therefore, we could have taken $\mathcal{N}$ instead of $\mathcal{I}$ for AMLS, but we observe in Section 9.6.3 that $\mathcal{I}$ has a significant computational advantage since Newton iteration for $\mathcal{I}$ has a much larger convergent domain than the one for $\mathcal{N}$. However, the function $\mathcal{N}$ has a simpler form to analyze. Hence, we analyze the zero-level set of $\mathcal{I}$ via the function $\mathcal{N}$.

9.3 Sampling Assumptions and Consequences

Our goal is to establish that the function $\mathcal{N}$ as defined in Equation 9.8 has the Hausdorff and gradient properties. This would require that the input point set P sample Σ densely though possibly with noise. Following the definition of noisy sample in Chapter 7 we assume that the input P is a $(\varepsilon, \varepsilon^2, \kappa)$-sample of Σ for some $\varepsilon < 1$ and $\kappa \geq 1$. In addition, we assume that each sample point is equipped with a normal with the following condition.

Normal assignment. The normal $\mathbf{v}_p$ assigned to a point $p \in P$ makes an angle of at most ε with the normal $\mathbf{n}_{\tilde{p}}$ at its closest point $\tilde{p}$ on Σ.

The sampling assumptions lead to the following result which would be used in our analysis.

Lemma 9.3. *For $\varepsilon < 0.01$ and any $x \in \mathbb{R}^3$, the number of sample points inside a ball $B_{x, \frac{\varepsilon}{2} f(\tilde{x})}$ is less than 10κ.*

Proof. Let p be any sample point in $B_{x, \frac{\varepsilon}{2} f(\tilde{x})}$. We have

$$\|x - p\| \leq \frac{\varepsilon}{2} f(\tilde{x})$$

$$\text{or, } \|x - \tilde{p}\| \leq \frac{\varepsilon}{2} f(\tilde{x}) + \varepsilon^2 f(\tilde{p})$$

and

$$\|\tilde{x} - \tilde{p}\| \leq \|x - \tilde{x}\| + \|x - \tilde{p}\|$$
$$\leq 2\|x - \tilde{p}\|$$
$$\leq \varepsilon f(\tilde{x}) + 2\varepsilon^2 f(\tilde{p}). \tag{9.9}$$

From the Lipschitz property of f and Inequality 9.9 we get

$$\frac{1 - \varepsilon}{1 + 2\varepsilon^2} f(\tilde{x}) \leq f(\tilde{p}) \leq \frac{1 + \varepsilon}{1 - 2\varepsilon^2} f(\tilde{x}). \tag{9.10}$$

By sampling condition the ball $B = B_{p,\varepsilon f(\tilde{p})}$ contains at most κ sample points. Thus, B can count for at most κ sample points in $B_{x,\frac{\varepsilon}{2}f(\tilde{x})}$. To count other sample points we can take a sample point, say q, outside B and again consider the ball $B_{q,\varepsilon f(\tilde{q})}$. We can continue this process each time choosing a center outside all the balls so far considered till we cover all sample points. We determine an upper bound on the number of such balls that are needed to cover all sample points.

We claim that the center, say p, of such a ball is at least $\varepsilon' f(\tilde{p})$ away from any other center q where

$$\varepsilon' = \frac{\varepsilon(1 - \varepsilon - \varepsilon^2)}{1 + \varepsilon^2}.$$

If q is introduced after p, we have $\|p - q\| \geq \varepsilon f(\tilde{p})$ which is more than the claimed bound. When p is introduced after q, it is at least $\varepsilon f(\tilde{q})$ away from q. If $\|p - q\| > \varepsilon f(\tilde{p})$ we are done. So, assume $\|p - q\| \leq \varepsilon f(\tilde{p})$. Then,

$$f(\tilde{q}) \geq f(\tilde{p}) - \|\tilde{p} - \tilde{q}\|$$
$$\geq f(\tilde{p}) - \|\tilde{p} - p\| - \|p - q\| - \|q - \tilde{q}\|$$
$$\geq f(\tilde{p}) - \varepsilon^2 f(\tilde{p}) - \varepsilon f(\tilde{p}) - \varepsilon^2 f(\tilde{q})$$

which gives

$$f(\tilde{q}) \geq \frac{(1 - \varepsilon - \varepsilon^2)}{1 + \varepsilon^2} f(\tilde{p}).$$

Since $\|p - q\| \geq \varepsilon f(\tilde{q})$, the claimed bound is immediate.

So, if we consider balls of half the size, that is, for a center p if we consider a ball of size $\frac{\varepsilon'}{2} f(\tilde{p})$ they will be disjoint. From Inequality 9.10 each such ball has a radius at least

$$r = \frac{\varepsilon'(1 - \varepsilon)}{2(1 + 2\varepsilon^2)} f(\tilde{x}).$$

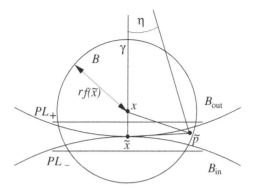

Figure 9.4. Illustration for Lemma 9.4: η is the angle between $\tilde{x}m$ and $\tilde{p}m$ where m is the center of the medial ball.

Also, each such ball will be inside the ball $B' = B_{x, \frac{\varepsilon}{2} f(\tilde{x}) + \frac{\varepsilon'}{2} f(\tilde{p})}$. Inequality 9.10 provides that the radius of B' is at most

$$R = \frac{\varepsilon(1 - 2\varepsilon^2) + \varepsilon'(1 + \varepsilon)}{2(1 - 2\varepsilon^2)} f(\tilde{x}).$$

One can pack at most $\frac{R^3}{r^3}$ balls of radius r inside a ball of radius R. This implies that there are at most $\frac{R^3}{r^3} \kappa$ sample points inside the ball $B_{x, \frac{\varepsilon}{2} f(\tilde{x})}$. We have

$$\frac{R^3}{r^3} \kappa = \left(\frac{(\varepsilon(1 - 2\varepsilon^2) + \varepsilon'(1 + \varepsilon))(1 + 2\varepsilon^2)}{\varepsilon'(1 - 2\varepsilon^2)(1 - \varepsilon)} \right)^3 \kappa$$

$$\leq 10\kappa \text{ for } \varepsilon < 0.01.$$

∎

For our proofs we need a result that all sample points near a point x in a small tubular neighborhood of Σ lie within a small slab centering $\tilde{x}$. Denote $S_{x,r}$ to be the boundary of $B_{x,r}$. Consider any point x on $\Sigma_{+\delta}$ or $\Sigma_{-\delta}$ and a ball $B_{x, rf(\tilde{x})}$ with a small radius $r < 1$. Let PL_+ and PL_- be two planes perpendicular to $\mathbf{n}_{\tilde{x}}$ and at a small distance $\omega f(\tilde{x})$ from $\tilde{x}$ (Figure 9.4). We show that if ω is of the order of $\varepsilon^2 + r^2$, all points of P within the ball $B_{x, rf(\tilde{x})}$ lie within the slab made by PL_+ and PL_-.

Lemma 9.4. *For $\delta < 0.5$ and $\varepsilon < 0.1$, let x be a point on $\Sigma_{+\delta}$ or $\Sigma_{-\delta}$ and p be any sample point inside $B_{x, rf(\tilde{x})}$ where $\delta < r < 1$. Let $R(r) = (\delta + r) + \frac{1 + r + \delta}{1 - \varepsilon^2} \varepsilon^2$. The following facts hold.*

(i) If $R(r) < \frac{1}{3}$ then $\angle(\mathbf{n}_{\tilde{x}}, \mathbf{v}_p) < \frac{R(r)}{1-3R(r)} + \varepsilon$.

(ii) p lies inside the slab bounded by two planes PL_+ and PL_- which are perpendicular to $\mathbf{n}_{\tilde{x}}$ and at a distance of $\omega(r)f(\tilde{x})$ from $\tilde{x}$ where $\omega(r) = \frac{R(r)^2}{2} + \frac{1+r+\delta}{1-\varepsilon^2}\varepsilon^2$.

Proof. Let B be the ball $B_{x, rf(\tilde{x})}$. We have

$$\|\tilde{p} - \tilde{x}\| \le (\delta + r)f(\tilde{x}) + \varepsilon^2 f(\tilde{p}). \tag{9.11}$$

From Lipschitz property of f, we obtain

$$f(\tilde{p}) \le \frac{1 + r + \delta}{1 - \varepsilon^2} f(\tilde{x}). \tag{9.12}$$

It follows from Inequalities 9.11 and 9.12 that

$$\|\tilde{x} - \tilde{p}\| \le R(r)f(\tilde{x}). \tag{9.13}$$

If $R(r) < \frac{1}{3}$, $\angle(\mathbf{n}_{\tilde{x}}, \mathbf{n}_{\tilde{p}}) < \frac{R(r)}{1-3R(r)}$ by the Normal Variation Lemma 3.3 which together with $\angle(\mathbf{n}_{\tilde{p}}, \mathbf{v}_p) < \varepsilon$ shows (i).

Let γ be the radius of either of the two medial balls B_{out} or B_{in} at $\tilde{x}$. Obviously, $\gamma \ge f(\tilde{x})$. Furthermore, we have

$$\sin\frac{\eta}{2} \le \frac{\|\tilde{x} - \tilde{p}\|}{2\gamma} \tag{9.14}$$

where η is the angle illustrated in Figure 9.4. The distance from $\tilde{p}$ to the tangent plane at $\tilde{x}$ is less than $\gamma(1 - \cos\eta) = 2\gamma\sin^2\frac{\eta}{2}$. Hence, the distance from p to the tangent plane at $\tilde{x}$ is less than $2\gamma\sin^2\frac{\eta}{2} + \varepsilon^2 f(\tilde{p})$, which shows (ii) by substituting Inequalities 9.12, 9.13, and 9.14.   ∎

9.3.1 Influence of Samples

We have formulated the implicit function $\mathcal{I}$ keeping in mind that, for any point $x \in \mathbb{R}^3$, the effect of the distant sample points on $\mathcal{I}(x)$ and hence on $\mathcal{N}(x)$ could be bounded. We establish this result formally in this section. For this result we will need an upper bound on the number of points that can reside inside a small ball $B_{x, \frac{\rho}{2}f(\tilde{x})}$ for some small ρ. Let $\lambda = \lambda(\rho)$ be this number. Notice that we have already derived an upper bound on λ for $\rho = \varepsilon$ in Lemma 9.3. We will use this specific value of ρ later in our proof. At this stage we work without specifying any particular value for ρ and use λ for the number of points inside $B_{x, \frac{\rho}{2}f(\tilde{x})}$.

In various claims, the contribution of a sample point p to the implicit function $\mathcal{N}$ or its derivative at a point x will be bounded from above by an expression

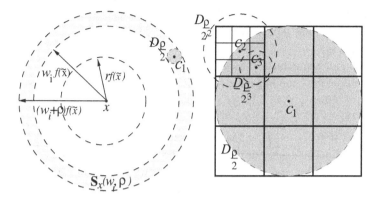

Figure 9.5. The nested shells and the hierarchical subdivision tree.

that involves the term

$$I_p(x) = \exp^{-\frac{\sqrt{2}\|x-p\|^2}{\rho^2\sigma(\tilde{p})\sigma(\tilde{x})}} \cdot \frac{\|x-p\|^s}{[\frac{\rho^2}{\sqrt{2}}\sigma(\tilde{p})\sigma(\tilde{x})]^t}.$$

The values of s and t will vary between 0 to 2 and 0 to 1 respectively in various equations where I_p is used. For instance, the contribution of a sample point p to the function $\mathcal{N}$ at x can be bounded by $I_p(x)$ with $s = 1$ and $t = 0$.

Our strategy for bounding $I_p(x)$ will be to decompose the space into spherical shells centering x. Theorem 9.2 shows that the total contribution from all sample points in the shells decreases as their distances from x increase. Let $\mathbb{S}_x(w, \rho)$ be the shell region between the spheres $S_{x,wf(\tilde{x})}$ and $S_{x,(w+\rho)f(\tilde{x})}$. For $i = 0, 1, \ldots$ consider the nested shells given by $\mathbb{S}_x(w_i, \rho)$ where $w_i = r + i\rho$ (Figure 9.5). To prove Theorem 9.2 we need a result that bounds the total contribution of the sample points lying within the intersection of a small ball of radius $\frac{\rho}{2}f(\tilde{x})$ and the shell $\mathbb{S}_x(w_i, \rho)$. Let $D_{\frac{\rho}{2}}$ be any such ball. We would like to bound the sum $\sum_{p \in D_{\frac{\rho}{2}} \cap \mathbb{S}_x(w_i, \rho)} I_p(x)$. The ball $D_{\frac{\rho}{2}}$ has a radius $\frac{\rho}{2}f(\tilde{x})$ though its center is not necessarily x. Therefore, we cannot use $\lambda = \lambda(\rho)$ to bound the number of sample points inside $D_{\frac{\rho}{2}}$. We overcome this difficulty by using a hierarchical subdivision of the smallest cube NC_1 containing $D_{\frac{\rho}{2}}$. The subdivision divides a cube unless it can be covered with a ball $B_{c,r}$ where r is a fraction of $f(\tilde{c})$. Then, one can use $\lambda = \lambda(\rho)$ to bound the number of sample points in $B_{c,r}$ and hence in the cubes of the subdivision. Therefore, we can bound the number of sample points in $D_{\frac{\rho}{2}}$ using the number of the leaf nodes in its corresponding subdivision tree. Notice that we do not have an explicit bound for the number of sample points in any $D_{\frac{\rho}{2}}$ since at different positions $D_{\frac{\rho}{2}}$ may have different subdivision trees adapting to the local geometry of the surface. However, we do have an explicit upper bound for the total weights from the sample points inside any $D_{\frac{\rho}{2}}$ as proved in Lemma 9.5.

Assume a hierarchical subdivision tree HST of NC_1 as follows. Let c_1 be the center of the bounding cube NC_1. Subdivide NC_1 into 27 subcubes of size $\frac{\rho}{3} f(\tilde{x})$ if $f(\tilde{c}_1) < f(\tilde{x})$. Let NC_2 be any such subcube. It can be covered by a ball $D_{\frac{\rho}{2^2}} = B_{c_2, \frac{\rho}{2^2} f(\tilde{x})}$ where c_2 is the center of NC_2. Subdivide NC_2 in the same way if $f(\tilde{c}_2) < \frac{1}{2} f(\tilde{x})$. In general, keep subdividing a subcube NC_k at the kth level if $f(\tilde{c}_k) < \frac{1}{2^{k-1}} f(\tilde{x})$ where c_k is the center of NC_k. Observe that NC_k is covered by $D_{\frac{\rho}{2^k}} = B_{c_k, \frac{\rho}{2^k} f(\tilde{x})}$. Figure 9.5 shows an HST in two dimensions. We use NC_k to also denote its intersection with $D_{\frac{\rho}{2^k}}$.

Lemma 9.5. *If $\rho \leq 0.4$, $\varepsilon \leq 0.1$, and $r \geq 5\rho$, then*

$$\sum_{p \in D_{\frac{\rho}{2}} \cap \mathbb{S}_x(w_i, \rho)} I_p(x) \leq \lambda \exp^{-\frac{rw_i}{(1+2r)\rho^2}} \cdot \frac{w_i^s}{\rho^{2t}} \sigma(\tilde{x})^{s-2t}$$

where $0 \leq s \leq 2$, $0 \leq t \leq 1$, $w_i = r + i\rho$ and λ is defined earlier.

Proof. Case 1: $f(\tilde{c}_1) \geq f(\tilde{x})$: HST has only one node NC_1. Let p be any sample point in $D_{\frac{\rho}{2}}$. Observe that $\|\tilde{p} - \tilde{c}_1\| \leq 2\|\tilde{p} - c_1\| \leq 2(\|\tilde{p} - p\| + \|p - c_1\|) \leq 2\varepsilon^2 f(\tilde{p}) + \rho f(\tilde{c}_1)$. By Lipschitz property of f,

$$f(\tilde{p}) \geq \frac{1 - \rho}{1 + 2\varepsilon^2} f(\tilde{x}).$$

From Inequality 9.6 we have

$$\sigma(\tilde{p}) \geq \frac{1 - \rho}{\beta'(1 + 2\varepsilon^2)} \sigma(\tilde{x})$$

where $\beta' = \frac{1+\beta}{1-\beta}$. Similarly, from condition $\|x - p\| \geq r f(\tilde{x})$ (p lies in $\mathbb{S}_x(w_i, \rho)$) and the fact $\|\tilde{x} - \tilde{p}\| \leq 2(\|x - p\| + \|p - \tilde{p}\|) \leq 2\|x - p\| + 2\varepsilon^2 f(\tilde{p})$ we obtain

$$\sigma(\tilde{p}) \leq (1 + \beta) \frac{1 + 2r}{r(1 - 2\varepsilon^2)} \|x - p\|.$$

Hence,

$$I_p(x) \leq \exp^{-\frac{\sqrt{2}(1-2\varepsilon^2)}{(1+\beta)(1+2r)} \frac{r\|x-p\|}{\rho^2 \sigma(\tilde{x})}} \cdot \left[\frac{\sqrt{2}\beta'(1 + 2\varepsilon^2)}{1 - \rho} \right]^t \cdot \frac{\|x - p\|^s}{[\rho\sigma(\tilde{x})]^{2t}}$$

which is a decreasing function of $\|x - p\|$ when $\|x - p\| \geq 4\rho\sigma(\tilde{x})$. Since $\|x - p\| \geq \frac{w_i\sigma(\tilde{x})}{1+\beta}$, we have

$$I_p(x) \leq \exp^{-\frac{\sqrt{2}(1-2\varepsilon^2)}{(1+\beta)^2(1+2r)}\frac{rw_i}{\rho^2}} \cdot \frac{[\sqrt{2}\beta'(1+2\varepsilon^2)]^t}{(1-\rho)^t(1+\beta)^s} \cdot \frac{w_i^s}{\rho^{2t}}\sigma(\tilde{x})^{s-2t}$$

$$\leq \exp^{-\frac{rw_i}{(1+2r)\rho^2}} \cdot \frac{w_i^s}{\rho^{2t}}\sigma(\tilde{x})^{s-2t}.$$

It is not hard to verify the second inequality under the given conditions. The lemma follows from the fact that $B_{c_1,\frac{\rho}{2}f(\tilde{c}_1)}$ covers $D_{\frac{\rho}{2}}$ and hence the number of sample points inside $D_{\frac{\rho}{2}}$ is less than λ.

Case 2: $f(\tilde{c}_1) < f(\tilde{x})$: Consider a leaf node NC_k at the kth level which is covered by $D_{\frac{\rho}{2^k}}$ in HST. We have $f(\tilde{c}_k) \geq \frac{1}{2^{k-1}}f(\tilde{x})$. Let p be any sample point inside the node. Since $\|\tilde{p} - \tilde{c}_k\| \leq 2\|\tilde{p} - c_k\|$, we obtain

$$\sigma(\tilde{p}) \geq \frac{1-\rho}{\beta'(1+2\varepsilon^2)} \cdot \frac{1}{2^{k-1}}\sigma(\tilde{x}).$$

On the other hand, p is also inside the parent node NC_{k-1} covered by $D_{\frac{\rho}{2^{k-1}}}$ in HST. Since $\|\tilde{p} - \tilde{c}_{k-1}\| \leq 2\|\tilde{p} - c_{k-1}\|$ and $f(\tilde{c}_{k-1}) < \frac{1}{2^{k-2}}f(\tilde{x})$, we obtain

$$\sigma(\tilde{p}) \leq \frac{\beta'(1+\rho)}{1-2\varepsilon^2} \cdot \frac{1}{2^{k-2}}\sigma(\tilde{x}).$$

Hence, for the given value of ρ and ε, we have

$$I_p(x)$$

$$\leq \exp^{-2^{k-2}\frac{\sqrt{2}(1-2\varepsilon^2)}{\beta'(1+\rho)}\frac{\|x-p\|^2}{[\rho\sigma(\tilde{x})]^2}} \cdot 2^{t(k-2)}\left[\frac{2\sqrt{2}\beta'(1+2\varepsilon^2)}{1-\rho}\right]^t \cdot \frac{\|x-p\|^s}{[\rho\sigma(\tilde{x})]^{2t}}$$

$$\leq \frac{1}{27}\exp^{-2^{k-2}\frac{rw_i}{(1+2r)\rho^2}} \cdot 2^{t(k-2)} \cdot \frac{w_i^s}{\rho^{2t}}\sigma(\tilde{x})^{s-2t}.$$

Since $B_{c_k,\frac{\rho}{2}f(\tilde{c}_k)}$ covers $D_{\frac{\rho}{2^k}}$ and hence the number of sample points inside the leaf node NC_k is less than λ, we have

$$\sum_{p\in NC_k} I_p(x) \leq \frac{1}{27} \cdot \lambda \exp^{-2^{k-2}\frac{rw_i}{(1+2r)\rho^2}} \cdot 2^{t(k-2)} \cdot \frac{w_i^s}{\rho^{2t}}\sigma(\tilde{x})^{s-2t}. \tag{9.15}$$

The above equation gives the bound for contributions of the sample points inside a single leaf node NC_k at any level $k \geq 2$. We use induction to establish that the bound also holds for any *internal* node. Let NC_k be an internal node. Then, by induction we can assume that each of the 27 children of NC_k satisfy Inequality 9.15 with $k = k + 1$. Summing over this 27 children and replacing

k with $k + 1$ in Inequality 9.15, we get

$$\sum_{p \in NC_k} I_p(x) \leq \lambda \exp^{-2^{k-1} \frac{r w_i}{(1+2r)\rho^2}} \cdot 2^{t(k-1)} \cdot \frac{w_i^s}{\rho^{2t}} \sigma(\tilde{x})^{s-2t}$$

$$\leq \frac{1}{27} \cdot \lambda \exp^{-2^{k-2} \frac{r w_i}{(1+2r)\rho^2}} \cdot 2^{t(k-2)} \cdot \frac{w_i^s}{\rho^{2t}} \sigma(\tilde{x})^{s-2t}.$$

The lemma follows from the fact that 27 NC_2s partition $D_{\frac{\rho}{2}}$. ∎

Theorem 9.2. *If* $\rho \leq 0.4$, $\varepsilon \leq 0.1$, *and* $r \geq 5\rho$, *then for any* $x \in \mathbb{R}^3$

$$\sum_{p \notin B_{x,rf(\tilde{x})}} I_p(x) \leq C_1 \lambda \cdot \frac{r^2 + r\rho + \rho^2}{\rho^2} \exp^{-\frac{r^2}{(1+2r)\rho^2}} \cdot \frac{r^s}{\rho^{2t}} \sigma(\tilde{x})^{s-2t}$$

where $0 \leq s \leq 2$, $0 \leq t \leq 1$, *and* $C_1 = 180\sqrt{3}\pi$.

Proof. The space outside $B_{x,rf(\tilde{x})}$ can be decomposed by $(\mathbb{S}_x(w_i, \rho))_{i=0}^{\infty}$ where $w_i = r + i\rho$. Each $\mathbb{S}_x(w_i, \rho)$ can be covered by less than $\frac{36\sqrt{3}\pi(w_i^2 + w_i\rho + \rho^2)}{\rho^2}$ balls of radius $\frac{\rho}{2} f(\tilde{x})$. From Lemma 9.5 the contribution from the sample points inside each of these balls are bounded. Hence,

$$\sum_{p \notin B_{x,rf(\tilde{x})}} I_p(x) = \sum_{i=0}^{\infty} \sum_{p \in \mathbb{S}_x(w_i, \rho)} I_p(x)$$

$$\leq \frac{C_1 \lambda}{5} \sum_{i=0}^{\infty} \frac{w_i^2 + w_i\rho + \rho^2}{\rho^2} \exp^{-\frac{r w_i}{(1+2r)\rho^2}} \cdot \frac{w_i^s}{\rho^{2t}} \sigma(\tilde{x})^{s-2t}$$

$$\leq C_1 \lambda \cdot \frac{r^2 + r\rho + \rho^2}{\rho^2} \exp^{-\frac{r^2}{(1+2r)\rho^2}} \cdot \frac{r^s}{\rho^{2t}} \sigma(\tilde{x})^{s-2t}.$$

The last inequality holds because the series is bounded from above by a geometric series with common ratio less than 0.8. ∎

9.4 Surface Properties

Although we prove Theorem 9.2 with the hypothesis that $\rho \leq 0.4$ and $\varepsilon \leq 0.1$ which is plausible in practice, our proof for topological guarantees uses the setting $\varepsilon \leq 4 \times 10^{-3}$ and $\rho = \varepsilon$. Also, we assume $\kappa = 5$ in our calculations. The requirement for such small ε is probably an artifact of the proof technique. There is room to improve these constants though the proofs become more complicated (see the discussion at the end of the section). We focus more on demonstrating the ideas behind the proofs rather than tightening the constants. In practice, AMLS surfaces work well on data sets sparser than the one required by theory, see some examples in Section 9.5.

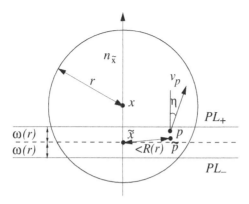

Figure 9.6. All marked distances are in unit of $f(\tilde{x})$. η is the angle between $\mathbf{n}_{\tilde{x}}$ and $\mathbf{v}_p$.

Recall that, for the homeomorphism claim, we only have to show that there exist δ and δ' with $\delta' < \delta < 1$ so that $\mathcal{N}$ has the Hausdorff property for some δ and δ' and the gradient property for δ'. We establish these properties for $\delta = 0.1$ and $\delta' = 0.3\varepsilon$. Then, by definition, $W = \mathcal{N}^{-1}(0) \bigcap 0.1\Sigma$ is the implicit surface of our interest. We establish the Hausdorff property in Lemma 9.7 and the gradient property in Lemma 9.8.

Since function values f and σ are very close to each other, the difference between the values of these two functions will not affect the result of the proof as we already demonstrate in the proof of Lemma 9.5. For the sake of simplicity, we make no difference between the values of these two functions for the proofs in the rest of this section.

9.4.1 Hausdorff Property

In our proof of the Hausdorff property, Lemma 9.4 plays a crucial role. We summarize the statement of the lemma once more here. As Figure 9.6 shows, for a point x on $\Sigma_{+\delta}$ or $\Sigma_{-\delta}$, all sample points inside $B_{x,rf(\tilde{x})}$ are inside a narrow slab bounded by two planes PL_+ and PL_- with $\omega(r)$ distance to $\tilde{x}$ if δ and r are small. In addition, the proof of Lemma 9.4 implies that the distance between $\tilde{x}$ and $\tilde{p}$ is less than $R(r)$ (see Lemma 9.4 for definitions of $R(r)$ and $\omega(r)$). For brevity write $R = R(r)$ and $\omega = \omega(r)$.

The following lemma is used in proving the Hausdorff property. Let $\tau = \frac{\sqrt{2}}{1-\varepsilon}$.

Lemma 9.6. *Let x be a point on $\Sigma_{\pm\delta}$ and p be any sample point inside $B = B_{x,rf(\tilde{x})}$ where $r = \sqrt{2\tau}\delta + 5\rho$. If $0.3\varepsilon \leq \delta \leq 0.1$ then*

$$(x - p)^T \mathbf{v}_p \geq (0.9\delta - 45\varepsilon^2)f(\tilde{x}) \quad \text{if } x \in \Sigma_{+\delta}$$

$$\leq (-0.9\delta + 45\varepsilon^2)f(\tilde{x}) \text{ if } x \in \Sigma_{-\delta}$$

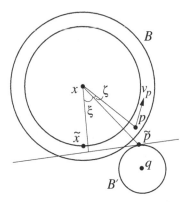

Figure 9.7. Illustration for Lemma 9.6.

Proof. We prove the first half. The second half can be proved similarly. Since $\tilde{x} - \tilde{p} \leq Rf(\tilde{x})$ (Inequality 9.13) we have

$$(1 - R)f(\tilde{x}) \leq f(\tilde{p}) \leq (1 + R)f(\tilde{x}).$$

Under the given values for the parameters, we have $R < 0.18$. In Figure 9.7, B' is the medial ball at $\tilde{p}$ on the side of Σ not containing x. Let q be the center of B'. We have $\|q - \tilde{p}\| \geq f(\tilde{p}), \delta f(\tilde{x}) \leq \|x - \tilde{p}\| \leq rf(\tilde{x}) + \varepsilon^2 f(\tilde{p})$, and $\|x - p\| \geq \|x - \tilde{p}\| - \varepsilon^2 f(\tilde{p})$.

Let ξ be the angle between $x\tilde{p}$ and the normal at $\tilde{p}$, and ζ be the angle between xp and $x\tilde{p}$. Hence, the angle between xp and $\mathbf{v}_p$ is less than $\zeta + \xi + \varepsilon$. Since $\|x - \tilde{p}\| \geq \|x - \tilde{x}\| \geq 0.3\varepsilon f(\tilde{x})$ and $\|p - \tilde{p}\| \leq \varepsilon^2 f(\tilde{p})$, we have $\zeta \leq 4\varepsilon$. In addition

$$\|x - q\|^2 = (\|x - \tilde{p}\| \cos \xi + \|q - \tilde{p}\|)^2 + \|x - \tilde{p}\|^2 \sin^2 \xi.$$

Since B' is on the side of Σ not containing x, we have $\|x - q\| \geq \|x - \tilde{x}\| + \|q - \tilde{p}\|$. Hence,

$$\cos \xi \geq \frac{2\|x - \tilde{x}\| \|q - \tilde{p}\| + \|x - \tilde{x}\|^2 - \|x - \tilde{p}\|^2}{2\|x - \tilde{p}\| \|q - \tilde{p}\|}.$$

Therefore,

$$\begin{aligned} (x - p)^T \mathbf{v}_p &\geq \|x - p\| \cos(\xi + 5\varepsilon) \\ &\geq (\|x - \tilde{p}\| - (1 + R)\varepsilon^2 f(\tilde{x}))(\cos \xi - 5\varepsilon) \\ &\geq \|x - \tilde{p}\| \cos \xi - 5\varepsilon \|x - \tilde{p}\| - 2\varepsilon^2 f(\tilde{x}) \end{aligned}$$

which leads to the first half of the lemma by carefully substituting the inequalities we derived. ∎

Lemma 9.7. *For $\rho = \varepsilon$, $\varepsilon \leq 4 \times 10^{-3}$, and $\kappa = 5$*

$$\mathcal{N}(x) > 0 \quad \text{if } x \in (0.1\Sigma \setminus 0.3\varepsilon\Sigma) \cap \Omega_O$$
$$< 0 \quad \text{if } x \in (0.1\Sigma \setminus 0.3\varepsilon\Sigma) \cap \Omega_I .$$

Proof. We prove the first half of the lemma. The other half can be proved similarly. Assume $x \in \Sigma_{+\delta}$ for $0.3\varepsilon \leq \delta \leq 0.1$. Let $r = \sqrt{2\tau}\delta + 5\rho$ and $B = B_{x,rf(\tilde{x})}$. For any sample point p inside B, we have from Lemma 9.6

$$((x - p)^T \mathbf{v}_p)\theta_p(x) \geq \theta_p(x) \cdot 0.09\varepsilon f(\tilde{x}) > 0. \tag{9.16}$$

From the sampling condition (i), there exists a sample point p_0 so that $\|\tilde{p}_0 - \tilde{x}\| \leq \varepsilon f(\tilde{x})$ and hence $f(\tilde{p}_0) \geq (1 - \varepsilon)f(\tilde{x})$. In addition we have $\|x - p_0\| \leq (\delta + \varepsilon_1)f(\tilde{x})$ where $\varepsilon_1 = (\varepsilon + \delta + \delta\varepsilon)$ obtained from the Close Sample Lemma 7.1. Thus,

$$\sum_{p \in B}((x - p)^T \mathbf{v}_p)\theta_p(x) > \exp^{-\frac{\tau(\delta+\varepsilon_1)^2}{\rho^2}} \cdot 0.09\varepsilon f(\tilde{x}).$$

Writing

$$\Delta = \frac{\left|\sum_{p \notin B}((x - p)^T \mathbf{v}_p)\theta_p(x)\right|}{\sum_{p \in B}((x - p)^T \mathbf{v}_p)\theta_p(x)}$$

we have

$$\mathcal{N}(x) > \sum_{p \in B}((x - p)^T \mathbf{v}_p)\theta_p(x)(1 - \Delta).$$

If we show $\Delta < 1$, we are done since $\mathcal{N}(x) > 0$ in that case.

Consider the sample points outside B. With $s = 1$ and $t = 0$ in Theorem 9.2 we have

$$\left|\sum_{p \notin B}((x - p)^T \mathbf{v}_p)\theta_p(x)\right| \leq \sum_{p \notin B}\exp^{-\frac{\sqrt{2}\|x-p\|^2}{\rho^2\sigma(\tilde{p})\sigma(\tilde{x})}} \|x - p\|$$

$$\leq C_1\lambda\frac{r^2 + r\rho + \rho^2}{\rho^2} \exp^{-\frac{r^2}{(1+2r)\rho^2}} \cdot r\sigma(\tilde{x}).$$

Hence,

$$\Delta \leq C_1\lambda\frac{r^2 + r\rho + \rho^2}{\rho^2} \exp^{-\frac{(\sqrt{2\tau}\delta+5\rho)^2}{(1+2r)\rho^2}+\frac{\tau(\delta+\varepsilon_1)^2}{\rho^2}} \cdot \frac{r}{0.09\varepsilon}$$

$$\leq C_1\lambda\frac{r^2 + r\rho + \rho^2}{\rho^2} \exp^{-\frac{(\sqrt{2\tau}\delta+5\rho)^2}{2\rho^2}+\frac{\tau(\delta+\varepsilon_1)^2}{\rho^2}} \cdot \frac{r}{0.09\varepsilon} \tag{9.17}$$

since $(1 + 2r) < 2$. Since the ball $B_{x,\frac{\rho}{2}f(\tilde{x})} = B_{x,\frac{\varepsilon}{2}f(\tilde{x})}$ contains at most 10κ sample points from Lemma 9.3 we have $\lambda \leq 10\kappa \leq 50$. The quantity on the right of Inequality 9.17 reaches maximum when δ attains its minimum 0.3ε. So, substituting all values we obtain

$$\Delta = \frac{|\sum_{p \notin B}\left((x-p)^T \mathbf{v}_p\right)\theta_p(x)|}{\sum_{p \in B}\left((x-p)^T \mathbf{v}_p\right)\theta_p(x)} < 1$$

as we are supposed to show.   ∎

9.4.2 Gradient Property

In the following lemma we prove the gradient property of $\mathcal{N}$ for $\delta = 0.3\varepsilon$.

Lemma 9.8. *Let z be any point on Σ, then for any $x \in \ell_{\mathbf{n}_z} \cap 0.3\varepsilon\Sigma$*

$$[\mathbf{n}_z]\mathcal{N}(x) > 0$$

for $\rho = \varepsilon$, $\varepsilon \leq 4 \times 10^{-3}$, and $\kappa = 5$.

Proof. Recall $\tilde{x} = \nu(x)$ and hence $\sigma(\tilde{x}) = f \circ \nu(x)$. Obviously, since x avoids the medial axis of Σ, $[\mathbf{n}_{\tilde{x}}](f \circ \nu)(x) = 0$. Since $z = \tilde{x}$, we have

$$[\mathbf{n}_z]\mathcal{N}(x) = \sum_{p \in P}[\mathbf{n}_z]((x-p)^T \mathbf{v}_p\theta_p(x))$$

$$= \sum_{p \in P}\theta_p(x)\left(\mathbf{n}_{\tilde{x}}^T \mathbf{v}_p - 2\frac{\sqrt{2}(x-p)^T \mathbf{v}_p \cdot (x-p)^T \mathbf{n}_{\tilde{x}}}{\rho^2\sigma(\tilde{p})\sigma(\tilde{x})}\right).$$

Let

$$r = \sqrt{2\tau(\delta + \varepsilon_1)^2 + 25\rho^2}. \tag{9.18}$$

and $B = B_{x,rf(\tilde{x})}$. For any sample point p inside B, we know it is inside the slab bounded by two planes from Lemma 9.4 as Figure 9.6 shows. In addition we have $f(\tilde{p}) \geq (1 - R)f(\tilde{x})$ from Inequality 9.13. We observe from Figure 9.6 that $|(x-p)^T \mathbf{n}_z| \leq (\omega + \delta)f(\tilde{x})$ and $|(x-p)^T \mathbf{v}_p| \leq (\omega + \delta + r\eta)f(\tilde{x})$. Under the given values for the parameters, we have $r < 5.68\varepsilon$ and $R < 6\varepsilon$. Hence, from Lemma 9.4 $\omega < 20\varepsilon^2$ and $\eta < 0.03$. Using these values we get

$$\theta_p(x)\left(\mathbf{n}_{\tilde{x}}^T \mathbf{v}_p - 2\frac{\sqrt{2}|(x-p)^T \mathbf{v}_p| \cdot |(x-p)^T \mathbf{n}_{\tilde{x}}|}{\rho^2(1-R)f^2(\tilde{x})}\right) \geq 0.4\theta_p(x). \tag{9.19}$$

Hence,

$$[\mathbf{n}_z](((x-p)^T \mathbf{v}_p)\theta_p(x)) \geq 0.4\theta_p(x) > 0.$$

In particular, there exists a sample point p_0 so that $\|\tilde{p}_0 - \tilde{x}\| \leq \varepsilon f(\tilde{x})$ and hence $f(\tilde{p}_0) \geq (1 - \varepsilon)f(\tilde{x})$. In addition we have $\|x - p_0\| \leq (\delta + \varepsilon_1)f(\tilde{x})$ where

$\varepsilon_1 = (\varepsilon + \delta + \delta\varepsilon)$ is obtained from the Close Sample Lemma 7.1. Hence,

$$\sum_{p \in B} [\mathbf{n}_z]((x - p)^T \mathbf{v}_p \theta_p(x)) > 0.4 \, \exp^{-\frac{\tau(\delta + \varepsilon_1)^2}{\rho^2}}.$$

Writing

$$\Delta = \frac{\left| \sum_{p \notin B} [\mathbf{n}_z]\big(((x - p)^T \mathbf{v}_p) \theta_p(x)\big) \right|}{\sum_{p \in B} [\mathbf{n}_z]\big(((x - p)^T \mathbf{v}_p) \theta_p(x)\big)}$$

we have

$$[\mathbf{n}_z]\mathcal{N}(x) > \sum_{p \in B} [\mathbf{n}_z]((x - p)^T \mathbf{v}_p \theta_p(x))(1 - \Delta).$$

If we show $\Delta < 1$ we are done since $[\mathbf{n}_z]\mathcal{N}(x) > 0$ in that case.
Consider the sample points outside B. We have

$$\left| \sum_{p \notin B} [\mathbf{n}_z]((x - p)^T \mathbf{v}_p \theta_p(x)) \right|$$

$$= \sum_{p \notin B} \theta_p(x) \left(\mathbf{n}_{\tilde{x}}^T \mathbf{v}_p - 2 \frac{\sqrt{2}(x - p)^T \mathbf{v}_p \cdot (x - p)^T \mathbf{n}_{\tilde{x}}}{\rho^2 \sigma(\tilde{p}) \sigma(\tilde{x})} \right)$$

$$\leq \sum_{p \notin B} \exp^{-\frac{\sqrt{2}\|x - p\|^2}{\rho^2 \sigma(\tilde{p}) \sigma(\tilde{x})}} \left(1 + 2 \frac{\sqrt{2}\|x - p\|^2}{\rho^2 \sigma(\tilde{p}) \sigma(\tilde{x})} \right). \tag{9.20}$$

From Theorem 9.2 the right side in Inequality 9.20 is no more than

$$C_1 \lambda \frac{r^2 + r\rho + \rho^2}{\rho^2} \cdot \exp^{-\frac{r^2}{(1+2r)\rho^2}} \left(1 + 2 \frac{r^2}{\rho^2} \right).$$

Therefore,

$$\Delta < \frac{C_1 \lambda}{0.4} \frac{r^2 + r\rho + \rho^2}{\rho^2} \cdot \exp^{-\frac{25}{1+2r}} \left(1 + 2 \frac{r^2}{\rho^2} \right)$$

which is less than 1 when r is evaluated for $\rho = \varepsilon \leq 4 \times 10^{-3}$ from relation 9.18 and λ is plugged in from Lemma 9.3. ∎

The requirement for small ε is mainly because of the following fact. Our proof requires that Inequalities 9.16 and 9.19 be true for all the sample points inside B. This means all the sample points inside B make positive contribution to the implicit function and its derivative. However, one can relax this requirement by further classifying the sample points inside B and allowing the sample points close to the boundary of B to make negative contributions. Since these sample points have small weights, their contributions do not change the positivity of the entire contribution from the sample points inside B.

We have proved that W and Σ are homeomorphic. It can also be proved that they are isotopic. Since W lives in a small tubular neighborhood of Σ and the segments normal to Σ intersect W in a single point within this tubular neighborhood, one can define an isotopy connecting W and Σ. This construction is exactly the same as the one used to prove that the power crust and the sampled surface are isotopic in the PC-Isotopy Theorem 6.4.

9.5 Algorithm and Implementation

In this section we summarize different steps of the algorithm for reconstructing with AMLS surfaces. We already know that the definition of AMLS involves the local feature sizes of the sampled surface Σ. In absence of Σ one cannot compute $f(\tilde{x})$ and hence $\sigma(\tilde{x})$ for a point x exactly. Due to this difficulty, we describe an implementation that can only approximate the AMLS surface. Recall that each sample point p is assumed to have an associated normal $\mathbf{v}_p$ that approximates the normal at $\tilde{p}$. So, for a sample P without any normal information, the approximation of the AMLS surface also needs to estimate the normals at the sample points.

9.5.1 Normal and Feature Approximation

In Chapter 7, we have already presented the algorithms for the normal and feature approximations from noisy point samples. The routine APPROXIMATENOR-MAL takes P and a threshold τ to decide which Delaunay balls in Del P are big enough to give good approximation of normals.

The normals computed by APPROXIMATENORMAL are not consistently oriented. The input points should be equipped with oriented normals for AMLS approximation. We orient the normals by walking over the points and propagating the orientation in the neighborhoods. We compute a minimum spanning tree of the points. It can be shown that any edge in the minimum spanning tree must connect two points p, q that are only $\tilde{O}(\varepsilon) \max\{f(p), f(q)\}$ distance apart. This means the true normals $\mathbf{n}_{\tilde{p}}$ and $\mathbf{n}_{\tilde{q}}$ differ only by a small amount and hence $\mathbf{v}_p$ and $\mathbf{v}_q$ should be similarly oriented. If during the walk we move from p to q where the normal $\mathbf{v}_p$ has been oriented, we orient $\mathbf{v}_q$ as follows. If a normal has not been computed by APPROXIMATENORMAL at q, we transport $\mathbf{v}_p$ to q. This means we set $\mathbf{v}_q$ to be parallel to $\mathbf{v}_p$ and orient it the same way as $\mathbf{v}_p$. In case APPROXIMATENORMAL has computed a normal at q, we orient $\mathbf{v}_q$ so that $\mathbf{v}_p^T \mathbf{v}_q$ is positive. One can show easily that this procedure orients the normal at any point p so that $\mathbf{v}_p$ and $\mathbf{n}_{\tilde{p}}$ make an angle less than $\frac{\pi}{2}$ thereby ensuring a consistent orientation.

ORIENTNORMAL(P,τ)

1   APPROXIMATENORMAL(P,τ);
2   compute a minimum spanning tree T of P;
3   let r be any point assigned a normal by APPROXIMATENORMAL;
4   carry out a depth-first search in T starting at r;
5   let q be a point reached from p by edge $pq \in T$;
6   if q is assigned normal $\mathbf{v}_q$ by APPROXIMATENORMAL
7   orient $\mathbf{v}_q$ so that $\mathbf{v}_p^T \mathbf{v}_q > 0$;
8   else
9       $\mathbf{v}_q = \mathbf{v}_p$;
10 endif.

We use the routine APPROXIMATEFEATURE from Chapter 7 to approximate the feature sizes. The routine APPROXIMATEFEATURE takes P and a user parameter k to determine the poles approximating the medial axis by searching the k-nearest neighbors of the sample points. Then, it estimates the local feature size by computing the distances of the sample points to these poles. We use ORIENTNORMAL and APPROXIMATEFEATURE to preprocess P and then apply a projection procedure to move a point in P to the AMLS surface.

9.5.2 Projection

The sample points are moved to the AMLS surface by the Newton projection method. It is an iterative procedure in which we move a point p to a new point p' along $\nabla\mathcal{I}(p)$ where

$$p' = p - \frac{\mathcal{I}(p)}{\|\nabla\mathcal{I}(p)\|^2}\nabla\mathcal{I}(p). \tag{9.21}$$

This iteration continues until the distance between p and p' becomes smaller than a given threshold τ'. To compute $\mathcal{I}(p)$ and $\nabla\mathcal{I}(p)$, one may take the sample points inside the ball with radius a small multiple of the width of the Gaussian weighting function since the sample points outside this ball have little effect on the function. We supply the parameter ρ which appear in the computations of $\mathcal{I}(p)$ and $\nabla\mathcal{I}(p)$. We see in the examples that the Newton iteration for AMLS surface converges quickly and has a big convergent domain in Section 9.6.

Finally, the projected set of points are fed to a reconstruction algorithm, say COCONE, to produce the output. Figure 9.8 shows the results of this algorithm applied on MAX-PLANCK and BIGHAND point clouds.

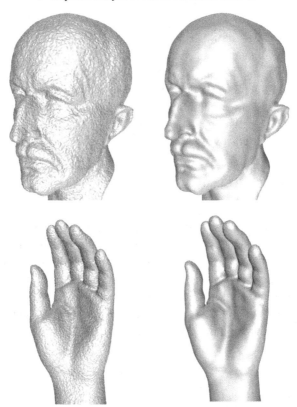

Figure 9.8. Reconstruction results before (left) and after (right) smoothing with AMLS. $\rho = 0.75$ for both models. The reason a bigger ρ is chosen than the one (0.4) we suggest in Section 9.2.1 is that the feature approximation method tends to compute a feature size slightly smaller than the exact one.

AMLS(P,τ,k,τ',ρ)

1   ORIENTNORMAL(P,τ);
2   APPROXIMATEFEATURE(P,k);
3   for each $p \in P$ do
4   compute p' by equation 9.21;
5   if $\|p - p'\| > \tau'$
6   go to 4 with $p := p'$;
7   endfor
8   let P' be the projected point set;
9   COCONE(P').

9.6 Other MLS Surfaces

9.6.1 Projection MLS

There is another implicit surface which is popularly known as an MLS surface in graphics. This surface was originally defined procedurally. Later an implicit formulation was discovered. To differentiate this surface from the one we just described, we call this surface *projection* MLS or PMLS in short.

The PMLS surface is defined as the stationary set of a map $\phi : \mathbb{R}^3 \to \mathbb{R}^3$, that is, the points $x \in \mathbb{R}^3$ with $\phi(x) = x$. The map ϕ at a point $x \in \mathbb{R}^3$ is defined procedurally. Let $\mathcal{E} : \mathbb{R}^3 \times \mathbb{R}^3 \to \mathbb{R}^3$ be the following map. Given a vector $\mathbf{v} \in \mathbb{R}^3$ and a point $y = x + t\mathbf{v}$ for some real $t \in \mathbb{R}$, $\mathcal{E}(y, \mathbf{v})$ is defined to be the sum of the weighted distances of all points in P from a plane with normal $\mathbf{v}$ and the point y. Specifically,

$$\mathcal{E}(y, \mathbf{v}) = \Sigma_{p \in P}((y - p)^T \mathbf{v})^2 \theta_p(y) \tag{9.22}$$

where θ_p is a weighting function. The nearest point to x where $\mathcal{E}$ is minimized over all directions v and all reals t defining y is $\phi(x)$.

This minimization procedure can be decomposed into two optimization steps. The first one finds an optimum direction and the second one uses this optimum direction to find the required minimum. For a point x let $\mathbf{n}(x)$ be the optimum direction found by the first optimization, that is,

$$\mathbf{n}(x) = \arg \min_{\mathbf{v}} \mathcal{E}(y, \mathbf{v}). \tag{9.23}$$

Let $\ell_{\mathbf{n}(x)}$ denote the line of the vector $\mathbf{n}(x)$.

For x let $\mathcal{E}(y, \mathbf{n}(x))$ achieve a local minimum at x_m over the set $y \in \ell_{\mathbf{n}(x)}$. Mathematically, this implies

$$\mathbf{n}(x)^T \left(\frac{\partial \mathcal{E}(y, \mathbf{n}(x))}{\partial y} |_{x_m} \right) = 0. \tag{9.24}$$

The following result is known.

Fact 9.1. *x is a stationary point of ϕ if $x = x_m$.*

From the above results one gets a projection procedure by which points can be projected onto a PMLS surface. Starting from a point x, the local minimum x_m is computed. Then x is replaced with x_m and the iteration continues till the distance between x and x_m drops below a threshold. Notice that the optimization is done over the set $y \in \ell_{\mathbf{n}(x)}$ where $\mathcal{E}$ depends on y. This makes the optimization procedure nonlinear and hence computationally hard.

One can conclude from Equation 9.24 and Fact 9.1 that the set of stationary points is actually the zero-level set of the implicit function

$$\mathcal{J}(x) = \mathbf{n}(x)^T \left(\frac{\partial \mathcal{E}(y, \mathbf{n}(x))}{\partial y} |_x \right).$$

One needs to be a little more careful. Equation 9.24 does not only hold for minima of $\mathcal{E}$ but also for all of its other extrema including the maxima. Therefore, in general, all components of $\mathcal{J}^{-1}(0)$ are not in PMLS surface. The ones where $\mathcal{E}$ reaches local minimum need to be identified for reconstruction purpose. One can verify that when the weighting function θ_p is a Gaussian as in Equation 9.5, the implicit function $\mathcal{J}$ takes the following form:

$$\mathcal{J}(x) = \sum_{p \in P} (x - p)^T \mathbf{n}(x) \left(1 - \left(\frac{(x - p)^T \mathbf{n}(x)}{h} \right)^2 \right) \theta_p(x). \qquad (9.25)$$

Notice that, instead of computing $\mathbf{n}(x)$ as in Equation 9.23, one may assume that the input points are equipped with some normals from which a normal field $\mathbf{n} : \mathbb{R}^3 \to \mathbb{R}^3$ can be derived, say by a simple linear interpolation.

9.6.2 Variation

The expression for $\mathcal{J}$ is a little cumbersome for projecting points as it leads to nonlinear optimizations. It can be simplified if we modify $\mathcal{E}$ slightly. Observe that the weighting function θ_p varies with y in the expression for $\mathcal{E}$ in Equation 9.22. Instead, we can vary θ_p with x. Then, we get a slightly different implicit function $\mathcal{G}$ than $\mathcal{J}$:

$$\mathcal{G}(x) = \sum_{p \in P} [(x - p)^T \mathbf{n}(x)] \theta_p(x). \qquad (9.26)$$

The surface given by $\mathcal{G}^{-1}(0)$ is a variation of the PMLS surface and hence we call it VMLS surface. An advantage of the VMLS surface is that, unlike the standard PMLS surfaces, its inherent projection procedure does not require any nonlinear optimization, which makes the algorithm faster, more stable and easier to implement.

9.6.3 Computational Issues

We have chosen $\mathcal{I}$ instead of $\mathcal{N}$ to define the AMLS surface though the topological and geometric guarantees can be worked out with both. The reason is mainly a practical consideration. Newton projections have larger convergent domain for $\mathcal{I}$ than $\mathcal{N}$. Figure 9.9 illustrates this fact.

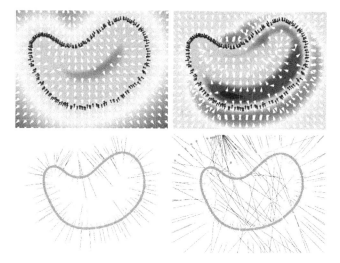

Figure 9.9. The left and right columns show the result of NP on $\mathcal{I}$ and $\mathcal{N}$ respectively. The top row shows the function values and the gradient field. The darker the shade, the higher the absolute value; it is negative inside and positive outside. In the bottom, the lines connect input gray points to their corresponding stationary points of NP.

Advantages of Newton Projections

Although the projection procedure of VMLS surfaces is more efficient than the PMLS surfaces, it turns out that the Newton projections are even better. The VMLS projection can be described as follows. Project x along $\mathbf{n}(x)$ to a new position

$$x' = x - \frac{\mathcal{G}(x)}{\sum_{p \in P} \theta_p(x)} \mathbf{n}(x) \tag{9.27}$$

and iterate until a stationary point is reached. Due to its linear nature we refer to this projection as Linear Projection or LP in short. The Newton projection for AMLS surfaces is referred to as NP in short. We argue that NP is better than LP in two respects: convergence rate and timing. As Table 9.1 shows, NP, in general, uses less iterations to project a point onto the implicit surface. This is not surprising as $\nabla \mathcal{I}(x)$ with x close to the implicit surface can estimate the normal more accurately at its closest point on the implicit surface. In addition, one has to compute $\mathbf{n}(x)$ before evaluating $\mathcal{G}(x)$. Hence to compute the new position using LP, one has to iterate twice over its neighboring points which makes LP slower than NP even in each iteration.

Table 9.1. *Time data for NP and LP. |P| is the number of points in the point cloud.*

Model	|P|	Method	#nb	#iter	Time
Max-	49137	NP	1000	3.1	94
planck		LP	1108	7.2	310
Bighand	38214	NP	1392	3.2	109
		LP	1527	8.6	400

#iter is the number of iterations in the average sense, i.e., we add up the number of iterations used to project all the input points and divide it by |P| to get #iter. Similarly, #nb is the average number of points considered as neighbors. $\tau' = 10^{-25}$ for these experiments. Times (second) are for projecting all the input points (PC with a 2.8 GHz P4 CPU and 1 GB RAM).

Figure 9.10. The leftmost and the middle pictures show zero-level sets of the standard PMLS under two different noise levels. The noise level in the middle is higher. Thicker curves represent the zero-level set $\mathcal{J}^{-1}(0)$ where $\mathcal{E}$ reaches minima while the thinner curves are zero-level sets where the energy function reaches maxima. The rightmost picture shows the zero-level set $\mathcal{I}^{-1}(0)$ under the same noise level as in the middle picture.

Zero-Level Sets

In the definition of PMLS, the actual PMLS surface is only a subset of the zero-level set $\mathcal{J}^{-1}(0)$ where the energy function $\mathcal{E}$ reaches a minimum along the normal direction. As one can deduce from Equation 9.25, there are two other layers of zero-level sets of the implicit function $\mathcal{J}$ on both sides of the PMLS surface, where the energy function $\mathcal{E}$ reaches the local maximum; see the left most picture in Figure 9.10. We refer to these two layers as *maxima layers*. The distance between these layers could be extremely small at places where either the local feature size is small or the noise level is high or both. In that case, computations on the PMLS surface become difficult.

First of all, many existing implicit surface techniques such as raytracing and polygonizing become hard to apply on the PMLS surface since one needs to distinguish different zero-level sets. When the maxima layers come close to the true PMLS surface, the marching step in a raytracer and the size of the cubes in a polygonizer may become impractically small.

Second, the projection procedure for the PMLS surface requires a non-linear optimization, specifically an one-dimensional minimization. The one-dimensional minimization algorithms usually begin with an interval known to contain a minimum guess m such that the function value at m must be less than the function values at the ends of the interval. Finding such a minimum guess m could be hard if the two maxima layers come close.

Third, the PMLS surface is more sensitive to the noise. When the noise level for position or normal or both increases, the three layers of the zero-level sets (one for minima and two for maxima) could easily interfere with each other. In the middle picture of Figure 9.10, the zero-level set for minima gets merged with those for maxima. As a result, the PMLS could give an implicit surface with holes or disconnectness. However, under the same level of noise, the AMLS still gives the proper implicit surface, see the rightmost picture in Figure 9.10.

9.7 Voronoi-Based Implicit Surface

There is a Voronoi diagram-based implicit surface that can be used for surface reconstruction. This method can also be proved to have output guarantees using the ε-sampling theory. We will briefly describe the function definition but will skip the proof of guarantees.

Given an input point set $P \subset \mathbb{R}^3$, the *natural neighbors* $N_{x,P}$ of a point $x \in \mathbb{R}^3$ are the Delaunay neighbors of x in $\mathrm{Del}\,(P \cup x)$. Letting $V(x)$ denote the Voronoi cell of x in $V_{P \cup x}$, this means

$$N_{x,P} = \{p \in P \mid V(x) \cap V_p \neq \emptyset\}.$$

Let $A(x, p)$ denote the volume stolen by x from V_p, that is,

$$A(x, p) = V(x) \cap V_p.$$

The natural coordinate associated with a point p is a continuous function $\lambda_p : \mathbb{R}^3 \to \mathbb{R}$ where

$$\lambda_p(x) = \frac{A(x, p)}{\Sigma_{q \in P} A(x, q)}.$$

Some of the interesting properties of λ_p are that it is continuously differentiable everywhere except at p and any point $x \in \mathbb{R}^3$ is a convex combination of its natural neighbors, that is, $\Sigma_{p \in N_{x,P}} \lambda_p(x) p = x$. Assume that each point p is equipped with a unit normal $\mathbf{n}_p$ which can either be computed via pole vectors, or be part of the input. A distance function $h_p : \mathbb{R}^3 \to \mathbb{R}$ for each point p

is defined as $h_p(x) = (p - x)^T \mathbf{n}_p$. A global distance function $h : \mathbb{R}^3 \rightarrow \mathbb{R}$ is defined by interpolating these local distance functions with natural coordinates. Specifically,

$$h(x) = \Sigma_{p \in P} \lambda_p(x) h_p(x).$$

One difficulty of working with such h is that it is not continuously differentiable everywhere as λ_p is not. To overcome this difficulty one may choose a smooth function arbitrarily close to λ_p and make h smooth everywhere. By definition, $h(x)$ locally approximates the signed distance from the tangent plane at each point $p \in P$ and, in particular, $h(p) = 0$.

When h is made continuously differentiable, $\hat{\Sigma} = h^{-1}(0)$ is a smooth surface unless 0 is a critical value. A discrete approximation of $\hat{\Sigma}$ can be computed from the restricted Delaunay triangulation Del $P|_{\hat{\Sigma}}$. All Voronoi edges that intersect $\hat{\Sigma}$ are computed via the sign of h at their two endpoints. The dual Delaunay triangles of these Voronoi edges constitute a piecewise linear approximation of $\hat{\Sigma}$. If the input sample P is a ε-sample of a surface Σ for sufficiently small ε, then it can be shown that $\hat{\Sigma}$ is geometrically close and is also topologically equivalent to Σ.

9.8 Notes and Exercises

The definition of MLS surfaces as described in Section 9.2 is taken from Shen, O'Brien, and Shewchuk [77]. The adaptive MLS surface definition and its proofs of guarantees are taken from Dey and Sun [40]. Historically, these definitions were proposed later than the PMLS definition. Levin [65] pioneered the PMLS definition. This definition and its variants such as the VMLS are popularly known as MLS surfaces in graphics. Alexa et al. [1] brought the PMLS surface to the attention of the graphics community in the context of surface reconstruction. Later, it was used for different modeling applications [75]. Zwicker, Pauly, Knoll, and Gross [83] implemented the VMLS definition in a modeling software called Pointshop 3D. The understanding of the PMLS surfaces became much more clear after the work of Amenta and Kil [8] who explained its relation to extremal surfaces and gave its implicit form.

Theoretical guarantees about the MLS surfaces in terms of sampling density were not proved until the work of Kolluri [63]. He showed that the MLS surface given by Equation 9.4 has same topology and approximate geometry of the sampled surface under a uniform sampling condition. Subsequently Dey, Goswami, and Sun [35] proved similar guarantees about the PMLS surface. Following these developments Dey and Sun [40] proposed the AMLS definition and proved geometric and topological guarantees using an adaptive sampling condition.

The natural neighbor-based implicit surface described in Section 9.7 was proposed by Boissonnat and Cazals [16]. The proof of geometric and topological guarantees for this surface is given for noise-free dense samples.

Other than MLS and natural neighbor surfaces, a few other implicit surfaces have been proposed for smooth surface reconstruction. The radial basis function of Carr et al. [18] and the multilevel partition of unity of Ohtake et al. [73] are examples of such surfaces, to name a few. Theoretical guarantees about these surfaces have not been shown.

Exercises

1. In Equation 9.3, we could take $\phi_p = 0$ in anticipation that $I^{-1}(0)$ fits the points in the input point sample P. What is the difficulty one faces with this choice? How can it be overcome?

2. Recall the definition of $\lambda(\rho)$ in Section 9.3.1. Prove that there is a constant c so that $\lambda(\rho) \leq \frac{c\rho^3\kappa}{\varepsilon^3}$ where ρ and ε are sufficiently small.

3^h. We assume P to be a $(\varepsilon, \varepsilon^2, -)$-sample to prove that the AMLS surface is isotopic to Σ. Show the same when P is a $(\varepsilon, \varepsilon, -)$-sample.

4. Prove Inequality 9.13.

5. Consider the minimum spanning tree T of a $(\varepsilon, \varepsilon^2, -)$-sample. Prove that for any edge $pq \in T$, the angle $\angle(\mathbf{n}_{\tilde{p}}, \mathbf{n}_{\tilde{q}})$ is $\tilde{O}(\varepsilon)$.

6^h. Prove that the projection method for PMLS converges [35].

7. Prove Fact 9.1.

8. Improve the bound on $\|\tilde{x} - \tilde{p}\|$ in the proof of Lemma 9.4. Specifically, show that

$$\|\tilde{x} - \tilde{p}\| \leq \sqrt{\frac{\|x - \tilde{p}\|^2 - (\delta f(\tilde{x}))^2}{1 - \delta f(\tilde{x})/\gamma}}$$

from which derive improved bounds on $R(r)$ and $\omega(r)$.

9^h. Carry out the entire proof of the homeomorphism between Σ and the AMLS surface with an improved ε, say $\varepsilon < 0.05$.

10°. Prove that the Newton projection for AMLS surfaces converges.

10

Morse Theoretic Reconstructions

In this chapter we describe algorithms for surface reconstruction that are based on Morse Theory, a well-known topic in differential topology. We describe two algorithms which are similar in principle though are different in details. We will not go over the proofs of geometric and topological guarantees of these algorithms as in previous chapters. Instead, we will emphasize their novel use of the Voronoi and Delaunay diagrams with Morse theoretic interpretations. In practice, for reasonably dense samples, these algorithms produce comparable results with other provable algorithms.

10.1 Morse Functions and Flows

Let $h\colon \mathbb{R}^3 \to \mathbb{R}$ be a smooth function. The smoothness means that h is continuous and infinitely often differentiable. The gradient ∇h of h at a point x is given by

$$\nabla h(x) = \left(\frac{\partial h}{\partial x_1}(x) \quad \frac{\partial h}{\partial x_2}(x) \quad \frac{\partial h}{\partial x_3}(x) \right).$$

This gradient induces a vector field $v\colon \mathbb{R}^3 \to \mathbb{R}^3$ where $v(x) = \nabla h(x)$. This vector field is smooth since h is so. A point x is *critical* if $\nabla h(x) = (0, 0, 0)$. The *Hessian* of h at x is the three by three matrix

$$\begin{pmatrix} \frac{\partial^2 h}{\partial x_1^2} & \frac{\partial^2 h}{\partial x_1 \partial x_2} & \frac{\partial^2 h}{\partial x_1 \partial x_3} \\ \frac{\partial^2 h}{\partial x_2 \partial x_1} & \frac{\partial^2 h}{\partial x_2^2} & \frac{\partial^2 h}{\partial x_2 \partial x_3} \\ \frac{\partial^2 h}{\partial x_3 \delta x_1} & \frac{\partial^2 h}{\partial x_3 \partial x_2} & \frac{\partial^2 h}{\partial x_3^2} \end{pmatrix} \text{ evaluated at } x.$$

A critical point of h is *nondegenerate* if the Hessian at that point is not singular. The function h is called a nondegenerate Morse function if all its critical points are nondegenerate. Nondegenerate critical points are necessarily isolated. They are characterized by the celebrated Morse Lemma which says that each critical point x has a local coordinate system with the origin at x so that

$$h(y) = h(x = 0) \pm x_1^2 \pm x_2^2 \pm x_3^2$$

for all $y = (x_1, x_2, x_3)$ in a neighborhood of x. The number of minus signs in the above expression is the *index* of x. The critical points of index 0 are the local minima, and the critical points of index 3 are the local maxima of h. The rest of the critical points are saddle points which may have index 1 or 2.

The gradient vector field v gives rise to an ordinary differential equation

$$\frac{d}{dt}\phi(t, x) = v(\phi(t, x)).$$

The solution of the equation is a map $\phi : \mathbb{R} \times \mathbb{R}^3 \to \mathbb{R}^3$ which has the following two properties:

(i) $\phi(0, x) = x$
(ii) $\phi(t, \phi(s, x)) = \phi((t + s), x)$.

The function ϕ is called a *flow* on $\mathbb{R}^3$. Its first parameter can be thought of as time and the mapping itself tells how points in $\mathbb{R}^3$ move in time with the vector field v. The first property says that points have not moved yet at time zero. The second property says that a point after time $t + s$ moves to a position where $\phi(s, x)$ moves after time t. The points which do not move at all, that is, where $\phi(t, x) = x$ for all $t \in \mathbb{R}$ are called the *fixed points* of ϕ. It turns out that the critical points of h are the fixed points of ϕ.

An embedding of the real line $\mathbb{R}$ into $\mathbb{R}^3$ can be obtained from ϕ for each x by keeping the second parameter fixed to x. The curve $\phi_x : \mathbb{R} \to \mathbb{R}^3$ where $\phi_x(t) = \phi(t, x)$ is called the *flow curve* of x. The flow curve ϕ_x describes how the point x moves in time which could be negative. This motion always follows the steepest ascent of the function h, that is the direction in which h increases the most. In other words, the flow curves are the integral curves of the gradient vector field v (see Figure 10.1). A natural orientation can be imposed on the flow curves with increasing value of h. The flow curves are open and as such do not have endpoints. However, if a flow curve is not flowing into infinity, its closure will have two critical points at the ends, one where it originates, the other where it terminates. The first one is called the *origin* and the second one is called the *destination* of the flow curve. To be uniform, we introduce a critical point p_∞ at infinity so that all flow curves have an origin and a destination.

Let $C(h)$ be the set of critical points of h. For a critical point $c \in C(h)$ we are interested in the points that are flowing into c. This means it is the set of points covered by the flow curves that have c as their destination. This motivates the

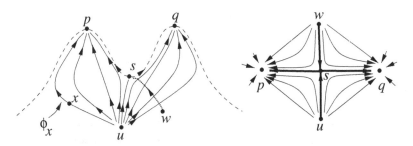

Figure 10.1. Flow curves drawn on the graph of a function from $\mathbb{R}^2$ to $\mathbb{R}$. The peaks of the two humps correspond to two maxima p and q. The point s corresponds to a saddle and u, w correspond to minima. The flow curve ϕ_x originates at u and terminates at p. On right the flow curves are drawn on the domain $\mathbb{R}^2$. The stable and unstable manifolds of s are drawn with thicker curves, $S(s) = us \cup ws$, $U(s) = ps \cup qs$.

definition of *stable manifold* of c as

$$S(c) = \{c\} \cup \{y \in \mathbb{R}^3 \mid c \text{ is the destination of } \phi_y\}.$$

If c is a minimum, that is, its index is 0, then $S(c) = \{c\}$ since no flow curve has c as a destination. If the index of c is $j > 0$, then the stable manifold $S(c)$ consists of c and a $(j-1)$-dimensional sphere of flow curves which means $S(c)$ is j-dimensional. For all c, $S(c)$ is the image of an injective map from $\mathbb{R}^j$ to $\mathbb{R}^3$. It is homeomorphic to $\mathbb{R}^j$ although its closure may not be homeomorphic to a closed ball $\mathbb{B}^j$. This exception can happen only if the closure of two flow curves coming into c share the starting point. The stable manifold $S(p_\infty)$ is the image of an injective map from the punctured three-dimensional sphere, $\mathbb{R}^3 \setminus \{0\}$, to $\mathbb{R}^3$. The stable manifolds are mutually disjoint open sets and they cover the entire $\mathbb{R}^3$, that is,

(i) $S(c) \cap S(c') = \emptyset$ for any $c \neq c'$,
(ii) $\bigcup_{c \in C(h)} S(c) = \mathbb{R}^3.$

Similar to the stable manifolds, one may define *unstable manifolds* for the critical points. These are the spaces of flow curves that originates at the critical points. Formally, the unstable manifold $U(c)$ for a critical point $c \in C(h)$ is given by

$$U(c) = \{c\} \cup \{y \in \mathbb{R}^3 \mid c \text{ is the origin of } \phi_y\}.$$

The dimensions of the stable and unstable manifolds add up to the dimension of the domain, that is, $U(c)$ is $(3-j)$-dimensional if c has index j. This means a minimum has an unstable manifold of dimension 3 and a maximum has an

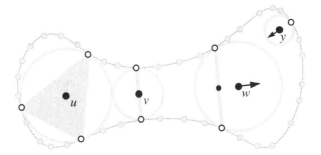

Figure 10.2. In this example the point set P is a sample from a curve $\Sigma \subset \mathbb{R}^2$. The sets $A(x)$ are shown with hollow circles for four points $x = u, v, w, y \in \mathbb{R}^2$. The convex hulls of $A(x)$ are lightly shaded. The driver of the point w is the smaller black circle. The driver of the point y is the single point in $A(y)$. The points u and v are critical since they are contained in $H(u)$ and $H(v)$ respectively. The points w and y are regular. The direction of steepest ascent of the distance function at w and y is indicated by an arrow.

unstable manifold of dimension 0. Similar to the stable manifolds, we have the following properties for the unstable ones:

(i) $U(c) \cap U(c') = \emptyset$ for any $c \neq c'$,

(ii) $\bigcup_{c \in C(h)} U(c) = \mathbb{R}^3$.

10.2 Discretization

In surface reconstruction from a point sample $P \subset \Sigma$, we have a distance function $d : \mathbb{R}^3 \to \mathbb{R}$ where $d(x)$ is the squared distance of x to the nearest point in P, that is, $d(x) = d(x, P)^2$. Unfortunately, we cannot use the setup developed for the smooth functions since d is not necessarily smooth. In particular, d is not smooth at the Voronoi facets, edges, and vertices of Vor P though it remains smooth in the interior of each Voronoi cell. Therefore, we cannot apply the theory of ordinary differential equations to get the flow curves and the associated stable manifolds. Nevertheless, there is a unique direction of steepest ascent of d at each point of $\mathbb{R}^3$ except at the critical points of d. This is what is used to define a vector field and the associated flow curves.

10.2.1 Vector Field

We need to determine the direction of the steepest ascent of d as well as its critical points. The following definitions are helpful to determine them. See Figure 10.2 for illustrations of the terms.

Definition 10.1. *For every point $x \in \mathbb{R}^3$, let $A(x)$ be the set of points in P with minimum distance to x, that is, $A(x) = \mathrm{argmin}_{p \in P} \| p - x \|$. Let $H(x)$ be the convex hull of $A(x)$. The point x is* critical *if $x \in H(x)$ and is* regular *otherwise.*

Definition 10.2. *For any point $x \in \mathbb{R}^3$, let $r(x)$ be the point in $H(x)$ closest to x. The point $r(x)$ is called the* driver *of x.*

The following lemma plays a key role in defining a flow from d. To keep the discussion simple we assume that no four points are co-circular.

Lemma 10.1 (Flow). *For any regular point $x \in \mathbb{R}^3$ let $r(x)$ be the driver of x. The steepest ascent of the distance function d at x is in the direction of $x - r(x)$.*

Proof. Let $v(x)$ be the vector along which d increases the most at x. Without loss of generality assume $v(x)$ is a unit vector. Let p be any point in $A(x)$. Let $d_p(x) = d(x, p)^2$. The directional derivative of $d_p(x)$ along $v(x)$ is given by $v(x)^T (x - p) = \| x - p \| \cos \theta_p$ where θ_p is the angle between $v(x)$ and $\mathbf{x}_p = x - p$. Since x is regular, $x \notin H(x)$ and thus $0 \leq \theta_p < \pi$. Also, $\| x - p \|$ is same for all $p \in A(x)$. These facts imply that $v(x)$ is along a direction that minimizes the maximum of the angles θ_p over all $p \in A(x)$. The negated vector, $-v(x)$, is along the direction which minimizes the maximum of the angles made by $-v(x)$ and vectors $-\mathbf{x}_p$ for each $p \in A(x)$.

Consider the ball $B = B_{x,d(x)}$. The ball B contains all points of $A(x)$ on its boundary. Let the ray of $-v(x)$ intersect the boundary of B at v'. Normalizing B to a unit sphere, the angle θ_p is given by the length of the spherical arc $v'p$. Therefore, v' minimizes the maximum spherical arc distances $v'p$ to each $p \in A(x)$.

Consider the unbounded polyhedral cone C_x formed by all rays originating from x and going through the points of $H(x)$. The convex hull of any subset $A'(x) \subseteq A(x)$ is projected radially on the boundary of B by this cone. Call this the spherical hull of $A'(x)$. In particular, the polytope $H(x)$ is projected on the boundary of B by this cone. Denote the spherical hull of $H(x)$ with $H'(x)$. Notice that the vertex set of $H(x)$ and $H'(x)$ is the same. From our previous discussion, it is clear that v' has to lie within $H'(x)$ to minimize the maximum arc distances to the vertices of $H'(x)$. Let the minmax distance of v' from the vertices of $H'(x)$ be realized by a subset $A'(x) \subseteq A(x)$ of vertices. We claim that v' lies on the spherical hull of $A'(x)$. If not, v' can be moved ever slightly to decrease the minmax distance. This means the ray of $-v(x)$

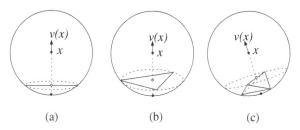

(a)   (b)   (c)

Figure 10.3. The vector $v(x)$ for one-, two-, and three-dimensional $H(x)$ is shown (from left to right). The hollow circle on $H(x)$ is the driver $r(x)$.

intersects the convex hull of $A'(x)$, say at z, where z is the center of the smallest disk circumscribing the vertices of $A'(x)$.

We claim that z is the closest point of $H(x)$ to x, that is, $z = r(x)$ and $v(x)$ is along the direction $x - r(x)$ as z lies on the ray $-v(x)$.

The spherical disk centering v' and with the vertices of $A'(x)$ on the boundary contains all other vertices of $A(x)$ inside. This means that the smallest (Euclidean) disk, say D, circumscribing the vertices of $A'(x)$ contains all other points of $A(x)$ (if any) on the side that does not contain x. Then, each point of $H(x)$ lies either on D or on the side of D which does not contain x. The center z of D is the closest point to x among all such points. ∎

The convex hull $H(x)$ can be zero-, one-, two-, and three-dimensional. Let us look at the Flow Lemma 10.1 for these different cases of $H(x)$ where $x \notin H(x)$.

(i) $H(x)$ is a single point p. In this case trivially $r(x) = p$.
(ii) $H(x)$ is one-dimensional, that is, $A(x) = \{p, q\}$. In this case $r(x)$ is the midpoint of the segment pq [Figure 10.3(a)].
(iii) $H(x)$ is two-dimensional. Consider the disk containing the points of $A(x)$ on the boundary. Let z be the center of this disk. If z is contained in $H(x)$, then $r(x) = z$ (Figure 10.3(b)). If z lies outside $H(x)$, then the midpoint of the edge of $H(x)$ which is closest to x is $r(x)$.
(iv) $H(x)$ is three-dimensional. The closest point to x on the boundary of $H(x)$ is $r(x)$. It is the circumcenter of either a facet or an edge of $H(x)$ (Figure 10.3(c)).

10.2.2 Discrete Flow

The Flow Lemma 10.1 prompts us to define a vector field $v \colon \mathbb{R}^3 \to \mathbb{R}^3$ as

$$v(x) = \frac{x - r(x)}{\|x - r(x)\|} \text{ if } x \neq r(x) \text{ and } 0 \text{ otherwise.}$$

Note that the vector field vanishes exactly at the critical points since $x \neq r(x)$ holds for all regular points. The flow induced by the vector field v is a function $\phi : \mathbb{R}^+ \times \mathbb{R}^3 \to \mathbb{R}^3$ such that the right derivative at every point $x \in \mathbb{R}^3$ satisfies the following equation:

$$\lim_{t \downarrow t_0} \frac{\phi(t, x) - \phi(t_0, x)}{t - t_0} = v(\phi(t_0, x)).$$

Notice that here we use $\mathbb{R}^+$ instead of $\mathbb{R}$ for the domain of t. The reason will be clear in a moment.

Let us explain how ϕ varies with t and x to obtain a more intuitive idea. For any critical point x

$$\phi(t, x) = x, \text{ for all } t \in \mathbb{R}$$

since $r(x) = x$ gives $v(x) = 0$. When x is not critical, let R be the ray originating at x and shooting in the direction $x - r(x)$. Let z be the first point on R where $r(z)$ is different from $r(x)$. If z does not exist, replace it by the point p_∞ at infinity. Then, for $t \in [0, \|z - x\|]$,

$$\phi(t, x) = x + t \frac{x - r(x)}{\|x - r(x)\|}.$$

When $t > \|z - x\|$ the flow is

$$\phi(t, x) = \phi(t - \|z - x\| + \|z - x\|, x)$$
$$= \phi(t - \|z - x\|, \phi(\|z - x\|, x)).$$

It can be shown that ϕ has the following properties as in the smooth case:

(i) ϕ is well defined on $\mathbb{R}^+ \times \mathbb{R}^3$
(ii) $\phi(0, x) = x$
(iii) $\phi(t, \phi(s, x)) = \phi(t + s, x)$.

The definition of $\phi(t, x)$ is valid only for positive t. In the discrete case, it may happen that flows overlap. As a result, for a point x there may not be a unique flow curve for negative t. This makes the definition of a flow curve a little more difficult. An open curve $\gamma : \mathbb{R} \to \mathbb{R}^3$ is a *flow curve* originating at a critical point c if the following holds. For any $\epsilon > 0$, there is a point $y \in B_{c,\epsilon}$ so that $\phi(t, y)$ is contained in γ. The critical point $\lim_{t \to \infty} \phi(t, y)$ is called the destination of the flow curve γ.

Our definition implies that the closure of a flow curve is a piecewise linear curve starting and ending at critical points. Each line segment of this flow curve is along the direction determined by any point on the segment and its driver. The flow curve changes the direction precisely at the points where driver changes

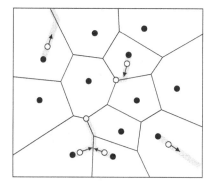

Figure 10.4. Some subsets of the flow curves induced by a set of points in $\mathbb{R}^2$. Flow curves originating at two bottom-most points merge and reach a Voronoi vertex which is a maximum after changing directions twice.

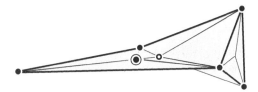

Figure 10.5. An example of an index 2 saddle point (doubly circled) whose stable manifold contains a Voronoi vertex (hollow circle). The points flowing to this Voronoi vertex constitute a three-dimensional region. So, the stable manifold contains both two- and three-dimensional parts. Solid circles are minima, that is, points from P.

(see Figure 10.4). Flow curves may overlap but never cross each other. Also, the Flow Lemma 10.1 implies that, once they overlap they remain so. This is because at each regular point, there is a unique direction along which v is defined. We can now talk about the stable manifolds of the critical points of d. For reconstruction, we will use stable manifolds in Section 10.3. In the sequel, we describe several properties related to the stable manifolds. The readers should observe that they also hold for unstable ones with appropriate modifications.

Just as in the smooth case we look into the regions whose points flow into a critical point of d. Recall that the critical points of d are the fixed points of ϕ. Let c be a critical point of d which means c belongs to the convex hull $H(c)$. The dimension of $H(c)$ is the index of c. The stable manifold $S(c)$ of c is again defined as the space of c and all flow curves with destination c. Let c have index j. We expect that $S(c)$ is j-dimensional. However, it may happen that $S(c)$ has points with neighborhoods homeomorphic to $\mathbb{R}^k$ where $k > j$, (see Figure 10.5). This is attributed to certain kind of nondegeneracies which we eliminate for simpler discussions.

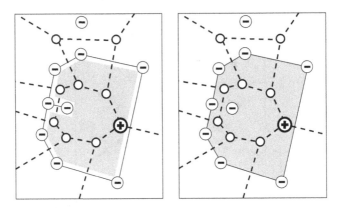

Figure 10.6. The stable manifold $S(c)$ where c is a maximum (marked as $\oplus$) is shaded on the left and $S^*(c)$ is shown on the right. The points of P are minima (marked as $\ominus$). Voronoi vertices are hollow circles.

Nondegeneracy Assumption

For any critical point c, $S(c)$ has no points with k-dimensional neighborhood where $k > j$, the index of c.

We will compute the closures of $S(c)$ in $\mathbb{R}^3$ which we denote as $S^*(c)$. We call $S^*(c)$ the *closed stable manifold* of c. Figure 10.6 illustrates the effect of taking these closures.

10.2.3 Relations to Voronoi/Delaunay Diagrams

The critical points of the distance function d and their stable manifolds associated with the discrete flow are intimately related to the Voronoi and Delaunay diagrams. This enables us to compute them from these diagrams.

Lemma 10.2 (Driver). *Let $x \in \mathbb{R}^3$ be any point and μ be the lowest dimensional Voronoi face in* Vor P *containing x. The driver $r(x)$ is the closest point to x on the Delaunay simplex dual to μ.*

Proof. It follows from the definitions that each point $p \in A(x)$ has x in V_p. This means $\mu = \bigcap_{p \in A(x)} V_p$. Also, Conv $A(x) = H(x)$ is the Delaunay simplex dual to μ by definition. The driver $r(x)$ is the closest point to x in $H(x) =$ dual μ. ∎

The following lemma is key in identifying the critical points and their stable manifolds.

Lemma 10.3 (Critical Point). *A point x is critical for the function d if and only if there is a Voronoi face $\mu \in$ Vor P and its dual Delaunay simplex $\sigma \in$ Del P so that $x = \sigma \cap \mu$. Also, the index of x is the dimension of σ.*

Proof. If $x = \sigma \cap \mu$, we have $x \in \mu$. For each point $x \in \mu$, $\sigma = $ dual $\mu \subseteq H(x)$. Since $x \in \sigma \subseteq H(x)$, x is critical by definition.

To show the other direction assume that x is critical and μ be the lowest dimensional Voronoi face containing x. By definition of critical points, $x \in H(x)$. Also, by definition, $H(x)$ is the dual Delaunay simplex σ of μ. Therefore, $x \in \sigma \cap \mu$.

The index of x is the dimension of $H(x) = \sigma$. ■

We can make the following observations about the stable manifolds of different types of critical points.

Index 0 *Critical Points*

These are the points of P which are local minima of the distance function d. They can also be thought of as intersections among Voronoi cells and their dual Delaunay vertices. The stable manifolds of these points are the points themselves.

Index 1 *Critical Points*

These are the critical points where a Delaunay edge intersects its dual Voronoi face. The interior of the Delaunay edge is the stable manifold of the corresponding critical point. These types of critical points are also called *saddles* of index 1. Recall that the Delaunay edges that intersect their dual Voronoi face (facet in three dimensions) are called Gabriel edges. Therefore, the closed stable manifolds of index 1 saddles are comprised of the Gabriel graph.

Index 2 *Critical Points*

These critical points are also called index 2 *saddles*. These are the points where a Delaunay triangle intersects its dual Voronoi edge. The stable manifold of such a saddle point is a piecewise linear surface bounded by the stable manifolds of the index 1 saddles together with the minima which are nothing but Gabriel edges. The stable manifolds of index 2 saddles play a vital role in the surface reconstruction procedure described in Section 10.3.

Index 3 *Critical Points*

These are the maxima of d. They are the Voronoi vertices contained in their dual Delaunay tetrahedra. The stable manifolds of these maxima are the

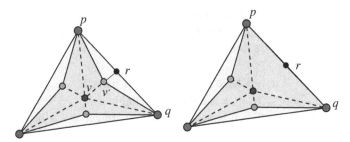

Figure 10.7. Construction of $S^*(c)$ when $v = c$. In the left picture pq is not Gabriel. In the right picture, pq is Gabriel.

three-dimensional cells bounded by the stable manifolds of index 2 saddles and their boundaries.

10.3 Reconstruction with Flow Complex

The surface reconstruction that we are about to describe uses the closed stable manifolds of the index 2 saddles. These stable manifolds are simplicial 2-complexes which decompose $\mathbb{R}^3$ into chambers, the stable manifolds of the maxima. This simplicial 2-complex is called the *flow complex* for P. The closed stable manifolds of index 2 saddles are best described procedurally which also leads to an algorithm to compute them.

10.3.1 Flow Complex Construction

Let c be an index 2 saddle. We will build $S^*(c)$ incrementally. At any generic step, it is a simplicial 2-complex where the vertices are points from P, the midpoints of the Gabriel edges, and some other points on the Voronoi edges. The boundary of $S^*(c)$ lies on the Gabriel edges. Let v be any vertex on the boundary of the 2-complex constructed so far where v is on a Voronoi edge e. Assuming general positions, e has three Voronoi facets incident on it. For each such facet μ, one or two triangles with its edges and vertices are added to the complex. Let $pq = \text{dual } \mu$ be the dual Delaunay edge of μ. Let r be the midpoint of the edge pq. If pq is a Gabriel edge, add the triangle pvq to $S^*(c)$, see the picture on right in Figure 10.7. Otherwise, the driver of the interior points of μ is r. In that case let v' be the point where the ray from r to v intersects μ for the first time. Add the triangles pvv' and qvv' with their edges and vertices to the 2-complex $S^*(c)$. See the picture on left in Figure 10.7. The process goes on as long as there is a point v on the boundary of the constructed

2-complex which is on a Voronoi edge. The above construction of $S^*(c)$ starts with $v = c$ and the Voronoi edge e containing c.

FLOWCOMPLEX(P)

```
1   T:=∅;
2   compute Vor P and Del P;
3   compute the set C of index 2 saddles;
4   for each c ∈ C do
5       σ:= Delaunay triangle containing c;
6       for each Delaunay edge e incident to σ do
7           push (c, e) into stack S;
8       endfor
9       while S ≠ ∅ do
10          (v, e):= pop S;
11          mark e processed;
12          p, q:= endpoints of e;
13          if e contains a saddle of index 1
14              T:=T ∪ {pvq};
15          else
16              μ:= dual e;
17              r:= driver of the interior of μ;
18              v':= the first point r⃗v intersects μ;
19              T:= T ∪ {vv'p, vv'q};
20              σ':= Delaunay triangle dual to the Voronoi edge containing v';
21              for each edge e' ≠ e incident to σ' do
22                  if (e' not processed) push (v', e') into S;
23              endfor
24          endif
25      endwhile
26  endfor
27  output Fl P:= 2-complex made by T.
```

10.3.2 Merging

The flow complex Fl P decomposes $\mathbb{R}^3$ into cells which are the closed stable manifolds of the maxima including the maximum p_∞ at infinity. We merge these cells in order to get a manifold surface.

We know that the closed stable manifolds have recursive structures in the sense that a closed stable manifold of index j critical point has the closed stable manifolds of the index $j - 1$ critical points on its boundary. We use this recursive structure of closed stable manifolds for merging. Let a and b be two maxima where $S^*(a)$ and $S^*(b)$ share a closed stable manifold $S^*(c)$ of an index 2 saddle. Merging a and b means to remove $S^*(c)$ from the flow complex Fl P. Of course it is not appropriate to merge maxima in arbitrary order nor does it make sense to merge every pair of adjacent maxima.

The order in which the pairs of maxima are merged is determined as follows. Let a and b be a pair with $S^*(c)$ on the common boundary of $S^*(a)$ and $S^*(b)$. Associate the value $\max\{d(a) - d(c), d(b) - d(c)\}$ with the pair (a, b) as its weight. The weight of a pair signifies how deep the maxima are relative to the boundary shared by their closed stable manifolds. Deep maxima capture the shape represented by P more significantly. Therefore, the merging process merges the pairs of maxima in the increasing order of their weights up to a threshold. The 2-complex resulting from the merging process is output. Clearly, this reconstruction depends on the user supplied threshold. The choice of a threshold is not easy in practice. Heuristics such as enforcing a topological disk neighborhood for each sample point while eroding the flow complex may be used to improve the output quality.

10.3.3 Critical Point Separation

The difficulty in merging the cells in the flow complex can be bypassed with a different approach that exploits the *separation* property of the critical points. This property says that the critical points are of two categories, ones that stay near the surface and the other ones that stay near the medial axis. This property holds when the sample P is sufficiently dense for a surface Σ. As before, we will assume Σ is compact, connected, C^2-smooth, and without boundary. Let M denote its medial axis.

Recall that, for a point $x \in \mathbb{R}^3 \setminus M$, $\tilde{x}$ denotes its closest point in Σ. Consider the medial ball at $\tilde{x}$ on the side of Σ as x is. Let $\rho(x)$ and $m(x)$ be the radius and the center of this medial ball. The following lemma states the separation property of the critical points. We will skip the proof (Exercise 5).

Lemma 10.4 (Separation). *Let d be the distance function defined for a ε-sample P of Σ where $\varepsilon \leq \frac{1}{3}$. A point $x \in \mathbb{R}^3 \setminus M$ is critical for d only if $\|x - \tilde{x}\| \leq \varepsilon^2 f(\tilde{x})$ or $\|x - m(x)\| \leq 2\varepsilon\rho(x)$.*

Motivated by the Separation Lemma 10.4, we call a critical point c of d *surface critical* if $\|c - \tilde{c}\| \leq \varepsilon^2 f(\tilde{c})$ and *medial axis critical* otherwise. Since a medial axis critical point c is far away from the surface, the vector $\overrightarrow{pc}$ from its closest sample point p makes a small angle with the normal $\mathbf{n}_p$ (Normal

Lemma 3.2) and hence with the pole vector $\mathbf{v}_p$. On the other hand, a surface critical point c being close to the surface makes the vector $\overrightarrow{pc}$ almost parallel to the surface (Exercise 5). This becomes the basis of the algorithm for separating the two types of the critical points.

Lemma 10.5 (Angle Separation). *Let c be a critical point of d and $p \in P$ be a sample point closest to c. For $\varepsilon \leq 0.1$, the angle $\angle_a(\overrightarrow{pc}, \mathbf{v}_p)$ is at least $75.5°$ if c is surface critical and is at most $28°$ if c is medial axis critical.*

The Angle Separation Lemma 10.5 motivates the following algorithm.

SEPARATE(Vor P,C)
1 for each $p \in P$ do
2   for all critical points $c \in C$ in V_p do
3   if $\angle_a(\overrightarrow{pc}, \mathbf{v}_p) < \frac{\pi}{4}$
4   label c surface critical;
5   else
6   label c medial axis critical;
7   endif
8   endfor
9 endfor.

Once the critical points are separated, one can take the closed stable manifolds of the medial axis critical points and produce the boundary of their union. Of course, one has to differentiate the critical points residing near the *inner* medial axis from those near the *outer* one. The boundary of $\bigcup S^*(c)$ approximates the surface where c is taken over any one of these two classes. We use a union-find data structure U on the set of medial axis critical points to collect either all inner medial axis critical points or the outer ones. Suppose c is a maximum near the inner medial axis. The boundary of $S^*(c)$ has the stable manifolds of index 1 and index 2 saddles. If any of these saddles are medial axis critical, we collect them in the same group using the union-find data structure.

The routine CRITSEP returns all outer medial axis critical points.

CRITSEP(Vor P)
1 compute the set of critical points C;
2 SEPARATE(Vor P, C);
3 let C_M be the set of medial axis critical points including p_∞;
4 initialize a union-find data structure U with all $c \in C_M$;
5 for each $c \in C_M$ do

```
6    for all c' ∈ (bd S*(c)) ∩ C_M do
7        U.union(c, c');
8    endfor
9    endfor
10   return the component of the union containing p_∞.
```

Once all outer medial axis critical points are collected, one can output the boundary of the union of their closed stable manifolds as the output surface.

SMRECON(P)

1   compute Vor P;

2   C:=CRITSEP(Vor P);

3   output bd $(\bigcup_{c \in C} S^*(c))$.

It can be proved that the output of SMRECON is homeomorphic to Σ if P is sufficiently dense and is locally uniform (Exercise 6).

10.4 Reconstruction with a Delaunay Subcomplex

The flow complex computes the stable manifolds for the index 2 saddles exactly from the Delaunay triangulation. Since these stable manifolds are not necessarily a subcomplex of the Delaunay triangulation, the output surface triangles are not necessarily Delaunay. The exact complexity of the flow complex is not known. Certainly, it introduces extra points in the output other than the input ones. However, it is not clear if the number of extra vertices could be too many. Also, computing the triangles for the index 2 saddles is somewhat cumbersome. From a practical viewpoint it is much simpler and sometimes desirable to compute the output as a Delaunay subcomplex. In this section we describe an algorithm called WRAP that computes the output surface as a Delaunay subcomplex. The Morse theoretic framework used for the flow complex remains the same though some different interpretations are needed.

10.4.1 Distance from Delaunay Balls

We will use a different distance function in this section. A Delaunay ball $B_{c,r}$ is treated as a weighted point $\hat{c} = (c, r)$. Recall from Section 6.1 that the power distance of a point x from a weighted point $\hat{c}$ is

$$\pi(x, \hat{c}) = \|x - c\|^2 - r^2.$$

For a point set $P \subset \mathbb{R}^3$, let C denote the centers of the Delaunay balls in Del P and $\hat{C}$ denote the set of weighted points corresponding to these Delaunay balls.

These Delaunay balls also include the ones that circumscribe the infinite tetrahedra in Del P. These infinite tetrahedra are formed by a convex hull triangle together with the point p_∞. Obviously, their centers are at infinity and they have infinite radii. Define a distance function $g : \mathbb{R}^3 \to \mathbb{R}$ as

$$g(x) = \min_{\hat{c} \in \hat{C}} \pi(x, \hat{c}).$$

Recall from Section 6.1 that the power diagram Pow $\hat{C}$ is the decomposition of $\mathbb{R}^3$ into cells and their faces determined by the power distance. When the weighted points are the centers of the Delaunay balls with their radii as weights, the power diagram coincides with the Delaunay triangulation. This means Pow $\hat{C}$ = Del P (Exercise 9). So, if a point $x \in \mathbb{R}^3$ lies in a Delaunay tetrahedron $\sigma \in$ Del P, $g(x)$ is exactly equal to $\pi(x, \hat{c})$ where c is the center of the Delaunay ball of σ. The distance function g is continuous but not smooth. The nonsmoothness occurs at the triangle, edges, and vertices of the Delaunay tetrahedra. Notice that the minima of this distance function occur at the centers of the Delaunay balls which are the Voronoi vertices. Not all Voronoi vertices but only the ones contained in their dual Delaunay tetrahedra are minima. The function g is negative everywhere except at the Delaunay vertices, that is, at the points of P. The points of P reside on the boundary of the Delaunay balls and thus have the value of g as zero. They become the maxima of the distance function g.

Similar to the distance function d defined in Section 10.2, we can introduce a flow induced by g. This calls for the notion of driver for each point under the function g.

Definition 10.3. *For every point $x \in \mathbb{R}^3$, let $H(x)$ be the convex hull of the points in C with the minimum power distance to x. The driver $r(x)$ of x is defined as the point in $H(x)$ closest to x. The point x is* critical *if $x \in H(x)$ and is* regular *otherwise.*

We have a counterpart of the Flow Lemma 10.1 for g.

Lemma 10.6 (Second Flow Lemma). *For any regular point $x \in \mathbb{R}^3$ the steepest ascent of g at x is in the direction of $x - r(x)$.*

We have a vector field $v : \mathbb{R}^3 \to \mathbb{R}^3$ as before defined by the steepest ascent direction of g and a flow $\phi : \mathbb{R}^+ \times \mathbb{R}^3 \to \mathbb{R}^3$ induced by it. Again, the flow curves derived from ϕ are piecewise linear curves and these flow curves have the property that they are either disjoint or overlap, but they never cross each other. Also, the Second Flow Lemma 10.6 implies that, once they join together

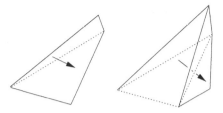

Figure 10.8. The dotted simplex is σ, an edge on the left, and a triangle on the right. The black arrow shows the flow direction from predecessor τ toward the successor ξ of σ.

they remain so. To be consistent with the smooth case we will denote a flow curve passing through a point x as ϕ_x.

The minima of g occur at a subset of Voronoi vertices. We are interested in the unstable manifold of these minima. In particular, we compute an approximation of the closed unstable manifold $U^*(p_\infty) = \text{Cl}\, U(p_\infty)$ of the minimum p_∞. The boundary of this approximation is the reconstructed surface. In general, this boundary is a subcomplex of Del P which we refer as the *wrap complex*.

10.4.2 Classifying and Ordering Simplices

The flow curves lead to an acyclic relation over the set of Delaunay simplices. The wrap complex is constructed by collapsing simplices following the order induced by this relation.

Flow Relation

Assume a dummy simplex σ_∞ that represents the outside, or the complement of Conv P. It replaces all infinite tetrahedra formed by the convex hull triangles and the point p_∞. All these tetrahedra have similar flow behavior and can be treated uniformly. Let $D = \text{Del}\, P \cup \{\sigma_\infty\}$. The flow relation $\prec$ on D mimics the behavior of the flow curves.

Definition 10.4. *We say $\tau \prec \sigma \prec \xi$ if σ is a proper face of τ and of ξ and there is a point $x \in \text{Int}\,\sigma$ with ϕ_x passing from $\text{Int}\,\tau$ through x to $\text{Int}\,\xi$. We refer this as τ precedes σ and σ precedes ξ. The condition implies that every neighborhood of x contains a nonempty subset of $\phi_x \cap \text{Int}\,\tau$ and a nonempty subset of $\phi_x \cap \text{Int}\,\xi$. We call τ a* predecessor *and ξ a* successor *of σ.*

Notice that predecessor successor relations are defined for σ. It is not true that if τ is a predecessor (successor) of σ, then σ is a successor (predecessor) of τ.

Figure 10.8 illustrates the predecessor and successor relation for an edge and a triangle. Based on the relation $\prec$ we also define the *descendents* and *ancestors*

Figure 10.9. Different types of flow through edges.

of a simplex. Basically, the descendents of a simplex are a set of simplices that can be reached from σ by transitive closure of $\prec$. The ancestors are the simplices which can reach σ by transitive closure of $\prec$.

Definition 10.5. *For a simplex σ, the descendents, Des σ, are defined as*

$$\text{Des}\,\sigma = \{\sigma\} \cup \bigcup_{\sigma \prec \xi} \text{Des}\,\xi.$$

The ancestors, Anc σ, are defined as

$$\text{Anc}\,\sigma = \{\sigma\} \cup \bigcup_{\tau \prec \sigma} \text{Anc}\,\tau.$$

The flow curves intersect the Delaunay simplices either in intervals or in single points. Any point x in the interior of a Delaunay simplex σ has the Voronoi face dual σ as $H(x)$. Therefore, all interior points in σ have the same driver $r(x)$. This means that the intersections of all flow curves with the interior of a Delaunay simplex are similar, that is, either all of them are points, or all of them are intervals. According to the pattern of these intersections and associated flows we classify the Delaunay simplices into three categories. The three categories are mutually exclusive and exhaust all possible Delaunay simplices.

Centered Simplices

A simplex $\sigma \in$ Del P is *centered* if and only if its interior intersects the interior of the dual Voronoi face $\mu = $ dual σ. The intersection point $y = $ Int $\sigma \cap$ Int μ is a critical point and its index is the dimension of μ. The flow curves intersecting centered simplices have the property that the portion of ϕ_x succeeding $x \in$ Int σ is contained in Int σ. Consequently, centered simplices do not have any predecessor or successor. The leftmost edge of Figure 10.9 and the leftmost triangle in Figure 10.10 are centered.

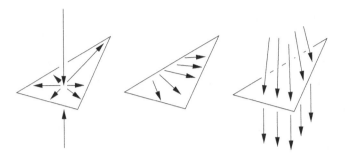

Figure 10.10. Different flow types for triangles.

Confident Simplices

A simplex $\sigma \in \text{Del } P$ is *confident* if and only if it is not centered and its affine hull intersects the interior of $\mu = \text{dual } \sigma$. Confident simplices are similar to the centered ones, in the sense that they would be centered if they covered large enough portion of their affine hulls. The neighborhoods of the flow curves succeeding any interior point of a confident simplex remain in the interior of the simplex. The edge in the middle of Figure 10.9 and the middle triangle in Figure 10.10 are confident.

All simplices that have a confident simplex σ as a predecessor or successor are faces of σ. We call them predecessor and successor faces of σ. The successor faces can be determined as follows. Let $z = \text{aff } \sigma \cap \text{Int } \mu$. The point z is the center of the smallest ball circumscribing σ. Let $k = \dim \sigma$. Consider each $(k - 1)$-dimensional face ξ of σ. The aff ξ either separates z from the interior of σ or both z and Int σ lie on the same side of aff ξ. We assume here the general positions which preclude z lying on aff ξ. A face ξ of σ is a predecessor if and only if the affine hulls of all $(k - 1)$-dimensional faces containing ξ separate z from the interior of σ. Each confident simplex has a unique lowest dimensional predecessor face υ contained in all predecessor faces of σ.

Equivocal Simplices

A simplex $\sigma \in \text{Del } P$ is *equivocal* if and only if its affine hull does not intersect the interior of the dual Voronoi face $\mu = \text{dual } \sigma$. The flow curves intersect equivocal simplices in a single point. The rightmost edge of Figure 10.9 and the rightmost triangle in Figure 10.10 are equivocal.

All predecessors and successors of an equivocal simplex σ are cofaces of σ. They are either centered or confident. An equivocal simplex can have more than one predecessors but only one successor.

Lemma 10.7 (Successor Lemma). *Each equivocal simplex has exactly one successor.*

Proof. Let σ be an equivocal simplex and $x \in \text{Int}\,\sigma$. Consider the flow curves passing through x. Because of the Second Flow Lemma 10.6, we know that all flow curves leave x along the same direction. Since after x all flow curves are the same in a sufficiently small neighborhood, consider the flow curve ϕ_x and a small portion immediately succeeding x. This portion is a line segment contained in the interior of a simplex ξ where $\sigma \prec \xi$. The simplex ξ is confident. Every flow curve that intersects ξ does so in a portion of a line passing through the center z of the smallest ball circumscribing ξ. It follows that for each point $x \in \sigma$, a sufficiently small portion of ϕ_x succeeding x lies on the line joining x and z and therefore in $\text{Int}\,\xi$. This implies that each x identifies the same simplex ξ which becomes the only successor of σ. ∎

The successor ξ of σ can be computed as follows. Let μ be the dual Voronoi face of σ. The closest point of μ to ξ is z which resides on the boundary of μ. Testing over all boundary Voronoi faces of μ, the Voronoi face μ' containing z can be determined. The successor ξ is the dual Delaunay simplex of μ'.

10.4.3 Reconstruction

The basic construction of the WRAP algorithm computes a subcomplex $\mathcal{X}$ from Del P whose boundary is output as the wrap surface $\mathcal{W}$. In general this surface is homotopy equivalent to $\mathbb{S}^2$ though other topologies can be accommodated with some postprocessing. It is constructed by peeling away simplices dictated by the flow relation.

A *source* is a simplex $\sigma \in$ Del P without any predecessor in the flow relation. The sources are exactly the centered simplices including σ_∞. We are interested in computing an approximation of the closed unstable manifold of p_∞. This approximation is obtained by following the flow relation. A very important property of the flow relation is that it is acyclic. A *cycle* is a sequence of simplices $\sigma_1 \prec \sigma_2 \prec \cdots \prec \sigma_\ell$, with $\ell \geq 3$ and $\sigma_1 = \sigma_\ell$.

Lemma 10.8 (Acyclicity). *The flow relation $\prec$ is acyclic.*

Proof. Let $\sigma_i \in$ Del P and $B_i = B_{c_i,r_i}$ be the smallest empty ball circumscribing σ_i. Consider $\sigma_i \prec \sigma_j$. Clearly, σ_j cannot be centered. If σ_j is confident then σ_i is equivocal and we have $B_i = B_j$ and $\dim \sigma_i < \dim \sigma_j$. If σ_j is equivocal then σ_i is centered or confident. Hence, $c_i \neq c_j$ and $r_i^2 > r_j^2$. We assign to each σ_i

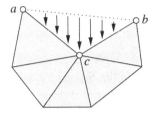

Figure 10.11. Collapsing an edge triangle pair.

the pair $(r_i^2, -\dim \sigma_i)$. The pairs decrease lexicographically along the chain preventing a cycle in it.   ∎

The sources and their descendent sets are analogous to the critical points and their unstable manifolds respectively. However, they are not exactly same. Approximations of the unstable manifolds with Delaunay subcomplexes face a difficulty with simplices that have more than one predecessor. Their existence causes possible overlap of the descendent sets. This is in contrast with the unstable manifolds of smooth functions which are necessarily disjoint though their closures may overlap. Equivocal edges may have more than one predecessor. Similarly, confident tetrahedra may have more than one predecessor face. Despite the possibility of overlapping descendent sets, a useful containment property for unstable manifolds holds. Let σ and τ be the centered simplices with the critical points $y \in \mathrm{Int}\,\sigma$ and $z \in \mathrm{Int}\,\tau$.

Lemma 10.9 (Descendent). $U(z) \subseteq \mathrm{Cl}\,U(y)$ *implies* $\mathrm{Des}\,\tau \subseteq \mathrm{Cl}\,\mathrm{Des}\,\sigma$.

The set $\mathcal{X}$ whose boundary is output as the wrapping surface is constructed from $\mathrm{Del}\,P$ by taking out a conservative subset of $\mathrm{Des}\,\sigma_\infty$. The simplices in $\mathrm{Des}\,\sigma_\infty$ which have more than one predecessor are eliminated to define the conservative descendent subset. By looking at the complement, we can say that $\mathcal{X}$ is exactly equal to the union of the descendent sets of all sources except that of σ_∞. In other words, the wrapping surface $\mathcal{W}$ is the boundary of

$$\mathcal{X} = \bigcup_{\text{sources } \sigma \neq \sigma_\infty} \mathrm{Des}\,\sigma.$$

10.4.4 Algorithm

The algorithm for constructing $\mathcal{W}$ removes simplices from $\mathrm{Del}\,P$ using collapses (see Figure 10.11). Let $\mathcal{K}$ be a simplicial complex and let σ be a simplex with exactly one proper coface $\tau \in \mathcal{K}$. The removal of the pair (σ, τ) from

$\mathcal{K}$ is called an *elementary collapse*. It is known that the underlying space of $\mathcal{K}_1 = \mathcal{K} \setminus \{\sigma, \tau\}$ is homotopy equivalent to that of $\mathcal{K}$.

An ℓ-simplex σ is *free* if there is a k-simplex τ in $\mathcal{K}$ with $k > \ell$ so that all cofaces of σ are faces of τ. The collapses shrink a subcomplex $\mathcal{Y}$ starting from the full Delaunay complex Del P. Call a simplex σ *collapsible* if

(i) $\sigma \in \mathcal{Y}$ is free and equivocal and
(ii) τ is the highest dimensional coface of σ in $\mathcal{Y}$ where $\sigma \prec \tau$ and σ is the lowest dimensional predecessor face of τ.

A *free collapse* is an operation where a collapsible simplex is removed together with its cofaces. Observe that a free collapse can be implemented with a sequence of elementary collapses. The following algorithm COLLAPSE carries out a sequence of free collapses on a given simplicial complex $\mathcal{Y} \subseteq$ Del P as long as there are collapsible simplices.

COLLAPSE $(\mathcal{Y}, \sigma)$
```
 1   for each face τ of σ do
 2       push τ into stack S;
 3   endfor
 4   while S ≠ ∅ do
 5       σ := pop S;
 6       if σ collapsible
 7           for each coface ξ of σ do
 8               𝒴 := 𝒴 \ ξ;
 9           endfor
10           Let τ be the highest dimensional coface of σ;
11           for each face ξ of τ that is not a coface of σ do
12               push ξ into S;
13           endfor
14       endif
15   endwhile
16   return 𝒴.
```

The algorithm WRAP uses the COLLAPSE routine on the Delaunay triangulation Del P. It starts the collapse with the faces of σ_∞ which are the simplices on the convex hull of P.

WRAP(P)
```
 1   compute Del P;
 2   output COLLAPSE(Del P, σ∞).
```

The following theorem asserts that no matter which free collapses are chosen among many, the final output $\mathcal{Y}$ of WRAP is actually $\mathcal{X}$.

Theorem 10.1. WRAP *outputs* $\mathcal{X}$.

The output $\mathcal{X}$ of WRAP is obtained from the Delaunay complex Del P through elementary collapses. Since each elementary collapse maintains the homotopy type, the underlying space $|\mathcal{X}|$ of $\mathcal{X}$ is homotopy equivalent to that of Del P and hence to a ball. Notice that $|\mathcal{X}|$ may not be homeomorphic to a three-dimensional ball though is homotopy equivalent to it. In case $|\mathcal{X}|$ is a ball, its boundary is homeomorphic to a sphere. This means that the basic construction of WRAP can reconstruct surfaces that are topologically 2-spheres. To accommodate other topologies, the basic construction needs some modifications.

The idea is to collapse simplices not only from the descendent set of σ_∞ but also from the descendent sets of other significant sources. For a source σ define its size $|\sigma|$ by the value $|g(y)|$ where $y \in \sigma$ is the corresponding critical point of the centered simplex σ. By definition, $g(y)$ is the negated squared radius of the diametric ball of σ. It is intuitive that large sizes of sources indicate the space through which the wrapping surface should be pushed. Keeping this in mind, we sort the sources in order of decreasing size $|\sigma_0| > |\sigma_1| > \cdots > |\sigma_m|$, where $\sigma_0 = \sigma_\infty$ and thus $|\sigma_0| = \infty$. For each index $0 \le j \le m$, define

$$\mathcal{X}_j = \bigcup_{i=j+1}^{m} \text{Cl Des } \sigma_i.$$

Define $\mathcal{W}_j = \text{bd } |\mathcal{X}_j|$. The $\mathcal{X}_j$ form a nested sequence of subcomplexes

$$\mathcal{X} = \mathcal{X}_0 \supseteq \mathcal{X}_1 \supseteq \cdots \supseteq \mathcal{X}_m = \emptyset.$$

Correspondingly, the $\mathcal{W}_j$ form a nested sequence of wrapping surfaces. The operation that removes a principal simplex from a simplicial complex $\mathcal{K}$ is called *deletion*. In contrast to a collapse, a deletion changes the homotopy type of $|\mathcal{K}|$. A particular $\mathcal{X}_j$ is constructed from Del P by a series of deletions and collapses. A source is deleted which is followed by a sequence of collapses taking out all simplices in the descendent set of the source. The complex $\mathcal{X}_j$ is computed by repeating these two operations $j + 1$ times, once for each of $\sigma_0, \sigma_1, \ldots, \sigma_j$.

Alternatively, one may resort to the separation property of the critical points as in Subsection 10.3.3. The distance functions d and g have the same set of critical points (Exercise 11). Therefore, we can use CRITSEP routine to obtain the set of outer medial axis critical points. All sources (Voronoi vertices) in this filtered set can trigger a deletion of its dual tetrahedron and a series of collapse thereafter.

MODIFIEDWRAP(P)

1   C:=CRITSEP(P);
2   $\mathcal{Y}$:=Del P;
3   sort sources containing $c \in C$ in decreasing order of size;
4   for each source σ in the sorted order
5     $\mathcal{Y}$:= COLLAPSE($\mathcal{Y}, \sigma$);
6   endfor
7   output $\mathcal{Y}$.

10.5 Notes and Exercises

Morse theory is a widely studied subject in mathematics. Milnor [70] and Guillemin and Pollack [60] are two standard books on the subject. The flow induced by distance functions as described in this chapter is relatively new and can be found in Grove [59]. The connection between Morse theory and the Voronoi diagrams was discovered by Edelsbrunner, Facello, and Liang [45] and Siersma [78] in different contexts.

Morse theoretic reconstruction was first discovered by Edelsbrunner in 1995 though it was not published until 2003 [44] due to propriety rights. In this work Edelsbrunner proposed the WRAP algorithm as described in Section 10.4. To circumvent the problem of nonsmooth vector field, he used the fact that a nonsmooth vector field can be approximated by a smooth one with arbitrary precision. Here we used the concept of driver introduced by Giesen and John [55, 56]. They used drivers to apply the idea of the flow in Grove [59] for distance functions induced by a set of discrete points. The flow complex computation as described in Section 10.3 is taken from this work [56]. The separation of critical points as described in Subsection 10.3.3 was discovered by Dey, Giesen, Ramos, and Sadri [32]. The Separation Lemma 10.4 and the Angle Separation Lemma 10.5 were proved in this paper. We took the leverage of this result to introduce MODIFIEDWRAP.

The idea of computing flow and their approximations through Delaunay subcomplexes was further investigated by Dey, Giesen, and Goswami [31] for shape segmentation and shape matching. The Flow Lemma 10.1 and a preliminary proof of it is included there.

Exercises

1. Let P be a set of points in $\mathbb{R}^2$. Characterize the flow complex Fl P when P is unweighted and weighted.
2. Consider the function d as used for the flow complex. Describe the unstable manifolds of the minima of this function.

3. Design an algorithm to compute the unstable manifolds of the index 2 critical points of d.

4. Consider the function d. Design an algorithm to compute the boundary of the stable manifold of p_∞. How should this boundary be modified to improve the reconstruction?

5. Prove the Separation Lemma 10.4 and the Angle Separation Lemma 10.5 [32].

6^h. Prove that the output of SMRECON is homeomorphic to Σ if P is locally uniform and is sufficiently dense [32].

7°. Prove or disprove 6 when P is a nonuniform sample.

8°. Determine the worst case optimal complexity of the flow complex.

9. Let $\hat{C}$ be the weighted points corresponding to the Delaunay balls in Del P. Show that Pow $\hat{C} = $ Del P.

10. Consider the function g used for the wrap complex. Describe the stable manifolds of the maxima of g.

11. Prove that the functions d and g have the same set of critical points.

12. Prove the Descendent Lemma 10.9 [44].

13. Give a proof of the Wrap Theorem 10.1 [44].

14°. Prove that the output of MODIFIEDWRAP is homeomorphic to Σ if the input P is sufficiently dense for Σ.

Bibliography

1. M. Alexa, J. Behr, D. Cohen-Or, S. Fleishman, D. Levin, and C. T. Silva. Point set surfaces. In *Proc. IEEE Visual.*, pp. 21–28, 2001.
2. E. Althaus. *Curve Reconstruction and Traveling Salesman Problem.* Ph.D. Thesis, Universität des Saarlandes, 2001.
3. E. Althaus and K. Mehlhorn. Traveling salesman-based curve reconstruction in polynomial time. *SIAM J. Comput.*, 31:27–66, 2002.
4. N. Amenta and M. Bern. Surface reconstruction by Voronoi filtering. *Discrete Comput. Geom.*, 22:481–504, 1999.
5. N. Amenta, M. Bern, and D. Eppstein. The crust and the β-skeleton: Combinatorial curve reconstruction. *Graph. Models Image Process.*, 60:125–135, 1998.
6. N. Amenta, S. Choi, T. K. Dey, and N. Leekha. A simple algorithm for homeomorphic surface reconstruction. *Int. J. Comput. Geom. Appl.*, 12:125–141, 2002.
7. N. Amenta, S. Choi, and R. K. Kolluri. The power crust, union of balls, and the medial axis transform. *Comput. Geom. Theory Appl.*, 19:127–153, 2001.
8. N. Amenta and Y. J. Kil. Defining point-set surfaces. In *Proc. ACM SIGGRAPH 2004*, pp. 264–270, 2004.
9. D. Attali. r-regular shape reconstruction from unorganized points. In *Proc. 13th Ann. Symp. Comput. Geom.*, pp. 248–253, 1997.
10. D. Attali, J.-D. Boissonnat, and A. Lieutier. Complexity of the Delaunay triangulation of points on surfaces: The smooth case. In *Proc. 19th Ann. Symp. Comput. Geom.*, pp. 201–210, 2003.
11. D. Avis and J. Horton. Remarks on the sphere of influence graph. In *Proc. Conf. Discrete Geom. Convexity*, J. E. Goodman et al. (eds.). *Ann. New York Acad. Sci.*, 440:323–327, 1985.
12. F. Bernardini and C. L. Bajaj. Sampling and reconstructing manifolds using α-shapes. In *Proc. 9th Can. Conf. Comput. Geom.*, pp. 193–198, 1997.
13. F. Bernardini, J. Mittleman, H. Rushmeier, C. T. Silva, and G. Taubin. The ball-pivoting algorithm for surface reconstruction. *IEEE Trans. Visual. Comput. Graph.*, 5:349–359, 1999.
14. H. Blum. A transformation for extracting new descriptor of shape. In *Models for the Perception of Speech and Visual Form*, W. Wathen-Dunn (ed.), MIT. Press, Cambridge, MA, pp. 362–380, 1967.
15. J.-D. Boissonnat. Geometric structures for three-dimensional shape representation. *ACM Trans. Graph.*, 3:266–286, 1984.

16. J.-D. Boissonnat and F. Cazals. Smooth surface reconstruction via natural neighbor interpolation of distance functions. In *Proc. 16th Ann. Symp. Comput. Geom.*, pp. 223–232, 2000.

17. J.-D. Boissonnat and B. Geiger. Three-dimensional reconstruction of complex shapes based on the Delaunay triangulation. In *Proc. Biomed. Image Process. Biomed. Visual.*, pp. 964–975, 1993.

18. J. C. Carr, R. K. Beatson, J. B. Cherrie, T. J. Mitchell, W. R. Fright, B. C. McCallum, and T. R. Evans. Reconstruction and representation of 3d objects with radial basis functions. In *Proc. ACM SIGGRAPH 2001*, pp. 67–76, 2001.

19. F. Chazal, D. Cohen-Steiner, and A. Lieutier. A sampling theory for compacts in Euclidean space. In *Proc. 22nd Ann. Symp. Comput. Geom.*, 2006.

20. F. Chazal and A. Lieutier. The λ-medial axis. *Graph. Models*, 67: 304–331, 2005.

21. F. Chazal and R. Soufflet. Stability and finiteness properties of medial axis and skeleton. *J. Control Dyn. Syst.*, 10:149–170, 2004.

22. S.-W. Cheng and T. K. Dey. Improved construction of Delaunay based contour surfaces. In *Proc. ACM Symp. Solid Model. Appl.*, pp. 322–323, 1999.

23. H.-L. Cheng, T. K. Dey, H. Edelsbrunner, and J. Sullivan. Dynamic skin triangulation. *Discrete Comput. Geom.*, 25:525–568, 2001.

24. L. P. Chew. Guaranteed-quality mesh generation for curved surfaces. In *Proc. 9th Ann. Symp. Comput. Geom.* pp. 274–280, 1993.

25. H. I. Choi, S. W. Choi, and H. P. Moon. Mathematical theory of medial axis transform. *Pac. J. Math.*, 181:57–88, 1997.

26. B. Curless and M. Levoy. A volumetric method for building complex models from range images. In *Proc. SIGGRAPH 96*, pp. 306–312, 1996.

27. L. H. de Figueiredo and J. de Miranda Gomes. Computational morphology of curves. *Vis. Comput.*, 11:105–112, 1995.

28. B. Delaunay. Sur la aphère vide. *Izv. Akad. Nauk SSSR, Otdelenie Mathematicheskii i Estestvennyka Nauk*, 7:793–800, 1934.

29. T. K. Dey, H. Edelsbrunner, and S. Guha. Computational topology. In *Advances in Discrete and Computational Geometry*, Contemporary Mathematics, B. Chazelle, E. Goodman, and R. Pollack (eds.), AMS, Providence, RI, 1998.

30. T. K. Dey and J. Giesen. Detecting undersampling in surface reconstruction. In *Proc. 17th Ann. Symp. Comput. Geom.*, pp. 257–263, 2001.

31. T. K. Dey, J. Giesen, and S. Goswami. Shape segmentation and matching with flow discretization. In *Proc. Workshop on Algorithms and Data Struct.*, LNCS 2748, pp. 25–36, 2003.

32. T. K. Dey, J. Giesen, E. A. Ramos, and B. Sadri. Critical points of the distance to an epsilon-sampling on a surface and flow-complex-based surface reconstruction. In *Proc. 21st Ann. Symp. Comput. Geom.*, pp. 218–227, 2005.

33. T. K. Dey and S. Goswami. Tight cocone: A water-tight surface reconstructor. *J. Comput. Inf. Sci. Eng.*, 3:302–307, 2003.

34. T. K. Dey and S. Goswami. Provable surface reconstruction from noisy samples. In *Proc. 20th Ann. Symp. Comput. Geom.*, pp. 330–339, 2004.

35. T. K. Dey, S. Goswami, and J. Sun. Extremal surface based projections converge and reconstruct with isotopy. Technical Report OSU-CISRC-4-05-TR25, Department of CSE, The Ohio State University, April 2005.

36. T. K. Dey and P. Kumar. A simple provable curve reconstruction algorithm. In *Proc. 10th Ann. ACM-SIAM Symp. Discrete Algorithms*, pp. 893–894, 1999.

37. T. K. Dey, G. Li, and J. Sun. Normal estimation for point clouds: a comparison study for a Voronoi based method. *Proc. Eurograph. Symp. Point-Based Graph.*, pp. 39–46, 2005.

38. T. K. Dey, K. Mehlhorn, and E. A. Ramos. Curve reconstruction: Connecting dots with good reason. *Comput. Geom. Theory Appl.*, 15:229–244, 2000.

39. T. K. Dey and J. Sun. Normal and feature approximations from noisy point clouds. Technical. Report OSU-CISRC-7/50-TR50, Department of CSE, The Ohio State University, July 2005.

40. T. K. Dey and J. Sun. An adaptive MLS surface for reconstruction with guarantees. In *Proc. Eurograph. Symp. Geom. Process.*, pp. 43–52, 2005.

41. T. K. Dey and R. Wenger. Fast reconstruction of curves with sharp corners. *Int. J. Comput. Geom. Appl.*, 12:353–400, 2002.

42. T. K. Dey and W. Zhao. Approximating the medial axis from the Voronoi diagram with a convergence guarantee. *Algorithmica*, 38:179–200, 2004.

43. H. Edelsbrunner. *Geometry and Topology for Mesh Generation*, Cambridge University Press, Cambridge, England, 2001.

44. H. Edelsbrunner. Surface reconstruction by wrapping finite point sets in space. In *Ricky Pollack and Eli Goodman Festschrift*, B. Aronov, S. Basu, J. Pach and M. Sharir (eds.), Springer-Verlag, New York, pp. 379–404, 2003.

45. H. Edelsbrunner, M. A. Facello, and J. Liang. On the definition and the construction of pockets in macromolecules. *Discrete Appl. Math.* 88:83–102, 1998.

46. H. Edelsbrunner, D. G. Kirkpatrick, and R. Seidel. On the shape of a set of points in the plane. *IEEE Trans. Inform. Theory*, 29:551–559, 1983.

47. H. Edelsbrunner and E. P. Mücke. Three-dimensional alpha shapes. *ACM Trans. Graph.*, 13:43–72, 1994.

48. H. Edelsbrunner and N. Shah. Triangulating topological spaces. *Int. J. Comput. Geom. Appl.*, 7:365–378, 1997.

49. J. Erickson. Nice point sets can have nasty Delaunay triangulations. *Discrete Comput. Geom.* 30:109–132, 2003.

50. S. Fortune. Voronoi diagrams and Delaunay triangulations. In *Handbook of Discrete and Computational Geometry*, J. E. Goodman and J. O'Rourke (eds.), (2nd edition), Chapman & Hall/CRC, New York, pp. 513–528, 2004.

51. H. Fuchs, Z. M. Kedem, and S. P. Uselton. Optimal surface reconstruction from planar contours. *Commun. ACM*, 20:693–702, 1977.

52. S. Funke and E. A. Ramos. Reconstructing curves with corners and endpoints. In *Proc. 12th Ann. ACM-SIAM Symp. Discrete Algorithms*, pp. 344–353, 2001.

53. S. Funke and E. A. Ramos. Smooth-surface reconstruction in near-linear time. In *13th ACM-SIAM Symp. Discrete Algorithms*, pp. 781–790, 2002.

54. J. Giesen. Curve reconstruction, the traveling salesman problem and Menger's theorem on length. *Discrete Comput. Geom.*, 24:577–603, 2000.

55. J. Giesen and M. John. Surface reconstruction based on a dynamical system. In *Proc. Eurographics 2002*, Vol. 21, No. 3, pp. 363–371, 2002.

56. J. Giesen and M. John. The flow complex: A data structure for geometric modeling. In *Proc. 14th Ann. ACM-SIAM Symp. Discrete Algorithms*, pp. 285–294, 2003.

57. C. Gitlin, J. O'Rourke, and V. Subramanian. On reconstruction of polyhedra from slices. *Int. J. Comput. Geom. Appl.*, 6:103–112, 1996.

58. C. Gold and J. Snoeyink. Crust and anti-crust: A one-step boundary and skeleton extraction algorithm. *Algorithmica*, 30:144–163, 2001.

59. K. Grove. Critical point theory for distance functions. *Proc. Symp. Pure Math.* 54(3): 357–385, 1993.

60. V. Guillemin and A. Pollack. *Differential Topology*, Prentice-Hall, New Jersey, 1974.

61. H. Hoppe, T. DeRose, T. Duchamp, J. McDonald, and W. Stützle. Surface reconstruction from unorganized points. In *Proc. SIGGRAPH 92*, pp. 71–78, 1992.

62. D. G. Kirkpatrick and J. D. Radke. A framework for computational morphology. In *Computational Geometry*, G. Toussaint (ed.), Elsevier, New York, pp. 217–248, 1985.

63. R. Kolluri. Provably good moving least squares. In *Proc. Ann. 16th ACM-SIAM Symp. Discrete Algorithms*, pp. 1008–1017, 2005.

64. R. Kolluri, J. R. Shewchuk, and J. F. O'Brien. Spectral surface reconstruction from noisy point clouds. In *Symp. Geom. Process.*, pp. 11–21, 2004.

65. D. Levin. Approximation power of moving least squares. *Math. Comp.* 67:1517–1531, 1998.

66. G. Matheron. Examples of topological properties of skeletons. In *Image Analysis and Mathematical Morphology, Vol. 2: Theoretical Advances*, J. Serra (ed.), Academic Press, London, pp. 217–238, 1988.

67. B. Mederos, N. Amenta, L. Velho, and H. de Figueiredo. Surface reconstruction from noisy point clouds. In *Proc. Eurograph. Symp. Geom. Process.*, pp. 53–62, 2005.

68. D. Meyers, S. Skinner, and K. Sloan. Surfaces from contours. *ACM Trans. Graph.*, 11:228–258, 1992.

69. N. Mitra, A. Nguyen, and L. Guibas. Estimating surface normals in noisy point cloud data. *Int. J. Comput. Geom. Appl.*, 14:261–276, 2004.

70. J. Milnor. *Morse Theory*, Princeton University Press, Princeton, NJ, 1963.

71. J. R. Munkres. *Topology, a First Course*, Prentice-Hall, Englewood Cliffs, NJ, 1975.

72. J. R. Munkres. *Elements of Algebraic Topology*, Addison-Wesley, New York, 1984.

73. Y. Ohtake, A. Belyaev, M. Alexa, G. Turk, and H.-P. Seidel. Multi-level partition of unity implicits. In *Proc. ACM SIGGRAPH 2003*, pp. 463–470, 2003.

74. A. Okabe, B. Boots, and K. Sugihara. *Spatial Tessellations: Concepts and Applications of Voronoi Diagrams*. John Wiley & Sons, Chichester, 1992.

75. M. Pauly, R. Keiser, L. Kobbelt, and M. Gross. Shape modeling with point-sampled geometry. In *Proc. ACM SIGGRAPH 2003*, pp. 641–650, 2003.

76. J. Ruppert. A Delaunay refinement algorithm for quality 2-dimensional mesh generation. *J. Algorithms*, 18:548–585, 1995.

77. C. Shen, J. F. O'Brien, and J. R. Shewchuk. Interpolating and approximating implicit surfaces from polygon soup. In *Proc. ACM SIGGRAPH 2004*, pp. 896–904, 2004.

78. D. Siersma. Voronoi diagrams and Morse theory of the distance function. In *Geometry in Present Day Science*, O.E. Barndorff-Nielsen and E. B. V. Jensen (eds.), World Scientific, Singapore, pp. 187–208, 1999.

79. J. Stillwell. *Classical Topology Combinatorial Group Theory*, Springer-Verlag, New York, 1980.

80. G. Voronoi. Nouvelles applications des paramètres continus à la théorie des formes quadratiques. *J. Reinne Angew. Math.*, 133: 97–178, 1907, and 134:198–287, 1908.

81. J. R. Weeks. *The Shape Space*, Marcel Dekker, New York, 1985.

82. F.-E. Wolter. Cut locus and medial axis in global shape interrogation and representation. MIT Design Laboratory Memorandum 92-2 and MIT Sea Grant Report, 1992.

83. M. Zwicker, M. Pauly, O. Knoll, and M. Gross. Pointshop 3d: An interactive system for point-based surface editing. In *Proc. ACM SIGGRAPH 2002*, pp. 322–329, 2002.

Index

Printed in the United States
By Bookmasters